This book

VOICES of RESISTANCE

VOICES
of
RESISTANCE
communication and
social change

By Mohan J. Dutta

Purdue University Press | West Lafayette, Indiana

Library of Congress Cataloging-in-Publication Data
Dutta, Mohan J.
 Voices of resistance : communication and social change / by
Mohan J. Dutta.
   p. cm.
 Includes bibliographical references and index.
 ISBN 978-1-55753-627-3 (pbk. : alk. paper) -- ISBN 978-
1-61249-238-4 (epdf) -- ISBN 978-1-61249-229-2 (epub) 1.
Communication in social action. 2. Communication--Political
aspects. 3. Mass media--Political aspects. 4. Social change. I. Title.
 HN18.3.D88 2012
 361.201'4--dc23
                    2012013713

Digital versions of this book are available (ePDF ISBN: 978-1-61249-238-4; ePUB ISBN: 978-1-61249-229-2). The screenshots included within the digital versions are linked to videos on YouTube. If your device supports this functionality and you are connected to the Internet, please click on the screenshot to access the associated video. In case of difficulty, you will find a URL for each video in the caption associated with the screenshot.

From a Bengali protest song from Indian People's Theater Association (IPTA):

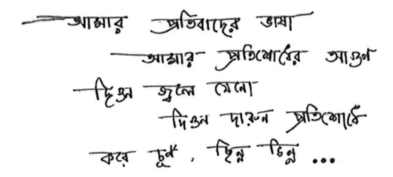

. . . The language of my protest
The fire of my resistance
May burn in conviction
In resistance
Breaking down barriers . . .

For Jethumoni, Shyamal Dutta, headmaster and schoolteacher

For Baba, Chanchal Dutta, foreman and union organizer

For Godaikaka, Monojit Dutta, teacher, union organizer, and activist

Contents

Preface

Your voices
Long unheard
By the beats of development
And progress
Share with me
The stories of hope
And sing to me
The songs of awakening.

—Paschim Midnapur, West Bengal, India, 2007

In this book, based on the culture-centered approach to social change (Dutta, 2011), we listen to the voices of resistance across the globe that foreground alternative rationalities of social, political, and economic organizing, challenging the hegemony of neoliberal ideology in organizing global economies. Primarily based on the economic substratum of resistance work, the book highlights the discourses, messages, and narratives of change that are articulated by the very people who are rendered invisible by the structures of neoliberalism. Drawing upon earlier work in Communication Studies that outlines the relationships between the discursive and material processes of resistance (Cheney & Cloud, 2006; Ganesh, Zoller, & Cheney, 2005; Dutta, 2008, 2011; Pal & Dutta, 2008a, 2008b; Zoller & Ganesh, 2012), the voices in this book engage with the possibilities of transformative politics as embodied in the agentic expression of those across the globe who are participating in varied forms of collective actions in order to be recognized and to resist the unequal policies promoted by neoliberalism. Drawing upon the Subaltern Studies framework (Guha, 1988; Spivak, 1988), on one hand, the book begins with the key

concepts of deconstruction that are embodied in the critical communication literature; on the other hand, the deconstructive turn is seen as an
opening for engaging with the positive sites of transformative politics that
depict subaltern struggles for recognition and representation.

Interrogating the academic expertise that is built into the production
and circulation of knowledge and making the argument that disenfranchisement from academic structures of knowledge production is intrinsically intertwined with the material disenfranchisement of the margins,
I seek to participate in the communicative processes of material transformations by attempting to co-construct the narratives of resistance with
the voices of social change articulated across various global sites of resistive struggles. My goal, therefore, is to foster spaces for the reader to listen
to the voices of resistance across the various sites of social change; however, these voices are constituted amidst dialogic engagements that also
foreground my own subjectivities as an academic and as a participant
(Dutta, 2008, 2011; Dutta & Pal, 2010; Dutta-Bergman, 2004a, 2004b; Pal
& Dutta, 2008a, 2008b). Whereas my involvement in directly engaging
these voices of change has in some instance been through active participation as an activist, engaging in performance as well as popular writing
through various platforms, in other instances, my involvement in these
struggles of resistance has been mediated through the new media, through
channels such as YouTube, Facebook, and my blog on the culture-centered
approach. My involvement as an academic in these sites of change is directed at transforming the very notions of academic work by centering
the voices of those who have been disenfranchised from such platforms
through the expertise-driven language of neoliberal governance; simultaneously, I seek to make visible the subjectivity of the academic and her/
his participation in the production of knowledge by referring to my own
journal entries, performative writings, and reflections. Furthermore, I seek
to engage with the voices of resistance that we hear through the pages of
the book by interrogating my own privilege and by reflecting on the communicative processes written into academic structures within which this
privilege is ensconced. For example, here is an entry that I wrote during
a 2008 trip to the Maliparbat Hills in the Kalahandi district of Orissa, lis-

tening to the voices of the indigenous activists in the region who were protesting the development of a mining project that would displace them and their livelihoods:

> Because I speak
>
> From this position of authority
>
> Your voice must be silenced
>
> And turned into a relic for codification.

The contribution of the culture-centered approach to the study of resistance in the communication literature lies in the foregrounding of listening as a tool for recognizing subaltern voices and for fostering spaces for representation of these voices in mainstream public spheres. Listening fosters spaces for meaning-making, which in turn offers alternative rationalities for organizing political, economic, social, and cultural spaces (Basu & Dutta, 2008a, 2008b, 2009; Dutta, 2008a, 2008b, 2008c, 2011; Dutta-Bergman, 2004a, 2004b; Kim, 2008; Pal, 2008). Meanings in the culture-centered approach are situated amidst the continuing relationships among culture, structure, and agency (for additional details, see Dutta, 2011) (see Figure 1). Structures refer to the systems of organizing that constrain and enable access to resources; agency is enacted in a dialectical relationship with structures, continually being shaped by structures and in turn working on structures to reproduce them, to challenge them, and to foster alternative configurations. Cultures are conceptualized as dynamic and refer to the local contexts within which localized meanings are articulated and understood. Structures are rendered meaningful through cultural rituals, codes, and beliefs; simultaneously, agency is enacted through the presentation of cultural symbols and narratives. Meanings emerge at the intersections of culture, structure, and agency, and through the enactments of agency that are intrinsically intertwined with the cultural logic, the structures of oppression and inequality are challenged.

In order to foster spaces of listening, the rules and logics of traditional academic processes have to be examined closely, especially as these rules and logics relate to the silencing of resistive voices. Therefore, throughout the pages of this book, I have sought to place emphasis on the active meaning-making amidst communities of resistance, and simultaneously engaged these meanings in conversations with my own subjectivities and reflections. The meanings that emerge from the spheres of disenfranchisement offer entry points for turning the lens inward, for interrogating the logics of the very processes that constitute the hegemony of academic expertise, and for questioning the nature of oppression that silences avenues for participation. Drawing upon the body of work in Subaltern Studies that documents the impossibilities of listening to subaltern voices (Spivak, 1988), the culture-centered project engages with the possibilities fostered by co-constructive participation through the presence of subaltern voices in discourse, situating itself amidst this dialectical relationship between the possibilities and impossibilities of recognition and representation (Dutta & Pal, 2010). I am deeply aware that even as I bracket out the voices of resistance and comment upon them through my academic insights and writing for an academic audience, my writing turns the voices of resistance into objects of analysis, and therefore turns subaltern agency into a subject of analysis. And yet it is this precise juncture of strategic essentialism that offers a collective base for enactments of resistance that connects various local sites of struggles into global counter-narratives.

Figure 1. The culture-centered approach to social change.

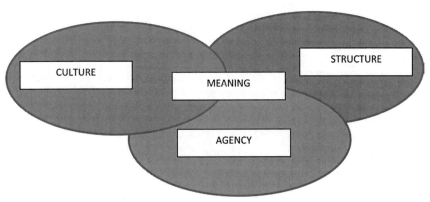

Acknowledgments

I dedicate this book to the activists, from the past to the present, and into the future, who carry on the light of hope with their tireless conviction that the world is going to be a better place through their active participation in the global politics of change. In imagining a world that is just and equitable, they work every day through ordinary forms of resistance, seeking to transform institutional structures of oppression that silence the voices of dissidence. This book repays a debt to all the lessons they have offered and to the collective wisdom they have created over generations through their networks of engagement and political action. The voices of resistance that we hear in the pages of this book are also the voices of courage and wisdom, offering us guidance for envisioning an alternative world outside the narrow confines of neoliberal greed.

Thanks to Kristen Hoerl for the invitation to speak at the lecture series at Butler University; thanks also to Paul McIvenny for inviting me to the opening seminar of the Center for Discourses in Transition (C-DiT), Denmark, to speak on the topic of "Communication for Social Change." The meeting in Denmark was inspiring for the conversations it opened up with Norman Fairclough, David Jaworski, Paul McIvenny, and the colleagues at Aalborg. Prasenjit Mitra and John Yen invited me to deliver a lecture on "Information Sciences and Organizing," and that lecture was central to developing some of my ideas that are expressed here. Most importantly, I express my gratitude to the Department of Communication and New Media (CNM) and the faculty of arts and social sciences at the National University of Singapore for the invitation to deliver the Lim Chong Yah lecture on "Voices at the Margins of Health." Thank you to Millie Rivera, Sun Sun Lim, Linda Perry, and Dean Brenda Yeoh for enabling the transition to Singapore.

Thanks to Shiv Ganesh and Heather Zoller for serving as sources of inspiration and for their engagement with many of the ideas that find expression in this book. Thanks to Bud Goodall, Larry Frey, Sarah Dempsey, Soyini Madison, Thomas Nakayama, and Jen Mercieca for co-authoring the *Communication Monographs* Café piece, entitled "What is the Role of the Communication Discipline in Social Justice, Community Engagement, and Public Scholarship?" Thank you to Kathy Miller for opening up the Café space on Facebook and for fostering Facebook as a forum for discussing the academic politics of social change and social justice. Thank you to Collins Airhihenbuwa, Arvind Singhal, Srinivas Melkote, and Krishnamurthy Sriramesh for your inspiration and continued support.

Thanks also to my colleagues at the Center on Poverty and Health Inequities (COPHI), Bart Collins, Haslyn Hunte, Titilayo Okoror, Cleve Shields, and Ayse Cifci for rigorously engaging with the social scientific study of inequities and for seeking to understand the creative role of interventions that would foster transformative spaces for policies and programs. Thanks to Steve Witz for the collaboration in creating the Center on Poverty and Health Inequities at Purdue. Thanks to Gary Kreps for collaborating on projects addressing health inequities, and for providing guidance through his engagement.

Thanks to our community partner, the Indiana Minority Health Coalition (IMHC) for the partnership and for the journey of transformative politics through collaboration; I have learned so much about advocacy and participation through our partnership on projects of health disparities. Thank you to Calvin Roberson, Nancy Jewell, Tony Gillespie, Tanya

Johnson, Tofur Bonu, and Tracy Robinson for your partnership in Indianapolis and in Gary, Indiana.

Thank you to my research teammates: Bart Collins, Titi Okoror, Gary Kreps, Steve Hines, Sydney Dillard, Rati Kumar, Shaunak Sastry, Uttaran Dutta, Agaptus Anaele, Christina Jones, Demarco Gray, and Loryn Wilson for your collaboration in developing a project of social change in some of the most disenfranchised contexts of the US. Thank you to our advisory board members and community workshop participants in Communities and Universities Addressing Health Disparities (CUAHD). Thank you also to Christina Jones, Agaptus Anaele, Abigail Borron, Soumitro Sen, and Haijuan Gao for your collaboration on the "Voices of Hunger" project in Tippecanoe County. Through each of these projects, I have learned about the role of listening in shaping the politics of social change.

Thank you to former advisees and current advisees, Debalina Mookerjee, Wonjun Chung, Rebecca DeSouza, Min Jiang, Ambar Basu, Iccha Basnyat, Induk Kim, Mahuya Pal, Chuck Morris, Kinnari Sejpal, Martina Mills, Nadine Yehya, Raven Pfister, Lalatendu Acharya, Raihan Jamil, Shaunak Sastry, Sydney Dillard, Zhuo Ban, Vicky Ortiz, Christine Spinetta, Rahul Rastogi, Rati Kumar, Christina Jones, Agaptus Anaele, Kacy Rodriguez, Soumitro Sen, and Daniel Teo for your friendship, for your conversations, and for your individual and collective journeys in carrying forward culture-centered projects of social change.

Thank you to Dean Irwin "Bud" Weiser in the College of Liberal Arts at Purdue University for being such an amazing leader to work with; your vision for diversity and inclusion has created a space that is vital to the politics of social change. I have enjoyed every aspect of working with you. Thank you to my colleagues JoAnn Miller, Song No, Barbara Dixon, and Joan Marshall for your kindness and support. Thank you to Molly Madison for your compassion and for protecting my time so that I could devote my energy to being in the field and writing amidst my role as associate dean. Beverly Sypher, Patrice Buzzannell, Stacey Connaughton, Felicia Roberts, Steve Wilson, Howard Sypher, Charlie Stewart, Jeong-Nam Kim, Sam McCormick, I have enjoyed working with each of you. Thank you to Robinda, Fullaradi, Joyontoda, Iradi, Alokeda, and Boudi for your friendship in West Lafayette, Indiana. Thank you to the Occupy Purdue and Occupy Lafayette groups for the local inspiration. Thank you to Charles Watkinson, director of Purdue University Press, for collaborating on innovating about design, co-presentation of voices, and the formats of delivery of the book. Many of the creative aspects of presentation were born out of conversations between Charles and me, and I am very appreciative of the leadership demonstrated by Purdue University Press in taking up challenging topics of public policy and social change, and for doing so in alternative formats. I am also very grateful to Katherine Purple for so diligently working through the words and the phrases, for co-constructing many aspects of the aesthetic representations, and for being ever so patient through our collaborative journey.

To Jethumoni, I am so excited to include you in my dedication because to you, my gratitude is enormous. For all those years of tireless dedication through which you built our local school and showed the possibilities of education to the many children that came through your door, you showed the value of voice. That voice is important was a lesson you brought home through your history lessons in school, and through your tireless striving to make education accessible to all. That the positions we stand from and the processes we engage in are deeply rooted in geography were lessons I learned under your tutelage.

To Baba, you taught me the earliest lessons in voice and the importance of lending your voice to issues that are meaningful. You also taught me how important it is to listen to voices that have otherwise been hidden or marginalized, and at the same time, to resist the voices of convenience that lay hidden in each one of us. Your work with the union, your everyday forms of activism, your letter-writing campaigns against things you considered unjust, your courage in trusting your voice especially at those times when others wanted you to simply join in their chorus, these are all sources of inspiration that have shown me the meaning of activism. I am lucky to have the opportunity to share this journey of activism with you, listening to these incredible voices of resistance that continue to emerge from across the globe. I remember how many years back you had expressed your conviction that change was going to come in the US—that one day people would rise up in resistance against the politics of inequality. As we live this moment of resistance in the US and across the globe, your thoughts fill me with hope and conviction. It was a treat to attend the Occupy protests with you as we traversed the US!

To Godaikaka, you taught me the dedication to be a teacher and you instilled in me the commitment to be an organizer of the poor and the dispossessed. In seeing you lend your voice of resistance time and again, I learned about the values of commitment and sustainability. In seeing you stand tall with your principles, I learned about the value of principled voices that are drawn to social change because of their conviction in building a just world.

To Alokaka, Badalkaka, Bhaikaku,Chotopishi, Pishimoshai, Pishimoni, and Boropishi, your value for learning taught me to listen for voices from elsewhere. Rangajethu, Notun jethu, and Moni kaka, the memories of your lively political discussions will continue to guide my political engagement. To Jethaimaa, Notunmaa, Rangamaa, Maa, Mishtimaa, and Kakimaa, your selfless love and undying support have always been my pillars of strength.

To Maa, you will continue to be my conscience, inspiring me to ask the difficult questions and putting your tremendous faith in my journey. Your rock solid confidence makes me trust the journeys ahead of me, and offers me the inner strength for pursuing my work.

To all my siblings, Dadabhai, Didibhai, Mejda, Sejda, Chordi, Bordi, Noda, Notunda, Rangada, Babidi, Betu, Munna, Tattu, Tuku, Babai, and Munia, what a collective we make! To my sister-in-laws, Boro Boudi, Mejo Boudi, Sejo Boudi, Nou Boudi, Ranga Boudi, Notun Boudi, and Piu, you complete our collective. To Munna, thank you for being my brother, for loving me unconditionally, and for keeping me grounded with your insights, jokes, and camaraderie. To Piu, thank you for being a sister, and for so generously sharing the spirit of our family.

To the Biswas family, my maternal uncles, aunts, and cousins, thank you for imparting in me the appreciation of performance as an avenue of expression. Thank you especially to Didibhai, Richard, Boudi, and Dadabhai. The four of you have played vital roles in my journey.

To my other family of the Banerjees in Gauhati, thank you for the great conversations, good food, love, and nurturance. To Thakuma, Baba, Ma, Mejka, Mejoma, Chotoka, and Chotoma, I am grateful for the home you have given me in Gauhati. Love to all the brothers and sisters in Gauhati for the laughter and joy.

To Debalina and Shloke, this journey, like all other journeys in life, are completed in your company, in solidarity with the two of you. Debalina, your friendship gives me the moral conviction that every single journey in life is worth embarking on, and every single issue is worth pursuing. You have shouldered this journey with me side-by-side, being a comrade at the protest marches and being an ally on the streets. You have opened up our home to friends, advisees, and students with the generosity of your spirit and with the warmth of your heart. If there is one other thing that parallels the strength of your support and the kindness of your friendship, it is the deliciousness of the food you make that sustains me and fuels my work. Shloke, playing with you is one of the most joyful moments of my life, and I enjoy every bit of our friendship. Thank you for accompanying us to our protest marches and performances on the street so enthusiastically. Thank you for joining in on the slogan "Whose house? Our house," accompanying the activists who sought to reclaim our courts and our democratic institutions through their protests. Thank you for your solidarity!

Mohan J. Dutta
West Lafayette, IN
February 1, 2012

Note Concerning URLs and Images: Due to the nature of the topic, this book references a large number of online sources, some of which are contested and may appear and disappear for political as well as technical reasons. URLs provided were working at the time of writing but readers will likely find that some links become broken over time. By providing full URLs and additional contextual information, it is hoped that most resources will still be discoverable with some creative online exploration. Image captions indicate the source of images. Photographs without credits were taken by the author.

Introduction:
Voices of Resistance

This book is set up as a primer that attempts to foreground the voices of social change that make up the current landscape of global politics of resistance, and that define the discursive spaces, processes, structures, and constructions of social change efforts across the globe. These current forms of social action spread throughout local sites in different parts of the globe offer us guiding frameworks for understanding the ways in which disenfranchised communities and the people residing in these communities are seeking to transform the political, economic, and social configurations that have excluded them. Although the issues that are taken up by these efforts of social change vary widely, what lies common to them is their emphasis on opening up opportunities for communication, recognition, representation, and community participation in local, national, and global decision-making processes (Bello, 2001; de Sousa Santos, 2008; della Porta, 2009; della Porta & Diani, 2006; Giugni, 2002, 2004; Giugni, McAdam, & Tilly, 1999; Guidry, Kennedy, & Zald, 2000; Johnston & Noakes, 2005; Langer & Muñoz, 2003; Lucero, 2008; Mayo, 2005; Meyer & Whittier, 1994; Moghadam, 2009; Smith, 2002, 2004; Smith & Johnston, 2002; Starr,

Chapter
One

2005; Tarrow, 2005; Waltz, 2005). Therefore, at the heart of the theoretical framework that I will elucidate throughout the different chapters of this book is the concerted emphases of these various social change processes on opening up communicative spaces for participation, recognition, representation, and dialogue, in ways that create possibilities for listening to the voices of subalternity[1] within mainstream structures of policy and program articulation, shaping the material realms of policy making and program planning (Bello, 2001; Dutta, 2011; Dutta & Pal, 2010, 2011; Ferree & Tripp, 2006; Frey & Carragee, 2007; George, 2001). Because the politics of representation lies at the very heart of these communicative struggles of resistance across the globe, the voices from the global margins seeking to transform the underlying communicative inequities are at the center of this book, working in solidarity to offer directions for structural transformation. As a strategy of disruption, I will seek to center the voices of resistance engaged in these various global struggles, although these voices are constituted in dialogue with my subjectivity as an academic interested in the emancipatory politics of social change.

Figure 1.1. South Korean farmers demonstrate against the World Trade Organization on December 15, 2005 (Photo by Guang Niu, iStockphoto, contributed by EdStock).

Communication Studies scholars have long studied resistance in various contexts of communication (Alvesson & Deetz, 2000; Cloud, 1994; Dutta & Pal, 2007; Dutta-Bergman, 2004a, 2004b; Mumby, 2005; Pal & Dutta, 2008), documenting the discourses and discursive processes at micro, meso, and macro levels that oppose the power and control written into the dominant structures of organizing. Whereas a large body of research on resistance has drawn on the fragmented discourses in everyday practices that resist the oppressions constituted in dominant structures, other lines of research have interrogated the emphasis on micro-practices of resistance and instead suggested the importance of examining the dialectical tensions between the discursive and material aspects of resistance against structures of oppression (Cheney & Cloud, 2006; Cloud, 1994; Dutta, 2009, 2011; Zoller, 2005). Yet more recent research in Communication Studies notes the Eurocentric logics that permeate scholarly examinations of resistance, and instead argues for the development of postcolonial and Subaltern Studies approaches to the study of communication that foreground the voices of resistance in the global margins (Broadfoot and Munshi, 2007; Dutta, 2009, 2011; Dutta-Bergman, 2004a, 2004b; Munshi, 2005; Pal & Dutta, 2008a, 2008b). The culture-centered approach joins the voices of postcolonial and Subaltern Studies scholars in Communication Studies and elsewhere to deconstruct the logics of erasure that silence subaltern representation in dominant public spheres in the global North/West where policies are configured and then carried out locally through collaborations with the local elite (Dutta, 2006, 2007, 2009, 2011). The politics of culture-centered work therefore lies in the precise moment of solidarity between academics at discursive sites of power with subaltern communities in the global margins in configuring a co-constructed politics of representation that opposes the dominant structures of oppression by rendering visible the hypocrisies underlying these structures and by articulating alternatives for local, national, and global organizing of resources that are based on alternative values and rationalities.

Therefore, resistance is understood in terms of the cultural, social, political, and economic processes that are directed at transforming the global structures of material inequities and the communicative inequities that accompany these global structures (Dutta, 2008, 2009, 2011, in press a, in press b; Dutta & Pal, 2010, 2011; Pal & Dutta, 2008a, 2008b). Particularly paying attention to the inequities in communicative structures and the efforts of change that are directed at fundamentally changing the processes and configurations of communication, the thesis of this book is driven by the culture-centered approach to communication for social change (Dutta, 2008a, 2008b, 2008c, 2011; Dutta-Bergman, 2004a, 2004b). The culture-centered approach to communication for social change focuses on the inequities in the opportunities for participation in communicative processes and spaces, and puts forth the argument that essential to the processes of structural transformation is the transformation of communicative structures, infrastructures, processes, rules, strategies and techniques that erase subaltern voices (Dutta, 2011, in press a, in press b; Dutta & Pal, 2011; Pal & Dutta, 2008a, 2008b).

Attending to the historic and contemporary differentials in access to communicative sites where articulations are made, policies are passed, and programs are implemented, culture-centered research documents the discursive processes and messages through which these differentials are maintained (Dutta, 2008c; Dutta-Bergman, 2004a, 2004b; Dutta & Basnyat, 2008a, 2008b, 2008c; Pal, 2008). Essential to the reproduction of these differentials is the privileging of certain forms of knowledge and knowledge claims and the simultaneous "othering" of other forms of knowledge claims as backward or primitive. Along with the primitivization of specific processes and forms of knowledge, the sites at which these processes and forms of knowledge are enunciated are marked off as outside the normal realm of participation. Discursive strategies of dichotomization are essential to the logics of (neo)colonization that carry out projects of marginalization by couching neoliberal projects in the languages of development, modernization, and in more recent times, liberalization and industrialization. The primitive other from the Third/South/Underdeveloped spaces emerges into discursive spaces of (neo)colonization as the agency-less subject in need for being saved by the dominant actors in the First/North/Developed sectors.[2] The language of culture emerges into the discursive spaces of development to describe and categorize the "other" as a subject to be managed and controlled under the logics of globalization (Dutta, 2011, in press a, in press b; Dutta & Pal, 2010, 2011; Sastry & Dutta, 2011a, 2011b; Escobar, 1995, 2003). It is this precise framing of culture as primitive and static underlying development interventions that is resisted in the culture-centered approach by foregrounding the dynamic, contextually situated, and active role of culture as a site for constructing alternative epistemologies that offer alternative rationalities for organizing life worlds (de Sousa Santos, 2008; de Sousa Santos, Nunes, & Meneses, 2008; Dutta, 2008, 2011, in press a, in press b; Shiva, 2001; Shiva & Bedi, 2002).

In the culture-centered approach, communication for social change seeks to change the inequitable structures that limit the possibilities for communication (Dutta, 2009, 2011; Dutta-Bergman, 2004a, 2004b, 2004c, 2004d, 2005a, 2005b; Dutta & Basu, 2007a, 2007b; Pal & Dutta, 2008a, 2008b). The material margins are defined, produced, and reproduced through communicative processes that mark the margins as backward and incapable of participation, and simultaneously erase those from the margins from the mainstream policy platforms, juridical structures, and platforms of decision making (Dutta, 2011; Kim, 2008; Pal, 2008). At the root of the processes of communicative marginalization is the economic inaccess to sites of power amidst mainstream structures that therefore dictate the rules, languages, techniques, and procedures for communicative participation. The consequence of communicative erasure is the further economic disenfranchisement of those in the margins, through the development of policies and programs that concentrate economic wealth in the hands of the dominant structures and simultaneously foster exploitative relationships with the margins. The relationship between symbolic and material marginalization therefore is twofold: on one hand, symbolic marginalization happens because of material marginalization; on the other hand, it is because of symbolic marginalization that material marginalization is perpetuated. Underlying the politics of resistance therefore is the necessity to disrupt this cyclical relationship between symbolic and material marginalization (Cheney & Cloud, 2006; Cloud, 2005; Dutta, 2011, in press a, in press b; Pal & Dutta, 2008b, 2010, 2011). These forms of resistance, I will argue through the presentation of examples that are woven throughout the book, are built on the idea that the margins are in essence fostered through logics of communication that limit the communicative opportunities for participation and voice. By listening to the voices of resistance constituted in the global margins, possibilities of structural transformation are introduced within the dominant spheres of knowledge production that have carried out the marginalization of the subaltern sectors through the delegitimization of the agency of local communities. Localized community participation emerges as a site for resisting the top-down control enacted by neoliberal forms of governance imposed through structural adjustment programs (SAPs) (Bello, 2001; Dutta, 2011, in press a, in press b; Johnston, 2009; Olivera, 2004; Shiva, 2001).

With the increasing inequities globally that have accompanied the processes of neoliberal reforms pushed across the various sectors of the globe (Millen & Holtz, 2000; Millen, Irwin, & Kim, 2000; Navarro, 1999), there have been increasing public participation in processes of social change, demanding for social justice and equity, evident in the Seattle protests in 1999, and the World Social Forums (Johnston, 2009; McAdam, McCarthy, & Zald, 1996a, 1996b; McAdam, Tarrow, & Tilly, 2001; Moghadam, 2009; Smith, 2002; Smith & Johnston, 2002; Tarrow, 2005). As the global centers of material wealth have increasingly consolidated powers in their hands through the co-optation of the state, civil society, and international networks to serve their agendas of wealth accumulation, the discursive spaces and communicative sites of participation have been dramatically reduced, having been constrained in the hands of the powerful political economic actors with access to global resources (Dutta, 2011). Under the name of promoting freedom and liberty, the language of the market has taken precedence, and has simultaneously carried out both physical as well as structural violence on communities at the margins through top-down programs of neoliberal governance that are imposed on communities without their participation (Dutta, 2008a, 2008b, 2011; Dutta & Basnyat, 2008a, 2008b). Communicative processes therefore have been increasingly limited in offering avenues for participation to the disenfranchised communities of the globe, ironically juxtaposed in the backdrop of the dramatic rise in participatory projects in international financial institutions (Bello, 2001; Dutta, 2011, in press a, in press b; Sachs, 2005; St. Clair, 2006a, 2006b; World Bank, 2001, 2002). The irony of neoliberal governance lies in the mismatch between the languages of participation and democracy that are widely circulated in order to push for neoliberal reforms that further disenfranchise the poor and the middle classes, and the ongoing erasures of actual opportunities for participation of the poor and the disenfranchised sectors in local, national, and global processes of decision making. Transformative politics of resistance therefore is constituted at this very juncture of erasure where voices of local communities from the global margins are continually being erased to push down monolithic logics of neoliberalism: In such instances, how then do communities from the margins create opportunities for participation?

Throughout this book, working through several case studies, we will actually listen to the voices of the men and women who have been violently rendered invisible in dominant structures of policy making and program planning under neoliberal hegemony. In weaving together the stories of resistance in the pages of this book, I will emphasize the processes of co-construction that lie at the heart of the culture-centered approach; the erasure of communities from the global South is resisted through the presence of those voices of change within the discursive spaces of knowledge production, representation, and circulation. Each of the examples that are woven into this book offer insights into the dignity and resilience with which communities at the margins seek to challenge structures of invisibility so that their voices may be heard; these struggles about economic justice, agricultural justice, environmental justice, political justice are each also struggles for voice. Through their voices, we listen to the stories of resistance through which local communities collaborate with other local communities dispersed across the globe to work toward fostering platforms where their voices would shape the realms of theorizing and praxis. We will begin this chapter by introducing the concept of resistance in the communication literature and by foregrounding the contributions of the culture-centered approach to this literature on resistance. We will then examine the foundational framework of globalization and attend to the basic premises of neoliberalism that constitute the political economy of globalization. Our deconstruction of neoliberalism will set the stage for understanding the paradoxes and hypocrisies that are embodied in conceptualizations of neoliberalism; it is through this journey of deconstruction that we will then outline some of the key themes that guide the culture-centered approach to social change communication.

Resistance and Communication

Communication scholars studying resistance emphasize the discursive elements of resistance, noting that resistance is constituted, constructed, negotiated, and enacted through discourse (Mumby, 2005; Pal & Dutta, 2008). Communication constitutes the framework for resistance through discourse, offering the template of meanings on which resistive acts are formulated (Dutta, 2009). Communicative approaches to resistance study the notion of everyday forms of resistance, understanding resistance in terms of the subjectivities of individuals negotiating structures (Alvesson & Deetz, 2000; Mumby, 1997), along with resistance studies that emphasize collective processes of organizing, and more recent emphases on understanding resistance in subaltern and postcolonial contexts (Broadfoot & Munshi, 2007; Dutta, 2008, 2009, 2011; Munshi & Kurian, 2007). The thread that runs through these various studies of resistance is the focus on the role of communication in constituting, reproducing, and enabling resistance in a wide variety of contexts (Dutta, 2009, 2011; Zoller, 2005). It is through communication that individuals and communities come to develop their resistive identities, and form the frameworks for resistive action (Dutta, 2011). Communication, in other words, creates the thread that weaves acts of resistance in relationship to the dominant structures of oppression, offering entry points for disrupting and/or transforming these structures. Communicative performances such as songs, speeches, slogans, poetry, and dances emerge as avenues for reshaping the contours of power by opening up new meanings and by recrafting existing meanings (Carawan & Carawan, 1963; Cohen-Cruz & Schutzman, 2006; Conquergood, 1986; Denzin, 2003; Deshpande, 2007; Foster, 1996; Gomez-Pena, 1993, 1996, 2000; Hashmi, 2007; Martin, 1998). These performative forms often emerge in communicative modes that challenge the essential rationalities of communication within dominant structures (Dutta, 2011). The messages that are constituted in these communicative acts, on the one hand, resist the very rationalities of communication that make up the expectations of dominant structures; on the other hand, they emerge in forms that disrupt the assumptions that underlie the perpetuation of resistance.

The emancipatory or the critical thrust in research on resistance, informed by Marxist theories, focuses on workers' interests and explores possibilities of worker revolution, drawing upon the role of discourses in mobilizing collective forms of resistance (Cheney & Cloud, 2006; Dutta, 2010; Pal & Dutta, 2008a, 2008b). Communication here is seen as the basis for the formation of identities, for the sharing of frames that comprise the basis for collective organizing, and for the development of the ambits of collective action (Dutta, 2009, 2011). In other critical work, the focus is on bringing about structural transformations through grassroots participation in processes of change; once again, communication forms the foundation of the grassroots processes of organizing (Dutta, 2011; Dutta-Bergman, 2004a, 2004b; Frey & Carragee, 2007; Zoller & Ganesh, 2012). Participatory processes of communication in local communities bring communities together in solidarity, set in opposition to oppressive structural forces. Through conversations, dialogues, and sharing of information and resources, these localized communities offer resistance to broader structures (Dutta, 2011). Resistance is fundamental to the processes of change in such localized grassroots movements, written in direct opposition to the structures of oppression. For the most part, this idea of resistance embodies the mobilization of a collective identity that opposes the exploitative goals of dominant social actors that control the sites of production. In the context of class-based acts of resistance, estranged from the ownership of production, laborers must abolish private ownership of production by organizing "class-based resistance" (Jermier, Knights, & Nord, 1994, p. 3). Members exert control through economically sustained access to discursive spaces and processes that serve as sites of power and control; resistance, therefore, is constituted in opposition to the materially located economic disparities within the system (Cloud, 1994; Marx, 1867 /1967). In this sense, in Marxist processes of organizing, the communica-

tion among workers, the formation of organized identities, and the fostering of collective demands through meetings and discussions become the
bases for economic organizing. The development of material strategies of
resistance is built upon communicative processes (Dutta, 2011). The resistive consciousness is formed and expressed through participation in
processes of communication. The relationship between material and discursive practices fosters possibilities of structural transformations (Artz,
2006; Cheney & Cloud, 2006; Pal & Dutta, 2008a, 2008b). When workers
develop strategies such as going on a strike, they do so through communication. Furthermore, the strategy of going on a strike is at once material
and communicative; it holds its economic power to disrupt by communicating its resistive message to the dominant structure. Organizing here
fosters a space for resistance. Furthermore, in the context of subalternity,
resistance in and of itself becomes a struggle for spaces of recognition and
representation (Dutta, 2011). The challenge to structures are constituted
amid the organized struggles of subaltern communities to seek out representation and recognition within those discursive spaces and processes
in the mainstream that have effectively erased them and carried out their
economic marginalization through these processes of erasure. In this sense,
transforming the very nature of the communicative processes and spaces
lies at the heart of resistance; it is through communication at the mainstream sites that subaltern communities disrupt the logics of oppression.

Within Communication Studies,, with the growing relevance of postmodern criticisms that drew attention to the ambiguities and fluidity in
the relationship between control and resistance, scholarly attention shifted
to studying the micropractices of resistance within a critical postmodern
framework (Mumby, 2005; Tretheway, 1997, 2000). In this sense, the literature on micropractices was directed toward disrupting the metanarratives
of modernist frameworks in resistance research. Contrary to totalizing collective consciousness of resistance in the realm of modernism, localized
forms of resistance and subjectivity are central to critical postmodernism,
where individuals socially constitute identities through discursive configurations that also open up spaces for resistance (Collinson, 2002; Murphy,
2001; Tretheway, 1997). Micropractices of resistance take place on a "lo-

cal, immediate and often informal level" (Gottfried, 1994, p. 107), which includes covert forms of resistance such as "sabotage and theft" (p. 107) that may not immediately be recognized as resistance. James Scott (1985) regarded such occasions of resistance as "routine resistances" (p. 23). Such routine and creative forms of resistance serve as "hidden transcripts" (p. 46) because they are neither documented in any public record, nor do they involve any collective action that is explicitly articulated in opposition to dominant structures. Prasad and Prasad (2002) suggested routine resistance can be deployed by means of subtle subversions of control systems through strategies such as gossiping, employee distance, and ambiguous accommodations. Most of these resistances are ubiquitous and manifest in mundane practices.

The everydayness of resistance shifted focus from what Mumby (2005) called the dualistic to a dialectical relationship between control and resistance, drawing attention to the discursive nature of resistance. Much of the current resistance literature in organizational research (Clair, 1994; Collinson, 2002; Murphy, 2001; Tretheway, 1997, 2000) examines the discursive practices in organizations to understand resistance as a routine yet complex social process that draws its meaning from the contextual aspects of organizing. Scholars have studied a variety of discursive practices such as humor and joking (Ezzamel, Wilmott, & Worthington, 2001), "bitching" and gossip (Sotirin & Gottfried, 1999), modes of dress (Gottfried, 1994), discursive distancing (Collinson, 1994), and whistle-blowing (Gabriel, 2008) as forms of resistance. Resistance redefines the same practices that it confronts and thus facilitates a point of change. However, this postmodern treatment of everyday forms of micropractices has also come under criticism for not engaging thoughtfully with the politics of structural transformations in the face of global oppressions, especially as they relate to collective forms of organizing and the charting out of terrains of solidarity between organizational workers and the various subaltern communities outside the organization that configure as the sites of oppression carried out by global organizations (Dutta, 2011; Dutta & Pal, 2010; Ganesh et al., 2005; Pal & Dutta, 2008b). In many ways, the emphasis on micropractices of resistance within the dominant resistance literature in Communication

Studies privileges US-based, white, middle class settings of dominant organizations that are often the very organizations and organizational settings
that perpetuate global inequities (Buzzanell, 2000), reflecting the US-centric biases of communication research and perpetuating the global structures of oppression without questioning them. The singular emphasis on
everyday forms of resistance within mainstream structures leave unques-
tioned and unmarked the terrains of power and control that are constituted amid the global divisions of labor at the intersections of the nation
state, transnational corporations (TNCs), and international financial institutions (IFIs). The assumptions of neoliberal hegemony go unchallenged
as the specific values embodied in many of these studies are the reconfig-
ured scripts of neoliberalism fashioned into discourses of fetishized liberty, identity performance, and individualized freedom achieved through
consumption, negotiation, and individualized performance. For instance,
the emphasis on resistance and resistive performance in the context of careers within globalized organizational settings often fail to interrogate the
locus of these careers within the dominant agendas of global hegemonic
structures such as TNCs, and therefore, remain oblivious to the gross inequities and the politics of inequities that are produced and perpetuated by
these structures. To frame the everyday practices of middle class workers
within TNCs as resistive and to solely focus on these everyday practices as
embodiments of resistance does violence to the experiences of the global
margins that are rendered invisible and economically exploited by those
very TNCs that employ the workers at globally attractive salaries. Most
fundamentally, the US-centric bias of communication research essentially
perpetuates a global hegemony of knowledge production that continues to
reify the dominance of the North/West as a site of knowledge production,
simultaneously undermining the resistive voices from the global South
that challenge this hegemony, and justifying the structural violence perpetrated on the global margins under the label of US supremacy (see, for
instance, Dutta, 2011, a discussion of the ways in which the narrative of
freedom was quintessential to the US-led imperialist occupation of Iraq).
Noting this point, McKie & Munshi (2005) share:

Much of the mainstream organizational communication scholarship, for example, remains largely US-centric and the "obsession with understanding, theorizing, and researching the skills and competencies of communication in largely American settings (and a vision of the U.S. way as the global way) tends to give American work . . . a parochial character." (p. 50)

These questions raised by critics point toward the need for engaging in understanding the relationship between discourses of change and the structural transformations that they could possibly open up in the context of transnational hegemony, especially attending to the voices of resistance from the global South and the calls for solidarity that emerge through the agentic expressions of these voices. Building on the earlier approaches to the study of resistance that note the structural aspects of collective organization, the fluid and dialectical relationships between control and resistance, the discursive processes through which resistance is enacted in organizational contexts, and the discourses of resistance in global social movements, communication scholars in recent years have called for research that examines the collective processes of bottom-up resistance in global politics that seek to transform the inequitable structures of neoliberalism (Dutta & Pal, 2010; Ganesh et al., 2005; Pal & Dutta, 2008a, 2008b; Zoller & Ganesh, 2012). The study of resistance itself, therefore, becomes a mark of solidarity in sketching out a politics of social change seeking to transform unjust global structures and policies. For instance, the scholarship by Peeples and DeLuca (2006) draws attention to the deployment of discourses in the environmental justice movement. The culture-centered approach described in earlier work and further developed in this book responds to this call for research on bottom-up organizing of social change by offering a theoretical framework that examines the role of communicative processes in fostering spaces of listening and in enabling social change through the processes of listening.

Globalization: Definition

Contemporary processes and practices of social change across the globe are situated on the landscape of globalization; the increasing presence of voices of resistance across local spaces distributed throughout the globe is positioned on the bedrock of the underlying economic and political processes that have marked the unequal contours of globalization as we understand it today (Algranati, Seoane, & Taddei, 2004; Ayres, 1999, 2001; Bennett, 2003a, 2003b, 2004; Bhattacharya, 2009; Brecher, Costello, & Smith, 2000; Choi, 1995; Cleaver, 1998; Cockburn, St. Clair, & Sekula, 2000; De, 2009; della Porta, 2009; della Porta, Kreisi, & Rucht, 1999; Donk, Loader, Nixon, & Rucht, 2004; Dutta, 2011; Dutta & Pal, 2011; Guidry, Kennedy, & Zald, 2000; Pal & Dutta, 2008a, 2008b; Robertson, 1992). Globalization is characterized by the increasing flow of goods, capital, labor, and services across national borders; economically, it is defined and marked by *neoliberalism* as the primary political and economic organizing framework for social relations, economic relations, relationships of production, institutional frameworks, policy making, and implementation of policies across various sectors of the globe (Dutta, 2009, 2011; Dutta & Pal, 2011; Harvey, 2005; Ganesh et al., 2005; Pal & Dutta, 2008a, 2008b; Sassen, 1998).

Neoliberalism, articulated in the visions of a global free market as an enabler of liberty, is embodied in the principles of privatization, liberalization of trade, and minimization of public services, and serves as the dominant logic of economic and political organizing that is exerted through international structures of power that shape the contours of policy making and programming on the global landscape, shaping national policies and determining internal political processes constituted around principles of economic organizing in the form of SAPs (Dutta, 2011; Ganesh et al., 2005; Harvey, 2001, 2005). As a social, cultural, economic, and political process, it has been marked by the hegemony of the neoliberal logic as the primary organizing framework for constituting relationships among nation states, key political actors in these nation states, non-governmental organizations (NGOs), transnational corporations (TNCs), global policy-making bodies, activist groups, and wider publics in the various sectors of the globe. The relationships of publics, civil society organizations, the state, and TNCs are negotiated through neoliberal frameworks of governance that operate on the basis of the principles of privatization of resources and the opening up of markets across the globe (Dutta, 2011; Khagram & Levitt, 2008; Sassen, 1998). Public structures, infrastructures, and programs are taken over by privatized entities and NGOs; simultaneously, the role of the nation state is reduced from the terrains of provision of social welfare to the terrains of ensuring of geostrategic security for global markets for TNCs. Notes Harvey (2006):

> The corporatization, commodification and privatization of hitherto public assets has been a signal feature of the neo-liberal project. Its primary aim has been to open up new fields for capital accumulation in domains hitherto regarded off-limits to the calculus of profitability. Public utilities of all kinds (water, telecommunications, transportation), social welfare provision (social housing, education, health care, pensions), public institutions (such as universities, research laboratories, prisons), and even warfare (as illustrated by the "army" of private contractors operating alongside the armed forces in Iraq) have all been privatized to some degree throughout the capitalist world. The intellectual property rights established through the so-called TRIPS agreement within the WTO defines genetic materials, seed plasma, and all manner of other products, as private property. Rents for use can then be extracted from populations whose practices had played a crucial role in the development of genetic materials. Biopiracy is rampant and the pillaging of the world's stockpile of genetic resources is well under way to the benefit of a few large pharmaceutical companies. (p. 44)

The framework of privatization takes over as the primary aspect of relationships, defining relationship with nature, social and cultural resources, public utilities, forms of social welfare, and so forth in terms of the private ownership of property. Resources, turned into the domain of private property, are transacted through the logics of the market, facilitated by the role of the State and the international financial institutions (IFIs) in defining them in the private domain. As a result, under neoliberal governance, the relationship of property bearing individuals with resources is mediated through the market.

Because neoliberalism operates on the essential premise that the deregulation of markets accompanied by the opening up of economies would free up markets, which would in turn free up social and political relations, it is the logic of the market that drives the basic premises of neoliberalism. Liberty is understood in terms of the liberty of the market; political and social liberties of expression are seen as arising out of the freedom of the market. The role of the State, therefore, is configured in terms of the protection of the freedom of the market. The State is seen as playing the function of securing the market and engaging with political structures globally to ensure that the barriers to the free market are minimized. State programs under the neoliberal framework are therefore directed at building a military-police base and strengthening it in order to ensure the security of the market. Terror emerges on the specter of neoliberalism as the essential threat to the market, to be adequately mapped out and controlled through anti-terror programs (Giroux, 2003). The development of the military and the police is tied to the primordial task of ensuring the security of the "free" market as a site of exchange.

As depicted in the rationality of the market that drives the basic premise of neoliberalism, the neoliberal logic is fundamentally an economic logic that operates on the basis of the idea that opening up markets to competitions among global corporations accompanied by minimum interventions of the State would ensure the most efficient and effective political economic system (Harvey, 2005). Politics and economics are interwoven in the role of the State as a catalyst of the efficient market; the language of efficiency and effectiveness is foregrounded in the narrative of governance (Brown, 2005; England & Ward, 2007; Miller & Rose, 2008). Efficiency mediates the effectiveness of the market in managing relationships and in achieving optimum effects; this is best accomplished through the role of experts in neoliberal governance, who through their expert knowledge, manage resources within the logic of the market. The welfare of the individual is achieved through the transference of rights and responsibilities at the level of the atomized individual, where the empowered individual is expected to optimize his/her health and well-being through rational choices enacted in the market. Duggan (2003) notes: ". . . neoliberalism is not presented as a particular set of interests and political interventions, but as a kind of nonpolitics—a way of being reasonable, and of promoting universally desirable forms of economic expansion and democratic government around the globe" (p. 10).

Participation in the neoliberal logic, therefore, is at the center of individualized management, as the role of the State in managing public infrastructures, education, and public health programs are transferred to communities comprising of loosely networked connectivities of individuals who are expected to optimize their participation in the market through individualized rational choices. Community participation and social capital are seen as ways of transferring the mechanics of governance into the hands of communities, with the assumption that loosely networked linkages of individuals within communities develop reciprocal relationships of support, thus shifting the burden of care from the state to the community and to the individual (Putnam, 1993, 1995). By extension, it is the atomized individual who becomes the rational subject of the neoliberal intervention; through the development of appropriate knowledge and expertise, and through participation in the market, this individual enacts his/her citizenship. In minimizing the role of the State, functions of social welfare are transferred into the mix of individuals and communities. Rational individuals participating in reciprocal relationships in communities are expected to take responsibility for the provision of services such as health and education. Empowerment is achieved through the unleashing of the entrepreneurial individual as a rational participant in the enactment of beneficial choices through reciprocal relationships guided by rational choice. Similarly, communities emerge as responsible sites for managing the delivery of services, fostered through community participation and partnership (Sharma, 2008).

Therefore, proponents of the neoliberal logic argue that the public sectors in nation states around the globe ought to be privatized so that these sectors could operate most efficiently and effectively. Global structures of privately funded infrastructure management emerge as mechanisms for efficient and effective management. In public health, for instance, global funding by corporate and private foundations such as the Bill and Melinda

Gates Foundation far exceed the funding infrastructures in public health for most national governments. As a result, the contours and mandates of global public health are increasing shaped by private entities and privatized spheres of control. In essence, then, the management of public programs becomes a profitable business for private entities; in other instances, public or collective resources such as water are turned into private commodities to be then exchanged in the marketplace (Dutta, 2011). Public-private partnerships become mechanisms for turning resources into the hands of privatized entities that treat specific societal problems that were previously envisioned to belong in the public domain through public-private partnerships (Miraftab, 2004; Mosley, 2001).

The advent of the neoliberal logic on the global stage has been marked by the power and control of global organizations such as the IFIs: World Bank and International Monetary Fund (IMF), as well as the General Agreement on Trade and Tariffs (GATT), which later evolved into the World Trade Organization (WTO), created with the goals of minimizing the barriers to global trade and maximizing trading opportunities for TNCs across national borders. The influential role of IFIs in fostering global neoliberal governance is carried out through loans offered by these programs, which are accompanied by specific configurations of structural adjustments that are imposed on nation states taking the loans. Top-down interventions of change within nation states are accomplished through the debt relief mechanisms and loan programs that are doled out by IFIs. Given the historic patterns of differentials between the global North and global South in the context of access to resources and access to IFIs, the policies of IFIs are largely shaped by the nation states of the global North. For instance, from the early days of the World Bank, the policies of the Bank were shaped by US interests, with the US having the largest stake in the Bank and being the major player in nominating the president of the Bank, who has always been an US citizen. Simultaneously, the mechanisms of SAPs implemented by the IFIs become mechanisms for exerting control on the global South by pressuring the South to open up their markets through policies of liberalization, privatization, and reduction of support from public infrastructures and resources. Essentially, then, organizations such as the World Bank utilize their international façade to push neoliberal policies that ultimately privilege the interests of the US and US-based corporations in the global arena (McKinley, 2004). The neoliberal logic of power and control has been and continues to be carried out through the linkages among TNCs, IFIs, WTO, national governments, and local elites, also referred to as neoliberal hegemony, with a critical role played by the debts doled out by the IFIs as mechanisms for setting up structural adjustment programs in nation states across the globe.

That globalization has resulted in the increasing inequalities in society, both within nation states as well as across nation states, is empirically documented (Millen & Holtz, 2000; Millen et al., 2000). Worth noting are the dramatic inequalities in the distribution of resources; simultaneously, certain segments of populations globally have been increasingly disenfranchised. The trickle-down logic of neoliberalism that was founded on the notion that the economic benefits accrued through the growth of the richest sectors would eventually trickle down to the lower sectors has been seriously questioned (Farmer, 1999, 2003; Farmer & Bertrand, 2000; Millen & Holtz, 2000; Millen et al., 2000), with empirical data pointing toward increasing disparities rather than reducing disparities Simultaneously, the distribution of communicative spaces and the opportunities to participate in these spaces are unequally distributed, with increasing gaps in access to communicative infrastructures between the rich and the poor (Dutta, 2008, 2009; Kim, 2008; Pal & Dutta, 2008a, 2008b). The poor are increasingly marginalized from discursive spaces where decisions of neoliberal development are taken (Dutta, 2011). The marginalization and erasure of the poor from policy and program platforms is particularly visible amidst those programs and policies of displacement, land-grab, industrialization, and mining that have tremendous effects on the lives of the poor (Dutta, 2008a, 2011; Farmer, 1988a, 1988b, 1992, 1999, 2003; Padhi, Pradhan, & Manjit, 2010; Pal, 2008; Rothman & Oliver, 1999, 2002). These disparities have been observed within local spaces, within nation states, as well as across the various sectors of the globe. Of particular interest here is the increasing marginalization of the poorer sectors of the globe with limited access to material resources as well as to platforms for articulating their voices within specific domains of policies and programs that have strong impact on their lives and livelihoods (Anuradha, Taneja, & Kothari, 2001; Bhattacharya, 2009; Das & Padel, 2010; Dutta, 2008, 2009; Dutta-Bergman, 2004a, 2004b; Kabeer, 1994; Padhi et al., 2010; Pal & Dutta, 2008a, 2008b; Survival International, 2008).

Marginalization is both communicative and material; communicative marginalization connotes the continued construction of a group, class, or sector as belonging at the bottom of a social system, often tied to the material location of the group, class, or sector, with limited opportunities for participation in discursive spaces and processes. The markers of marginalization vary widely, including categories such as class, caste, race, gender, nationality of origin, sexual orientation, and so forth, although almost all forms of marginalization carry an economic logic with them, with the emphasis on the inaccess to basic resources; subalternity is expressed in the forms of marginalization that completely erase the presence of the raced, classed, sexed subject from the discursive spaces of participation. The question of the margins has become of increasing interest to communication scholars as globalization processes have actively participated in creating these margins and in sustaining them through top-down structural adjustment programs embodied in trade liberalization, privatization, and exploitation of natural resources, and often operating on the basis of violence to delegitimize the rights of the communities at the margins to have a voice or to establish their stake on the resources that are introduced into the logic of the market (Amnesty International, 2010; Bhattacharya, 2009; Das & Padel, 2010; De, 2009; Dutta, 2009, 2011; Dutta & Pal, 2011; Farmer, 2003; Millen et al., 2000). For instance, under the name of SAPs and development initiatives, collective lands belonging to indigenous people worldwide are being usurped for the purposes of developing mining projects, hydroelectric projects, manufacturing plants, industrialization zones etc. (De, 2009; Morales, 2008; Padhi et al., 2010; Navlakha, 2010).

In Orissa in India, a location that is rich with mineral resources, the state-sponsored Operation Green Hunt is utilizing police and military violence to thwart tribal resistance to projects of mining and industrialization in the region (Das & Padel, 2010; Padhi et al., 2010; Survival International,

2008). The frames of terrorist threat and geo-security are deployed to justify the use of violence on tribal populations in order to make way for projects of neoliberal development. Similar stories of state-enacted violence against local resistance are also evident in the US, in the Middle East, in Africa, in Europe, and in the Andean region countries of Ecuador, Peru, Bolivia, Colombia, and Venezuela (Burt & Mauceri, 2004). The use of the military and the police under the framework of geo-security ensures that power is retained in the hands of neoliberal hegemony, and furthermore works toward the colonization of global resources in the hands of TNCs (Dutta, 2011). The military-police nexus also works to retain neoliberalism as an organizing framework of society, politics, economics, and culture.

In conceptualizing the question of resistance in the framework of neoliberalism, the culture-centered approach draws attention to the role of listening to the margins as a process for creating the possibilities for transforming the globalization processes that continually participate in the creation of the margins, and in the enactment of violence on the margins through the labels of development and industrialization (Agacino & Escobar, 1997; Basu & Dutta, 2008a, 2008b; Bennett, 2004; Beverly, 2004a, 2004b; Boal, 1979, 1992, 1995, 1998; Dutta, 2008a, 2008b, 2008c, 2009, 2011; Dutta & Pal, 2011; Guidry et al., 2000; Kim & Dutta, 2009). Listening offers an entry point for change by essentially returning the gaze on those structures of neoliberalism that have perpetrated the violence on subaltern communities through languages of development, modernization, democracy, and participation. The act of listening to subaltern voices interrogates these structures of oppression and renders open the constructs of democracy and participation, questioning their rhetoric in the backdrop of the reality of the lived experiences of subaltern communities under the programs of reform. For the purposes of this book, we will engage with those margins of contemporary societies that are systematically erased from dominant discursive spaces of knowledge production, co-constructing alternative frameworks of organizing for change. Even as the increasing power and control in the hands of neoliberal hegemony are carrying out the exploitation of the subaltern[3] sectors, communicative processes and practices of change are being articulated among the subaltern spaces in the midst of these very structures of oppression. These processes of change are directed at transforming the specific programs of trade liberalization, privatization, and minimization of public resources that have been brought about by neoliberalism. Voices of resistance shared across the globe demonstrate the ways in which communicative practices of social change are enacted in combination with material practices to disrupt the oppressive and exploitative structures of neoliberalism (Dutta, 2011; in press a, in press b; Pal & Dutta, 2008b). The overall purpose of this book is to listen to these voices of resistance at the margins that seek to disrupt dominant structures of neoliberalism and bring about transformations in these structures through local politics of participation. The culture-centered approach reviewed in the book as an organizing framework for co-constructing the narratives of resistance departs from the dominant approaches to communication for social change by fundamentally noting the capacity of marginalized communities to consciously and strategically participate in processes of change that are meaningful to them and that threaten to disrupt neoliberal structures that marginalize them (Basu & Dutta, 2008a, 2008b; Desmarais, 2007; Dutta, 2008b, 2008c; Reed, 2005; Stoller-McAllister, 2005). From other participatory approaches to communication, it differs in the explicit identification of the variety of ways in which participation is co-opted into dominant structures to serve their agendas (Dutta & Basnyat, 2008a, 2008b, 2008c); instead, participation in culture-centered work foregrounds the agency of local communities in articulating knowledge claims that render impure the categories of neoliberalism, and instead offer alternative frameworks of organizing social, political, and economic process.

Neoliberalism: An Interrogation

The global hegemony of neoliberalism is accomplished through the articulation of neoliberalism as a marker of human progress, treating it as a universally advanced stage of progress in the development of global modes of governance (World Bank, 2000a, 2000b, 2000c, 2001, 2002). However, closer scrutiny of key concepts of neoliberalism draw attention to the Eurocentric roots of the concept, tied to Eurocentric notions of progress and

global development, situated in individualistic understandings of freedom
and participation. Neoliberalism, therefore, is a cultural artifact that is tied
to specific sets of values located within specific historical-political contours of Eurocentric thought, primarily within the context of Europe and
the US. Neoliberalism was popularized by Hayek and Friedman with its
roots in Austria and the US, respectively, and was globally positioned in
the aggressive push of the Washington Consensus during the presidency
of Ronald Reagan in the US and Margaret Thatcher in the UK (Harvey,
2005). This Eurocentric foundation of neoliberalism is eloquently elucidated by Duggan (2003, pp. xi-xii):

> Neoliberalism developed primarily in the U.S., and secondarily in Eu-
> rope, in response to global challenges that challenged the dominance
> of Western institutions . . . Generated by the International Monetary
> Fund, the World Bank and the U.S. Treasury, and also implemented
> through the World Trade Organization, neoliberal policies of fiscal
> austerity, privatization, market liberalization, and governmental sta-
> bilization are pro-corporate capitalist guarantors of private property
> relations. They were designed to recreate the globe in the interests of
> the unimpeded operation of capitalist "free markets," and to cut back
> public, noncommercial powers and resources that might impeded or
> drain potential profit making.

The critique offered by Duggan brings forth the tremendous political influence exerted by neoliberal institutions such as the World Bank and the
IMF in securing the global hegemony of the neoliberal logic. Through their
loans and debt programs, these IFIs created a global neoliberal presence,
turning nation states into sites of neoliberal governance through their
top-down SAPs imposed on nation states (Duggan, 2003; Harvey, 2005).
Furthermore, the IFIs, World Bank, and IMF played key roles in diffusing
the US agenda of neoliberalization through international loans given out
to governments in the global South, which were in return required to sign
into opening up their markets to US capital (Harvey, 2005). Implicit then
in the global diffusion of neoliberalism were the neo-imperial functions
played out by IFIs in shaping and dictating national policies in the global
South, and in opening up markets in the global South to US-based TNCs.

Embedded in the economic logic of neoliberalism is its imperialistic desire to impose a narrowly defined cultural logic on a global scale; this becomes possible through the framing of the Eurocentric value system as a universal metric of progress and development. Postcolonial interrogations attend to this relationship between the specific and the universal, raising questions such as: What is the discursive move entailed in the conversion of the Eurocentric specific into the a-cultural universal? Engaging the concept of neoliberalism from a postcolonial lens suggests that neoliberal economic policies are predicated on the Eurocentric logic of economic and political organizing that privileges the individual, and therefore, brings to question the taken-for-granted bases for the cultural roots of neoliberal ideas that are superimposed on the globe through top-down programs described earlier (Dutta 2011; A. Prasad, 1997, 2003, 2006). Consider for instance what Harvey (2005) notes about the theoretical core of neoliberalism:

> Neoliberalism is in the first instance a theory of political economic practices that proposes that human well-being can best be advanced by liberating individual entrepreneurial freedoms and skills within an institutional framework characterized by strong private property rights, free markets, and free trade. (p. 2)

The basic values at the core of neoliberal theory are culturally rooted in the celebration of individual rights and the individualistic ownership of property (Dutta, 2011; P. Prasad, 1997). Therefore, the individual emerges as the unit of analysis; it is through the enactment of individualistic choices that the individual participates as a citizen within the neoliberal framework. These cultural values, I argue, result in specific, culturally based sets of practices ingrained in the Protestant roots of US-style capitalism, simultaneously erasing other ways of livelihood (P. Prasad, 1997; Weber, 1988). The logics of free market and free trade are ultimately founded on this specific Eurocentric cultural articulation of the individual as the unit of analysis and decision making, with an emphasis on the effectiveness and efficiency of the individual as a knowledge agent that is empowered to make her or his choices.

Especially worth noting is the process through which neoliberalism is established as a global form of governance. The global hegemony of neoliberalism, much like the earlier theories of development, is achieved through the obfuscation of this specific cultural logic and through the representation of neoliberalism as a marker of universal human desire. It is precisely this move that erases the cultural substratum of universalized Eurocentric concepts of individually directed freedom and ownership of property that underlie the neoimperial character of neoliberalism (Dutta, 2011, in press a, in press b; Banerjee & Linstead, 2001; P. Prasad, 1997). This Eurocentric logic is sold globally under the narrative of progress and modernization to serve the interests of Western power elites. Duggan (2003, p. 11) notes:

> In world politics, Western political leaders and economic elites have supported neoliberal policies as the apogee of private freedoms and maximum wealth expansion within a neutral regulatory framework. But in practice, the institutions promulgating neoliberal solutions to global problems have advanced the specific interests of Western financial, commercial, and trade centers with coercive tools—especially through offering conditioned loans to needy nations, and by negotiating biased trade agreements.

The underlying cultural logic of neoliberal governance is accompanied by an economic logic that privileges the economically powerful actors in the global North exercising their powers through the IFIs and their instruments of top-down SAPs. Through the loans and debt relief programs, IFIs imposed SAPs on the global South, carrying out a form of neo-imperialism that exhumed resources from the global South to enhance the wealth of TNCs located in the global North, constituting "a reinvention of Western imperialism, not the worldwide democratization and broad-based enrichment promised by neoliberal globalization's promoters" (Duggan, 2003, p. 11). Financialization of economies and the development of lending mechanisms emerge as extractive tools that further accumulate the wealth of the rich. This upward redistribution of resources facilitated by the IFIs is captured poignantly by Harvey (2005, p. 74):

> The extraction of tribute via financial mechanisms is an old imperial practice. It has proven very helpful to the restoration of class power,

particularly in the world's main financial centres, and it does not always need a structural adjustment crisis to work. When entrepreneurs
in developing countries borrow money from abroad, for example,
the requirement that their own state should have sufficient foreign
exchange reserves to cover their borrowings translates into the state
having to invest in, say, US Treasury bonds. The difference between
the interest rate on the money borrowed (for example 12 percent) and
the money deposited as collateral in US Treasures in Washington (for
example 4 percent) yields a strong net financial flow to the imperial
centre at the expense of the developing country.

Loans serve as key mechanisms for the global dominance of transnational
capital, setting up structures that extract wealth into the centers of capital. These patterns of wealth extraction, favored through the unregulated
global markets, work toward redistributing wealth upwards, making the
rich richer while simultaneously impoverishing the poor. In other instances, global sites of neoliberalism perpetuate the agendas of neoliberalism through efforts of democracy promotion that are directed at civil
society organizations in the global South with the aim of fostering public
opinion that would enable the opening up of markets (Dutta-Bergman,
2005a, 2005b, 2005c). In yet other instances, support for dictatorships,
military coups, and local elite are offered as mechanisms for instituting
neoliberal states. Finally, in the ultimate expression of the imperial character of global neoliberal dominance, nation states are invaded through
military operations framed in the language of "democracy building" to
establish neoliberal states elsewhere in the globe (as in the case of Iraq,
see Dutta, 2011; Dutta-Bergman, 2005c).

   The global hegemony of neoliberal governance has been accompanied
by rising inequalities across the globe, both within nation states as well as
across nation states (Coburn, 2000, 2004; Harvey, 2005; Gershman & Irwin, 2000; Millen & Holtz, 2000; Millen et al., 2000; Navarro, 1999; Nixson & Walters, 2003; Payer, 1974; Peet, 2003). As poverty has increased
globally, wealth has become increasingly concentrated in the hands of the
economic elite, who exercise their power through their interpenetrating
relationships with the political elite. The development of global policies
that favor privatization and liberalization has led to the minimization of

public resources, accompanied by rising unemployment, food insecurity, and poverty. The poor are increasingly disenfranchised through public policies that favor the privatization of resources; as a result, resources that were publicly available now have to be purchased as commodities in the marketplace.

Essential then to the politics of social change is the identification and analysis of neoliberal strategies, attending to the assumptions that recycle in global practices of neoliberal transformations, and returning the gaze to the dominant structures of neoliberalism situated in the global North. Emphasizing this need for critique that originates from the global South, Banerjee & Prasad (2008) note that:

> there is a need to "anthropologize the West" to show how organization, practices and knowledge become translated into universal categories despite their European origin. Perhaps, 'provincializing Europe' to borrow a phrase from Dipesh Chakrabarty can reveal the historical peculiarity of taken-for-granted universal truths and allow the emergence of human narratives that interrupt and defer the universalizing and totalizing discourses of management and organization theory in an attempt to reclaim historical difference. (p. 96)

With this goal of returning the gaze to the structures of global economic and political control, this book seeks to listen to the voices of resistance spread across the globe that organize in solidarity, seeking out spaces of social change and structural transformation. The culture-centered approach is offered as a theoretical entry point for dialogue that deconstructs the neoliberal rhetoric of democracy, participation, and community and simultaneously seeks to co-construct narratives of resistance with communities at the global margins that actively enact their agency in participating in a politics of change that is directed at transforming those very structures that marginalize them.

Culture-Centered Approach: Voices of Resistance

As noted in the introduction to this chapter, in the face of the increasing consolidation of power in the hands of TNCs, the opportunities for articulations of voices have been increasingly constrained, with political and juridical platforms increasingly being taken over by corporate interests (Dutta, 2008, 2011, in press a, in press b; Dutta & Pal, 2011). Policy platforms and public spaces have increasingly been turned as sites of privatized control, playing out the agendas of TNCs and economic elites; the culture-centered approach is offered precisely in this backdrop as an entry point for participation that foregrounds the roles of communities as entry points to the articulations of alternative rationalities that resist the dominance of neoliberalism. With the guiding observation that access to juridical, legislative, and executive spaces of governance have been predicated upon the economic access to resources, with these spaces primarily serving the interests of transnational hegemony, the culture-centered approach explores the processes of meaning-making at the margins that sustain themselves in spite of the marginalizing efforts of the dominant structures (Dutta, 2011). What then are the possibilities of resistance for communities at the margins that have been disenfranchised through the communicative structures of neoliberalism that have minimized the opportunities of meaningful participation in spite of the rhetoric of participation, democracy, and community empowerment?

The culture-centered approach begins with a critical analysis of the discursive structures and processes that limit the opportunities of participation. The mainstream structures of communication serve the interests of the dominant actors in society, maintaining and propagating the goals of these dominant actors, and perpetuating their political and economic agendas. In the contemporary global scenario, communicative processes in the mainstream are constituted with the goals of maintaining the interests of the power elite, and continuing to reinforce the increasing class differentials within the neoliberal framework (Dutta & Pal, 2011). These existing processes, commitments, and philosophies of dominant actors are situated within the rules, roles, and goals of structures. Structures here refer to ways of organizing institutional processes and resources that enable or constrain access to resources. Social change, therefore, is conceptualized in the context of the goals of communicative process, strategies and tactics directed at changing these structures in contemporary globalization that are primarily driven by the neoliberal logic, thus increasing global inequities and facilitating the upward transfer of wealth into the hands of the wealthy.

It is on the basis of the principle of transformation in social structures that the culture-centered approach is proposed as an organizing principle for engaging with the communicative processes, strategies, and tactics that lie at the heart of contemporary efforts of social change (Basu & Dutta, 2008a, 2008b; Dutta, 2008, 2009; Dutta & Pal, 2011; Kim & Dutta, 2009). For example, the World Social Forums (WSF) have emerged as popular sites of resistive politics against neoliberalism, bringing together over 5,000 activists from 117 countries at the first WSF meeting in Porto Alegre, Brazil, in 2001, and increasing that number to 155,000 activists from 135 countries by the 2005 meeting (Moghadam, 2009). The WSF is an exemplar of participatory consciousness of local collectives, communities, and networks as they articulate alternate values and principles of organizing in their dialogic engagement at global sites. Similarly, multiple efforts of resistance have emerged from the global South that challenge the key definitions and implications of neoliberal policies (see Dutta, 2011). The ultimate goal of this book is to offer a framework for understanding communicative principles of resistance set on the canvass of the articulations of local-national-global structures that continue to perpetuate inequities, injustices, and silences across the globe. Attending to the ways in which marginalized communities across the globe participate in processes of structural transformation, the book documents various instances of culture-centered processes of social change communication in the backdrop of globalization that are directed at creating points of access and justice for the poor, underserved, and marginalized sectors of the globe.

Hypocrisies and Paradoxes

Critics of neoliberalism document the hypocrisies that are embodied in the definition of neoliberalism and in the application of neoliberal principles that are carried out in the names of freedom and liberty (Duggan, 2003). Culture-centered politics of social change are constituted at these very sites of hypocrisies. Because specific arguments and logics of progress, modernity, enlightenment, and emancipation lie at the heart of the knowledge claims and public relations tactics that are utilized by transnational hegemony to diffuse "free" market reforms in the global South, it is through the foregrounding of the hypocrisies in the logics of neoliberalism that discursive spaces and sites are opened up for engaging in dialogues about alternative rationalities of global organizing (Dutta, 2011).

Whereas in the definition and rhetoric of neoliberalism, the liberty of the individual is foregrounded as the key driving force in pushing ideas of neoliberalism in global markets, what remains absent from the articulations of liberty is the critique of top-down use of force in instituting neoliberal reforms globally (Dutta, 2011; Dutta-Bergman, 2005c; Harvey, 2005). The hypocrisy of neoliberal expansionism lies in its use of force to carry out transnational imperialism under the very language of liberty. Whereas neoliberalism is instituted globally through appeals to the logics of democracy and freedom, the implementation of neoliberal experiments in the global South have often taken place through the use of explicit imperial force such as in the case of Iraq (Dutta-Bergman, 2005c; Harvey, 2005); through the use of manipulative strategies such as USAID sponsorships of local elites and the simultaneous undermining of populist forces in the global South (Dutta-Bergman, 2005c); through the explicit undermining of democratic processes in order to promote pro-market reforms, often in the form of support for pro-market dictatorships (Dutta-Bergman, 2005c); and through the use of economic tactics of exertion of power (Harvey, 2005). Therefore, the rhetoric of democracy in neoliberalism is juxtaposed in the backdrop of the actual practices of violence that are carried out in the name of democracy, often thwarting local democratic and populist processes. Therefore, essential to a culture-centered critique is an interrogation of Eurocentric notions of democracy constituted within neoliberal frameworks, opening up the space theoretically and practically for the local ideas and ideals of democracy as voiced by local communities from the global South.

Similarly, the theorizing and the rhetoric of neoliberalism are fundamentally based on the concept of the non-interventionist state that frees up the market as a rational actor. Freedom in this sense is achieved through competition in the market, devoid of the hand of the state. The role of the state is conceptualized as minimal, thus allowing for the freedom of the market and for competition to play out. It is this logic of neoliberalism that is utilized to push neoliberal reforms globally; public programs in the global South are forcibly cut back under structural adjustment programs, the public sector is increasingly privatized, and the state is forced to open up its markets to foreign capital, simultaneously minimizing the subsidies that are paid to the local sectors. In the backdrop of these top-down programs imposed on the global South through the SAPs that are pushed by IFIs and mostly by the US in its role in influencing the IFIs, we observe the largely protectionist policies that are applied by the US to promote certain sectors, such as the agro sector within its domestic confines. Furthermore, as recently, when financial institutions fail, the state is expected to bail out these financial institutions. The hypocrisy of neoliberal governance, therefore, lies in the internal contradictions of the logic, and the large-scale gaps between what is preached as an argument for justifying neo-imperial interventions of resource grab and the actual practice of neoliberalism. Whereas on one hand, the role of the state is minimized in regulating financial capital and in promoting public welfare, on the other hand, the role of the state becomes fairly important when it comes to supporting financial institutions and ensuring a market for these institutions.

The liberty of the market is equated with the attainment of individual liberties. Yet, in multiple instances, these individual liberties are governed in the domain of the state. Whereas the state, on one hand, promotes economic principles of free market, on the other hand, it develops fairly draconian policies for governing private lives. Individual liberties become constituted within the logics of the market and may be sacrificed if the security of the market is threatened. The military-police apparatus within the neoliberal state serves to maintain the security and stability for the market. When this stability is potentially threatened, individual liberties may be sacrificed and brought under the surveillance of the military-police state as observed in the post-9/11 climate in the US or with the large-scale police atrocities that have been carried out on peaceful protestors to thwart the Occupy movement. The interrogation of these contradictions in the value systems in neoliberalism opens up the discursive space to the possibilities of listening to voices from the global South, especially in the backdrop of the systematic erasure of the South as an entry point to the creation of knowledge.

Listening to Voices from the Global South

Because the global hegemony of the neoliberal logic is accomplished through the capacity of dominant global political-economic actors to turn a fundamentally Eurocentric logic into a universal, accomplished through the forceful role of the IFIs including the IMF and the World Bank in pushing specific top-down programs of governance based in Eurocentric values, resistance to the global hegemony needs to be understood in the context of those voices and rationalities from the global South that have been rendered invisible through the use of structural, physical, political, and epistemological violence. Especially worth noting in the various forms of violence is the key role of epistemological violence, which is fundamental to the project of imperialism. It is through the depiction of the traditional knowledge of colonies as backward and in need of uplifting that the colonizer carries out the act of colonization. Embodying this very logic, the colonization of the global South is carried out under neoliberalism in the guise of development, promising to bring enlightenment and progress in the form of economic growth while actually fostering further marginalization and exploitation of the global South. It is on this landscape of silences in development policy and program platforms that the voices from the global South emerge into dominant discursive spaces, rendering impure the underlying logics of neoliberalism and the accompanying programs and policies that arise out of neoliberal thought. Although we will engage with the narratives of resistance offered across global spaces, particularly relevant in my treatment of resistance in this book is the engagement with the resistive epistemologies that emerge from the global South.[4]

In listening to the voices of resistance from the global South, the culture-centered approach seeks to foster openings for the articulations of alternative rationalities that offer entry points into imagining an alternative framework for organizing the social, political, and economic systems across world. At the center of culture-centered theorizing is the impetus to provincialize Europe, and in doing so, to open up possibilities of theorizing from other worlds that offer alternative visions for how we come to understand the world and relate to it. Culture is adopted in a strategically essentialist sense as a vantage point for organizing, as a way to turn the lens on the dominant structures of political and economic organizing in neoliberalism, and as a legitimating ground for the voicing of alternative arguments. The concept of culture co-opts the Eurocentric notions of culture and cultural aggregates to offer issue frames and to mobilize participation in the politics of resistance against the narrow definitions of liberty, democracy, and free market that guide neoliberalism. Culture emerges in discursive sites of social change to offer frameworks of learning and praxis from the global South.

The impetus to listen to the voices of and from the global South also disrupts the hegemony of US-centric and Eurocentric processes and frameworks of knowledge production. When actors from the global South talk back to the dominant structures of knowledge production, they do so by taking into task the very processes of knowledge production through which theories are judged and applications are carried out. They also interrogate the fundamental rules of the game that are applied in the production of knowledge and the values that are intertwined with these rules. Therefore, in attending to the many voices from the global South that find their way into discursive spaces, we will pay attention to the ways in which these voices negotiate their structural marginalization, identify the structural marginalization, and specifically articulate explicit forms of resistance to their structural marginalization. What are the discourses and discursive processes through which these voices from the global South seek to invert the hegemony of the neoliberal logic? What are the meanings that circulate in global politics of resistance that open up possibilities for structural transformations on a global scale, enabled through the presence of the voices from the global South that render impure the dominant logics of neoliberalism (Dutta & Pal, 2011)?

Networks of Solidarity: Local and Global

The organizing framework of neoliberalism is formulated around the global frameworks of neoliberal governance that shape the landscape of inequalities locally and globally. Because neoliberalism operates through the powerful linkage between the global and the local, the resistance to neoliberalism is also built on this relationship between the local and the global. Top-down interventions in neoliberalism are carried out through global policies that are developed by the IFIs such as the World Bank and the IMF, then imposed on the nation states, and furthermore carried out at local sites, producing specific effects of oppression and exploitation on local communities. Resistance is mobilized through the reversal of these top-down processes, with local voices driving the politics of change. However, because of the top-down nature of globalization politics of neoliberalism, the domains of influence also lie within national and global sites.

Solidarity networks among local, national, and global sites carry on the messages of resistance from local sites of change to national networks and then to global sites of social change through transnational networks of organizing. The networks of solidarity between local voices of resistance with national and global voices create entry points for collaboration that disrupt national and global policies that carry out oppressions. Many of the struggles presented through the pages of this book are highly localized, resisting the specific forms of oppression that have been carried out by local elites. Yet as we listen to these narratives of resistance, the voices of the activists and community members make us aware of the global nature of the policies and reforms that are pushed nationally and locally; it is through these frameworks of awareness of the interpenetration of local, national, and global issues that activist groups organize their resistance simultaneously at multiple sites of protest.

Communities in Resistance

As noted earlier throughout this chapter, communities are the key sites of neoliberal governance and are also the entry points to the politics of social change. With the transfer of responsibility and entrepreneurial skill sets to the level of the community, the provision of social services, such as education and health, is moved into the realm of the community. Community participation is utilized to serve the privatization agenda through the use of the language of empowerment to minimize the role of the state in supporting public programs and in offering programs of welfare. In the framework of neoliberal governance, whereas on one hand, communities as sites of social capital become key players in carrying out the roles of service provision that were earlier handled by the state, on the other hand, communities play minimal roles in influencing state-level decisions of governance and in guiding political and economic decisions of the state that favor transnational hegemony.

The language of empowerment of communities is tied to the disempowerment of communities as sites of decision making regarding the use, maintenance, allocation, and regulation of resources. Programs of community relations, private-public partnerships, and participatory planning are utilized as tools within the framework of neoliberal governance to secure buy-in for top-down interventions and for carrying out the corporatization of public sectors and resources. For instance, public-private partnerships emerge as instruments of privatizing public programs of HIV/AIDS prevention that were earlier constituted in the hands of the community (Dutta, 2011; Sastry & Dutta, 2011). Participation at the level of the community emerges as a tool of co-optation, where the role of the community is played out in carrying out the agendas of neoliberal governance. In neoliberalism, local agency is co-opted as a strategic tool for enhancing the consolidation of resources in the hands of transnational hegemony and for the upward transference of resources to the power elite. Agency and the expression of agency in community settings are configured within the goals of the powerful economic and political actors. Programs of community participation and participatory research are driven toward the goals of serving transnational agendas, thus enhancing the reach of transnational hegemony within communities.

The culture-centered approach interrogates this co-optation of community participation to explore the local level processes of resistance and social change in communities that are directed toward challenging the inequitable policies written into the global political and economic structures. These processes of enactment of agency stand in opposition to the dominant structures that seek to consolidate decision-making powers in the hands of transnational hegemony. Resistance to dominant configurations becomes the guiding framework for understanding community participation, and attention is paid to those grassroots processes of community organizing that are directed at transforming the inequitable structures of control of global resources. Essential to these forms of community participation is the resistive capacity of participatory communication in challenging the communicative inequities that render communities as silent in global structures of decision making. Throughout the different case studies that are utilized in this book, we will engage with voices of resistance in local communities that fundamentally challenge the inequitable distribution of resources and communicative opportunities. Community participation, therefore, will be approached from the standpoint of communities in resistance, seeking to understand those communicative processes that are enacted within local communities, which are directed at transforming the symbolic and material inequities that are written into the sites of neoliberal governance (Cheney & Cloud, 2006; Cloud, 2005, 2006, 2007; Dutta, 2011; Dutta & Pal, 2011).

Throughout the chapters presented in this book, the foregrounding of communities as sites of resistance attends to the agentic capacity of community members and community coalitions as active participants in shaping the realms of policy making and program planning. The purposeful theorizing of communities as sites of resistance to dominant structures is critical to culture-centered theorizing, and this is accomplished through the representation of the voices from communities across the globe that organize explicitly in resistance to transnational neoliberal policies and the specific uptake of these policies in nation states and in local communities. The role of resistance as a defining characteristic of social change, therefore, is foregrounded. Communities as sites of resistance ultimately offer us alternative theories, methodologies, and applications that create entry points for alternative ways of thinking about the world, for organizing the world politically and economically, and for offering frameworks of social justice that attend to the voices of the margins instead of carrying out legal processes and frameworks that disenfranchise those without access to resources. The articulation of community agency in resisting structures of top-down globalization takes place in global sites of resistance, seeking to enact change through participation in processes of direct action and performance, and creating avenues for change through dialogues locally as well as in conversation with solidarity networks across various local sites spread throughout the globe.

Returning the Gaze

Ultimately, the arguments throughout the various chapters of this book are put together in a theoretical framework that explores the possibilities of transformative politics directed at changing the ways in which neoliberalism has redefined the organizing of political, economic, social, and cultural spaces of the globe. The hegemony of the neoliberal project has been accomplished by the discounting of the voices from local communities and by essentially eliminating the accountability of the state to the public, instead turning the processes of decision making under the dictates of powerful TNCs. The essential removal of democratic opportunities of participation under the very name of democracy has defined the specter of neoliberalism and redefined the role of communication in democratic spaces and processes. Democracy has been narrowly constructed within Eurocentric ideals of the market and has been used as a tool under democracy promotion programs to attain the expansionist goals of TNCs, opening up foreign markets to their interventions.

It is in this backdrop that *Voices of Resistance* attends to those voices dispersed throughout the globe that seek to reclaim the fundamental human dignity of local communities and their members to communicate and to participate in the realms of decision making. In doing so, because of the large-scale co-optation of communicative possibilities under the Eurocentric definitions of democracy that privilege the market, the resistive voices of local communities return their gaze at the very structures of neoliberalism, identifying the parameters of neoliberalism that minimize the opportunities for participation and narrating the stories of oppression that are written into neoliberal reforms.

From stories voiced in the struggles for water rights in Cochabamba to stories of resistance against World Bank-imposed mega-dams in Narmada, local communities seek change by pointing out the hypocrisies in the languages of neoliberalism and by explicitly articulating skeptical stances toward projects of global expansionism narrated under the guise of altruism. In the stories of resistance, we see the continued deconstruction of the age-old narrative of "lifting the burden of the soul" that has lied at the heart of Western expansionism through the deployment of the frames of altruism. This very act of redefining the so-called frames of development, participation, growth, and progress that constitute the bulwark of neoliberal expansion is an act of returning the gaze, of talking back to the very structures that have hidden the agentic capacity of communities (Snow & Benford, 1992, 1998). As we will see throughout the many examples and the many voices that emerge throughout this book, the voices of resistance expressed at various sites of global oppression and exploitation achieve their legitimacy by returning their gaze at the communicative processes of neoliberal organizing that have exhumed their agency in justifying neoliberal expansion.

Conclusion

In the rest of the book, we will listen to the voices of resistance that offer us alternative entry points into the dominant discursive spaces, rendering them impure through their articulations. Through the issues and frames they foreground into the discursive space, these voices resist the narratives of individualism and greed that mark the landscape of the neoliberal agenda carried out on a global scale. With the commitment to listening to these voices as they narrate stories of change, I will mostly co-construct narratives that engage the local voices in dialogue, simultaneously paying attention to minimizing my interruptions so that you, the reader, can listen to these voices mediated through the texts. Although the narratives that emerge through these spaces are fundamentally rooted in the impossibilities for representation, they nevertheless seek to offer storied frameworks for understanding and appreciating the resistive processes and movements through which individuals, communities, and networks of solidarity are expressing their resistance to the inherently unequal global organizing of resources.

Chapter two, titled "Resisting Global Economic Policies," will open up the book with voices of resistance that explicitly conceptualize the economic policies of neoliberalism and offer resistance to it. Chapter three will examine the communicative processes of change that make up global resistance efforts against inequitable agricultural policies and the effects of these policies on the agricultural sectors of the globe. In chapter four, we will listen to the voices of resistance that emerge in the politics of social change that is directed at transforming the environmental policies globally that have produced large-scale effects on the environment. Chapter five will specifically discuss the processes of social change in the context of politics, attending to the resistive struggles that seek to redefine the terrains of political decision making amidst neoliberalism. Chapter six will offer us insights into the voices of resistance that construct a narrative of transformation within the realm of development, a key marker of neoliberal expansionism. Finally, we will wrap up with an epilogue that will synthesize the threads that weave together a broader politics of resistance, connecting local, national, and global voices of change. Because the metatheoretical commitments of the culture-centered approach are to listening to the voices at the margins, throughout the book, we will listen to these voices engaged in co-constructions with my theoretical understandings as I seek to make sense of these voices in joining with them in solidarity, seeking out alternative frameworks for understanding and organizing our relationships with the globe, and the policies and programs that construct the stories of these relationships.

Notes

1. Subalternity is depicted in the historic erasure from the dominant discursive spheres.
2. Even as the historic divisions of knowledge structures and material relationships have been reconstituted under contemporary frames of globalization,

the marginalization of the global South in the hands of economic policies and programs dictated from the global North continue to constitute the landscape of globalization. The erasure of communities from the global South is carried out in programs of neoliberalization that use the languages of development and modernization to impose top-down projects of industrialization, mining, and urbanization. The language of development and modernization plays a crucial role in defining the ambits of global economic programs, with the deployment of liberalization and privatization agendas through the precise language of development. As patterns of globalization have deployed and concentrated resources in the hands of global capital, the inequities in distribution of resources have been carried out globally, with pockets of the global South/impoverished situated amidst the global North, and with pockets of global North/rich with concentration of power and economic resources rapidly taking up the material spaces of the global South. The North as well as the South are punctuated by large-scale inequities within nation states. In spite of these ruptures in concentration of power that have fostered a global economic elite across nation states accompanied by the impoverishment of the subaltern sectors across nation states, the rhetoric of globalization continues to carry out the logics of modernization to justify the large-scale adoption of neoliberal policies. Furthermore, the access to international structures of decision making and policy making among TNCs situated in the global North foregrounds the value of theorizing that continues to attend to the nuanced yet fairly powerful differentials in geographic distributions of power.

3. The term "subaltern" refers to the condition of being under, played out in the context of race, class, gender, caste, nationality, occupation, and position within the social structure. Although most of the examples that we work through in this book will focus on the experiences of subaltern communities in the global margins, many other communities discussed in these pages might be considered marginalized because although they are visible in policy platforms, their participatory capacity has been dramatically reduced. The term "subaltern" is framed under a key debate that suggests that to the extent a community can be heard, it is no longer a subaltern (Beverly, 2004a, 2004b; Spivak, 1988). The line of argument I build in this book engages at its base with the above notion, and yet departs from it in charting out a politics of social change, seeking to document the efforts of these groups who have historically been erased (and therefore subaltern) and continue to be erased from policy platforms, and yet make concerted efforts of resistance, putting

their bodies on the line, urging dominant structures to listen. For instance, in the eastern part of India, the Dongria Kondh tribe may be considered a subaltern community because of their historic erasure from dominant discursive sites and spaces and the current erasure of the community from industrialization policies in the region that threaten to displace them (Amnesty International, 2010). It is in this backdrop that the community, which has traditionally been situated amidst subalternity, emerges in mainstream discourses, offering various strategies that disrupt the silences that are perpetuated by the logics of the mainstream. The resistance that we hear in the voices of the Dongria Kondh is accompanied by voices of protests by actors in the mainstream, building local-global linkages of solidarity. Yet other voices that are presented in the pages of this book are voices of resistance emerging out of popular movements of social change such as the Occupy World Street movement that bring together students, teachers, union workers, farmers, and so forth in their protests against neoliberal structures of global governance.

4. Because the South is symbolically reflective of the margins that are left out of dominant discursive spaces, I conceptualize voices of resistance in movements such as the Occupy movement as voices from the global South; these voices belong to the South of the dominant North that frames neoliberal policies to guide political and economic decision making based on specific Eurocentric visions of liberty and market rationality. Furthermore, many of the conceptual categories and resistive strategies that emerge in movements such as the Occupy movement are derived from broader conceptual categories and strategies put forth in Egypt, in Oaxaca, and in Cochabamba. The concepts that emerge in the WSF, for instance, are also largely shaped by resistive articulations in the global South that initially originated the calls for global resistance against neoliberalism.

Resisting Global Economic Policies

Introduction

As noted in chapter one of this book, at the heart of global inequities are neoliberal economic policies that continue to foster the increasing inequalities between the haves and have-nots by pushing forth policies of trade liberalization, privatization of resources, minimization of subsidies, and the minimization of state-based support for the poor across nation states. With globalization, the gaps between the rich and the poor have increased dramatically on a global scale, with the increasing concentration of economic resources in the hands of the rich (Dutta, 2008, 2011; Harvey, 2005). Simultaneously, the interpenetrating relationships between economically strong actors and political players have led to the further consolidation of power in the hands of the economically powerful. Communicative spheres have been increasingly concentrated in the hands of the dominant social, political, and economic actors, with limited opportunities for public participation and with increasingly intertwined relationships between privatized media public spheres, businesses, economic entities, and political actors. Mediated

Chapter Two

spheres are owned by the same actors that own the economic spheres of production and exchange (McChesney, 1997, 1999). These limited communicative spheres then have carried out the structural violence on the margins through the deployment of communicative resources and processes to serve the interests of the rich, and simultaneously erasing the opportunities for public participation (Dutta, 2008, 2011).

Chapter two attends to the politics of resistance constituted globally in opposition to the inequitable economic policies, particularly paying attention to the concentration of power in the hands of the financial sector and the deep-seated interlink between the sites of global capital and the political realms of economic decision making. What are the alternative rationalities and forms of organizing that are put forth by these global movements of social change that are seeking to transform inequitable economic policies? Through the case of the Occupy Wall Street (OWS) movement in this chapter, I seek to offer conversational entry points into the voices of resistance that directly seek to transform economic policies and the political realms of decision making about global economic policies. Whereas OWS serves as the primary basis of this chapter, I will also refer to other movements of economic justice as they relate to OWS, depicting a global network of solidarity that seeks out alternative forms of global economic organizing.

Occupying Communicative Spaces

The privatization of the economic spheres of production is resisted through the physical occupation of spaces, which also is a reflection of the occupation of symbolic spaces. The OWS movement in the US began on September 17, 2011, with the occupation of Liberty Square in Manhattan's Financial District. The initial Wall Street occupation in New York City sparked a number of occupations across cities and towns in the US and globally. The occupation of Wall Street in New York City as a space is both symbolic and material, being embodied in the slogan "Wall Street is our street." In constructing Wall Street as the site of US and global economic decision making, OWS seeks to recapture the site, and through the process, challenge the privatized nature of US and global economic decision making. The material presence of the protestors at the financial center of the globe disrupts the hegemony of the logic of neoliberalism by interrogating its taken-for-granted assumptions about the privatized processes involved in economic decision making. In this sense, the privatization of the economy is resisted through the rupturing of the privatized spaces (such as Wall Street) where economic decisions take place. Here is the description of OWS on the website titled "Occupy Wall Street: The revolution continues worldwide!" (http://occupywallst.org/), which is connected to the link http://www.occupytogether.org/):

> Occupy Wall Street is leaderless resistance movement with people of many colors [link to http://pococcupywallstreet.tumblr.com/], genders and political persuasions. The one thing we all have in common is that We Are The 99% [link to http://wearethe99percent.tumblr.com/] that will no longer tolerate the greed and corruption of the 1%. We are using the revolutionary Arab Spring [link to http://en.wikipedia. org/wiki/Arab_Spring] tactic to achieve our ends and encourage the use of nonviolence to maximize the safety of all participants.

> This #ows movement empowers real people to create real change from the bottom up. We want to see a general assembly [link to http://ta-kethesquare.net/2011/07/31/quick-guide-on-group-dynamics-in-peoples-assemblies/] in every backyard, on every street corner because we don't need Wall Street and we don't need politicians to build a better society.

The identity of the OWS collective as the 99% is positioned in opposition to the 1% that control resources and the decisions regarding how these resources are to be allocated. In voicing the power of real people to enact real change from the bottom up, the OWS movement seeks to resist what it terms as the greed and the corruption of the 1%. The localized general assemblies, with their local textures and avenues of participation, become the global relics of symbolic resistance as avenues for the voicing of oppositional narratives that interrogate the taken-for-granted assumptions of neoliberal governmentality, seeking to render redundant the traditional structures of decision making in the globalized political economy, namely Wall Street and politicians. Central to OWS, therefore, is the occupation of the public sphere as the site of decision making, at once rendering it impure by questioning the taken-for-granted logics that constitute neoliberal configurations of public spheres where decisions are made by experts through expert-based and expert-driven processes, and simultaneously opening up the discursive sites of public spheres to alternative modes and processes of voicing that serve as avenues for listening to the concerns and thoughts of the 99%. This grassroots occupation of communicative spaces is constituted in resistance to the top-down forms of decision making embodied in neoliberal structures, where communicative processes and discursive spaces have been continuously constrained in the hands of the powerful elite. The "About" section describing the OWS movement on the Occupy Wall Street website (http://occupywallst.org/about/) states that:

> Occupy Wall Street is a people-powered movement that began on September 17, 2011 in Liberty Square in Manhattan's Financial District, and has spread to over 100 cities in the United States and actions in over 1,500 cities globally. #ows is fighting back against the corrosive power of major banks and multinational corporations over the democratic process, and the role of Wall Street in creating an economic collapse that has caused the greatest recession in generations. The movement is inspired by popular uprisings in Egypt and Tunisia, and aims to fight back against the richest 1% of people that are writing the rules of an unfair global economy that is foreclosing on our future.

The symbolic occupation of physical spaces in Manhattan's Financial District is a communicative act, one that seeks to draw attention to the corrosive power of major banks and multinational corporations in shaping political processes. In voicing its resistance to the rules and processes that are dictated by the richest 1% of the globe in fostering an unfair and unequal global economy, OWS seeks to rewrite the rules of neoliberal governmentality that have fostered the inequities.

Simultaneously, the building of interconnected networks at the grassroots lies at the heart of OWS, and this is accomplished through multiple synergistic linkages of solidarity, evident in the multiple hyperlinks to outside resources that are presented within the Occupy posts, and that simultaneously draw upon OWS posts and concepts to build the network of grassroots communicative spaces. For instance, the description of the OWS movement refers to the Arab Spring and to movements elsewhere globally. In offering peaceful, nonviolent general assemblies as communicative spaces of decision- making, it offers a link to the "Take the square" website, specifically pointing to a text prepared by the Commission for Group Dynamics in Assemblies of the Puerta del Sol Protest Camp in Madrid, that sets up guidelines for how to conduct general assemblies:

> This text has been prepared by the Commission for Group Dynamics in Assemblies of the Puerta del Sol Protest Camp (Madrid). It is based on different texts and summaries which reached consensus in the internal Assemblies of this Commission (and which will be made available on the official webs of the 15th May Movement) and from the experiences gained in the General Assemblies held in this Protest Camp up until 31st May 2011. (http://takethesquare.net/2011/07/31/quick-guide-on-group-dynamics-in-peoples-assemblies/)

The grassroots-driven nature of communication articulated in the voices of resistance also means that the procedures and processes of conducting general assemblies are organically developed, incorporating learning curves and flexibility as general assemblies locally work out their communicative practices and processes for setting up collective decision making. This point is further elucidated in the description of the quick guide:

> The purpose of this Quick Guide is to facilitate and encourage the development of the different Popular Assemblies which have been created since the beginning of the 15th May Movement. This Quick Guide will be periodically revised and updated. On no account is it to be considered a closed model which cannot be adapted through consensus by any given Assembly. From the Commission for Group Dynamics in Assemblies of the Puerta del Sol Protest Camp we invite our friends and comrades to attend and take part in the meetings, work plans and internal Assemblies of this Commission, which are open to anyone who wants to come to them and actively participate in maintaining, perfecting and developing them. (http://takethesquare.net/2011/07/31/quick-guide-on-group-dynamics-in-peoples-assemblies/)

Worth noting here is the working out of the processes and procedures of the general assemblies on the principles of collective decision making. The processes and principles, however, are themselves organic, attending to the grassroots nature of decision making through which frameworks for participation and collective decision making emerge. Once again, in addition to the communicative messages that are directly put forth in resistance to the dominant structures of neoliberal governmentality, what is pivotal in the voicing of resistance here is the fundamental resistance in the articulation of collective-based thinking and decision making, positioned as an open-ended, adaptive, and changing process based on the participation of grassroots social actors. Under the heading "Open Reflection on Collective Thinking," the introduction to the general assembly guide states the following:

> While we would like to share our impressions so far, we encourage you to continue to reflect on and debate these impressions as we feel that Collective Thinking is an essential part of our movement.
>
> To our understanding, Collective Thinking is diametrically opposed to the kind of thinking propounded by the present system. This makes it difficult to assimilate and apply. Time is needed, as it involves a long process. When faced with a decision, the normal response of two people with differing opinions tends to be confrontational. They each defend their opinions with the aim of convincing their opponent, until their opinion has won or, at most, a compromise has been reached.
>
> The aim of Collective Thinking, on the other hand, is to construct. That is to say, two people with differing ideas work together to build something new. The onus is therefore not on my idea or yours; rather it is the notion that two ideas together will produce something new, something that neither of us had envisaged beforehand. This focus requires of us that we actively listen, rather than merely be preoccupied with preparing our response.
>
> Collective Thinking is born when we understand that all opinions, be these opinions our own or others', need to be considered when generating consensus and that an idea, once it has been constructed

indirectly, can transform us. Do not be discouraged: we are learning; we'll get there: all that's needed is time. (http://takethesquare.
net/2011/07/31/quick-guide-on-group-dynamics-in-peoples-assem-
blies/)

At the heart of the process of solidarity building is the emphasis on collective thinking. Collective thinking, which is the goal of the general assemblies, is positioned in opposition to top-down decision making that
constitutes political and economic decision-making processes under
neoliberalism. The competition-based framework of argumentation in
communicative processes is displaced by an alternative narrative of collaboration and consensus. Articulating collective thinking as oppositional
to the thinking that constitutes the present system, the general assembly
guidelines offer the framework of collaboration as the basis of communication. The voicing of collective thinking then points to the notion that
communication can be built on the foundation of active listening, seeking to build something new through communication rather than being
framed within a confrontational framework where the participants focus
on preparing their responses to each other. Also worth noting is the inter-
textuality articulated above as the "Take the square" website links to the
OWS website under a "Do It Yourself" section, both offering information
on the OWS as well as sharing strategies learned from the OWS.

The occupation is a symbolic marker of resistance that disrupts the
hegemony of neoliberalism and its economic assumptions. Consider the
following posting by Chris on the OWS website under the heading "Why,"
seeking to offer a rationale for the movement:

> Contemporary society is commodified society, where the economic
> transaction has become the dominant way of relating to the culture
> and artifacts of human civilization, over and above all other means of
> understanding, with any exceptions being considered merely a tem-
> porary holdout as the market swiftly works on ways to monetize those
> few things which stubbornly remain untouched. Perhaps the most
> pernicious aspect of this current setup is that it has long ago co-opted
> the very means of survival within itself, making our existence not an
> inherent right endowed to us by the simple fact of our humanity but

a matter of how much we're all worth—the mere act of being alive has a price tag. Some pay it easily. Others pay for it with their submission. Others still can't pay it at all. Regardless, though, like cars, TVs and barrels of oil, our lives are commodities to be bought and sold on the open market amid the culture of ruthlessness and desperation that has arisen to accommodate it. This is the natural consequence of a society built around entities whose purpose it is to always, always minimize costs and maximize profits. It is the philosophy of growth for the sake of growth, the same ideology that drives a cancer cell. An economy in a steady state is not healthy. It needs to expand, constantly, perpetually . . .

The people coming to Wall Street on September 17 come for a variety of reasons, but what unites them all is the opposition to the principle that has come to dominate not only our economic lives but our entire lives: profit over and above all else. Those that do not embrace this principle: prepare to be out-competed. They will lose the race to the bottom and the vulture will swoop down to feast. It is indicative of a deep spiritual sickness that has gripped civilization, a sickness that drives the vast deprivation, oppression and despoliation that has come to cover the world.

The world does not have to be this way. A society of ruthlessness and isolation can be confronted and replaced with a society of cooperation and community. Cynics will tell us this world is not possible. That the forces arrayed against us have won and will always win and, perhaps, should always win. But they are not gods. They are human beings, just like us. They are a product of a society that rewards the behavior that has led us to where we are today. They can be confronted. What's more, they can be reached. They just need to see us. See beyond the price tags we carry. (http://occupywallst.org/article/why/)

As the movement spread, web resources started being created and shared that addressed different aspects of occupations, providing resources for collectives locally to organize their occupations. Here is an example of a collective resource hosted at a website titled "How to Occupy: Grassroots practices for global change":

HowToCamp/HowToOccupy is conceived to promote and spread the methods, techniques and knowledge about peaceful occupation of public spaces while developing sustainable ways of living based on participatory democracy. We are an open community *based on free information,* we believe in the power of synergy applied to creative commons and copyleft for the benefit of the many.

Our goal is to establish an universal and accessible database made up of documents related to peaceful civil disobedience and grassroots practices, spreading it physically and on-line to the very assemblies, occupations and groups around the whole world.

We hope to put together all the experiences the older camps have had in order to put them to the service of new occupations in a successive way, creating a collaborative chain of information. These are necessary tools for a peaceful rising up.

We plan to install more features to this platform soon, as we develop and unite. (http://occupycentral.wordpress.com/2011/12/17/how-to-camp-for-a-global-revolution-just-another-take-the-square-sites-site/)

The website provides a variety of resources on occupations, thus offering guidance for collective action and for the physical occupation of spaces. The broader objectives of the site are to serve as resources for learning about the methods and techniques for occupations, as well as establishing databases that draw upon lessons from older camps. In establishing a universal and accessible database comprised of documents on civil disobedience and grassroots practices, the OWS website seeks to develop into a resource or a repository on occupying tactics and strategies, sharing tools for strategies of peaceful rising up.

Consider for instance the following post with the heading "10 days until #OCCUPYWALLSTREET":

#OCCUPYWALLSTREET is all about breaking up that cosy relationship between money and politics and bringing the perpetrators of the financial crash of 2008 to justice.

On September 17, 20,000 of us will descend on Wall Street, the iconic financial center of America, set up a peaceful encampment, hold a people's assembly to decide what our one demand will be, and carry out an agenda of full-spectrum, absolutely nonviolent civil disobedience the likes of which the country has not seen since the freedom marches of the 1960s.

From our encampment we will launch daily smart mob forays all over lower Manhattan . . . peaceful, creative happenings in front of Goldman Sachs; the SEC; the Federal Reserve; the New York Stock Exchange . . . and maybe even, if we can figure out where they're being held, at the sites of Obama's private $38,500 per person fundraising events happening somewhere in Manhattan on Sept. 19 and 20.

Our strategy will be that of the master strategist Sun Tzu: "appear at points which the enemy must hasten to defend; march swiftly to places where you are not expected." With a bit of luck, and if fate is on our side, we may be able to turn all of lower Manhattan into a site of passionate democratic contestation—an American Tahrir Square.

We will do all this with peace in our hearts. Our unshakable commitment to nonviolence will give us the spiritual strength we need to inspire the nation and to ultimately triumph in the weeks and maybe months of struggle that will unfold after September 17. (http://occupywallst.org/article/adbusters-ten-days-until-occupywallstreet/)

In discussing the strategies of resistance, OWS voices the importance of occupying the very sites of the corporate-government nexus, thus disrupting the taken-for-granted assumptions that underlie that relationship and at the same time, making this nexus evident within the public discursive space. The symbolic occupation of Wall Street, the financial capital of America, is articulated as the right of the public to have a voice in shaping economic policies that affect their lives. The launching of smart mob forays in front of the sites of corporate capitalism embodied in the forms of Goldman Sachs, the SEC, the Federal Reserve, the New York Stock Exchange, among others, is seen as an act of rupturing the logic of privatiza-

Figure 2.1. Uploaded by "tender2be." http://youtu.be/ayUGOgFaCs8

tion of communicative spaces and the deployment of these spaces to serve the economic and political interests of the dominant power structures. For instance, the envisioning of smart mob forays at the sites of Obama's private $38,500 per person fundraising events happening in Manhattan offers an alternative narrative that seeks to disrupt the corporate-political nexus in the US.

As noted earlier in this section, the occupation of public spaces as symbolic spaces of protest against privatization is central to the message of OWS. In a post titled "Occupy Wall Street Test Run (Video)," a video of the police harassment of protestors (http://youtu.be/ayUGOgFaCs8) is accompanied by the following message:

> On Thursday, Sept. 1st, a small group of demonstrators were met with police intimidation while performing a peaceful and legal occupation of a public sidewalk on Wall Street for a single night. Nine were arrested for disorderly conduct and later released without charge. One

demonstrator was held for 24 hours because he was unable to provide proof of residency.

This demonstration was intended to serve as a one night test run for
the September 17th occupation using the "legal encampment" strategy. According to a federal court ruling in 2000, the use of "public
sleeping as a means of symbolic expression" is allowed on public
sidewalks in New York City. (METROPOLITAN COUNCIL, INC.,
Plaintiff, -against- HOWARD SAFIR, Commissioner of the New York
City Police Department, et al., June 12, 2000 [99 F. Supp. 2d 438; 2000
U.S. Dist.]). The demonstrators of Bloombergville also employed this
tactic for an occupation that lasted a few weeks.

Despite fully obeying the law, demonstrators were still met with police harassment and intimidation. This event serves to remind us that
we're living in a police state with absolutely no respect for the right
of the people to peacefully assemble and exercise their constitutional
free speech. But we will not be scared away or deterred. This abuse
of authority by the NYPD only serves to strengthen our resolve and
reinforce our belief that corruption and injustice in America must
be fought.

More will be coming September 17th. (http://occupywallst.org/ar-
ticle/occupy-wall-street-test-run-video/)

Once again, evident in this narrative of resistance is the performance of
public sleeping as a means of symbolic expression. The interaction with
the police as depicted in the video is constituted around the occupation
of public spaces around the movement, with the movement participants
drawing attention to their right to freely assemble and to constitutional
free speech. The depiction of police harassment and intimidation draws
attention to the state-police-privatization linkage in neoliberalism, and
serves as an argument for the reason why corruption and injustice in
America needs to be fought, thus serving to mobilize public participation
and support for OWS.

The Narrative of Greed

The voices of resistance against economic injustices continually point toward the greed of the rich underlying the large-scale economic inequities and economic inaccess. In a piece titled "OWS Snapshot" posted on the one-month anniversary of the Occupy movement, resisting corporate greed is defined at the core of the movement:

> OWS vibrates with activity. In every corner of Liberty Square people are organizing against corporate greed, refusing to be afraid, to be silenced. The local community center, the nearby atrium, the surrounding parks and cafes pulse with working groups planning actions, coordinating with community groups, engaging with the press, supporting each other, and strengthening solidarity within the movement. We are growing change in the shadow of the wealth, greed, and thievery that is Wall Street. (http://occupywallst.org/archive/Oct-19-2011/page-1/)

The vibrancy of activity against economic injustices is positioned in relationship to greed. The organizing of people at Liberty Square is set in motion in resistance to corporate greed. Pointing to the hegemonic nature of corporate greed and its role in silencing voices of dissent, OWS is built on the notion of resistance. In other words, the resistive voices in OWS exist in a dialectical relationship with the structural oppressions and corruptions of corporations. OWS finds meaning through the articulation of the frame of corruption. The change that defines the character of the OWS movement exists in the broader backdrop of corporate corruption, greed, and wealth. The post further continues under the subheading "No Hate":

> No Hate: Many people from different places have been affected by the greed of the 1% and by the false solutions of corporate greed, union busting, and the slashing and privatization of social services. The 99% is varied and broad—but we have principles of solidarity, and we are working together to make a better world—a world of inclusion, dignity, love and respect. #OWS has no space for racism, sexism, transphobia, anti-immigrant hatred, xenophobia, and hatred in general. (http://occupywallst.org/archive/Oct-19-2011/page-1/)

The fabric of solidarity of OWS is made up of collective experiences of marginalization experienced by people from different places. These experiences of marginalization are noted as having been produced by the false solutions proposed by corporations. The solidarity of the movement is articulated in resistance to the neoliberal solutions of union busting, privatization, and the minimization of social resources. The post further goes on to note the following:

> Demands: A group claiming to be on the verge of issuing demands for #OWS has gotten the attention of a story hungry media. We are our demands. #OWS is conversation, organization, and action focused on ending the tyranny of the 1%. On Saturday we marched in solidarity against corrupt banking systems, against war, and against foreclosure. We discussed how to break up the "too big to fail" financial companies and end excessive wall street executive bonuses, we were arrested [link to http://youtu.be/fdeuuzXS_sY] while trying to remove our money from the grasp of these dangerous institutions, we occupied the boardrooms of the 1% [link to http://www.occupythe-boardroom.org/] so they wouldn't feel so sad and alone, we occupied foreclosure court rooms [link to http://www.o4onyc.org/] where they use a broken system to legally steal the homes of the 99%, rallied in front of military recruitment centers demanding an end to US wars, and tens of thousands of us marched into the times square, the neon heart of consumerism, demanding economic justice.

> *Occupy Wall Street is a people-powered movement that began on September 17, 2011 in Liberty Square in Manhattan's Financial District, and has spread to over 100 cities in the United States and actions in over 1,500 cities globally. #OWS is fighting back against the corrosive power major banks and unaccountable multinational corporations wield against democracy, and the role of Wall Street in creating the economic collapse that has caused the greatest recession in nearly a century. The movement is inspired by popular uprisings in Egypt and around the world, and aims to expose how the richest 1% of people are writing the rules of a dangerous neoliberal economic agenda that is stealing our future.* (http://occupywallst.org/archive/Oct-19-2011/page-1/)

The greed of the 1% is set as the framework within which the resistance of the OWS movement is organized. In noting the issues that constitute the organizing of OWS, the post refers to fighting the corrosive power concentrated in the hands of banks and multinational corporations. In solidarity with other movements globally, the OWS takes as its agenda the fighting of corporate greed. In seeking to change the rules of economic organizing in the US and globally, the OWS movement aims to make visible the rules of the neoliberal agenda that are written by the richest 1% people and are driven by the goals of the richest 1% to accumulate wealth while simultaneously depriving the 99%. The post also utilizes the frame of greed to refer to the role of Wall Street in bringing about the economic collapse in the US.

Specific strategies that refer to the framework of greed are then outlined around the notion of fighting both corporate and consumerist greed. They include actions such as removing personal money from greedy financial institutions, occupying the boardrooms of the 1%, occupying foreclosure courtrooms, rallying in front of military recruitment centers, and protesting in front of Times Square—the heart of consumerism. Each of these strategic actions is accompanied by a hyperlink to actual demonstrations and reports of these actions shared through text, video, and audio. For instance, the reference to occupation of foreclosure courtrooms links to the "Organizing for Occupation" (O4O) website, which describes the movement as constituted around the human right to safe and affordable housing. Similarly, the reference to the occupying of the boardrooms is linked to the "Occupy the Board Room" website at http://www.occupythe-boardroom.org/, which serves as a resource for communicating back to the top 1%, providing information and resources on Wall Street elites, and also serving as an avenue for delivering messages to Wall Street elites through demonstrations, performances, direct delivery of mail, and other activities.

Not only does greed emerge in collective acts of protest against the structures of greed in neoliberalism, but also through calls for changes in lifestyles that are founded on greed and consumption. The framing of Black Friday as "Buy Nothing Day" draws on the narrative of greed:

You've been sleeping on the streets for two months pleading peacefully for a new spirit in economics. And just as your camps are raided, your eyes pepper sprayed and your head's knocked in, another group of people are preparing to camp-out. Only these people aren't here to support occupy Wall Street, they're here to secure their spot in line for a Black Friday bargain at Super Target and Macy's.

Occupy gave the world a new way of thinking about the fat cats and financial pirates on Wall Street. Now lets give them a new way of thinking about the holidays, about our own consumption habits. Lets' use the coming 20th annual Buy Nothing Day to launch an all-out offensive to unseat the corporate kings on the holiday throne.

This year's Black Friday will be the first campaign of the holiday season where we set the tone for a new type of holiday culminating with #OCCUPYXMAS. As the global protests of the 99% against corporate greed and casino capitalism continues, lets take the opportunity to hit the empire where it really hurts . . . the wallet.

On Nov 25/26th we escape the mayhem and unease of the biggest shopping day in North America and put the breaks on rabid consumerism for 24 hours. Flash mobs, consumer fasts, mall sit-ins, community events, credit card-ups, whirly-marts and jams, jams, jams! We don't camp on the sidewalk for a reduced price tag on a flat screen TV or psycho-killer video game. Instead, we occupy the very paradigm that is fueling our eco, social and political decline.

Historically, Buy Nothing Day has been about fasting from hyper consumerism—a break from the cash register and reflecting on how dependent we really are on conspicuous consumption. On this 20th anniversary of Buy Nothing Day, we take it to the next level, marrying it with the message of #occupy . . . (http://www.adbusters.org/campaigns/bnd)

The greed of the fat cats and pirates on Wall Street offers a broader framework for articulating alternative ways of living in resistance. By questioning individual consumption habits, the OWS movement urges community members to use the Buy Nothing Day to enact their protest against corporate greed and casino capitalism. Flash mobs, mall sit-ins, and community events become means for re-occupying the framework of greed embodied in the consumerist occupations of sidewalks to secure a spot in line for a Black Friday bargain.

The Stories of Suffering

The narratives of greed that point toward the concentration of global material resources in the hands of the few are accompanied by the stories of suffering and deprivation being experienced by Americans as a result of the economic policies dictated and determined by the top 1% of US society. Participants in the movement discuss their personal experiences of loss; these stories of loss offer a framework for depicting the lack of access to basic resources experienced by the 99%, and constitute the basis for action. These narratives of loss and suffering offer a platform for constituting the identity of the 99% as a collective, serving as the entry points for organizing against social injustices and for seeking to bring about transformations in the US political, economic, and cultural systems.

In discussing the experiences of the 99% under the heading "We are the 99 percent" (http://wearethe99percent.tumblr.com/), the OWS movement seeks to resist the greed and corruption of the richest 1%. The "We are the 99 percent" site becomes the space for narrating the experiences of the disenfranchised majority at the hands of oppressive policies that serve the interests of the powerful sections of the US society. The site offers collections of voices narrating the specific experiences of oppression and suffering in the hands of the global economic policies. Each story is accompanied by an image of the person narrating her or his story. Usually, the narrative is written by hand on a piece of paper, and the author holds the narrative in front of her/him like a placard, often completely or partially covering her/his face. The narratives disrupt the taken-for-granted assumptions and discourses of trickle-down neoliberal economics and an economically solvent middle class by bringing forth the experiences of suffering connected to the material absences of resources and economic opportunities for everyday Americans. Consider for instance the story of her experience of disenfranchisement as articulated by a 24-year-old woman:

> I am 24 years old. I have lived in the U.S. since I was 10. I am $30K in debt because one day I went to the doctor . . . He could not tell me why I was sick. I attend community college full time and have a 4.0 . . . I struggle to pay for tuition, books and my living expenses. I bar tend in the evenings and make about $17K each year. In 2 years my Green Card expires, citizenship costs about $600 (sometimes more). I can't afford this (and this is home). I also do not know if my American Education is enough for me to pass the citizenship test . . . I AM THE 99% (http://wearethe99percent.tumblr.com/post/14430766470/i-am-24-years-old-i-have-lived-in-the-u-s-since)

In this instance, the experience of suffering is constituted amidst the high cost of health care that put patients in debt. For this participant, going for a visit to the doctor ended up with $30,000 in debt. Similarly, consider the following story:

> I am 27 yrs old. I have a Bachelors of Social work and have about $50,000 in student loans. I also have a spinal injury from 8 years ago. Since I could not afford health insurance for most of those 8 years, I was not able to seek treatment for my back. I now have chronic back pain and my pain has forced me to pay out of pocket for treatment.
>
> My weekly medical bills and my monthly student loan payments add up to an amount that makes it hard for me to cover my daily living costs of food, much less anything else I should be enjoying in life at this moment and yet I make too much to qualify for food stamps.
>
> I am currently applying to grad school so that I can further my education and hopefully obtain a better paying job. But I am horrified that I will not be able to afford grad school or will go further into debt from any loans I have to take. (http://wearethe99percent.tumblr.com/post/14353066977/i-am-27-yrs-old-i-have-a-bachelors-of-social-work)

In this narrative, the participant discusses her $50,000 debt in student loans. Her suffering is further enunciated by her inability to seek out treatment for spinal injury because she could not afford health insurance. As a result, the chronic back pain she experiences has forced her to pay out of pocket for treatment. Due to her high medical bills and student loan payments, the participant is barely able to make a living, unable to cover the expenses of food. This inaccess to food is juxtaposed in the backdrop of the notion that she makes too much money to qualify for food stamps. Her desire to go to grad school is interrupted by the high cost of education and by her doubts regarding her (in)ability to pay for graduate school.

The stories of suffering provide the personal reasons for the occupation. Consider the following story that is narrated by Akuabba:

> I grew up in a single parent home in a basement apartment. The government has refused to give my family any type of financial help since '95. My playgrounds were surrounded by rapists. My schools were filled with drug dealers. My apartment building was taken over by gang-bangers. And many of my friends have been shot/murdered. I am an African-American female. I have been told that I am at 'the bottom of the list' . . . as in the government's list of concerns. My family has never been on vacation and we still can not afford a car. BUT THAT HAS NOT STOPPED US! My mother has been ill for almost 10 years, but that has not stopped her. My brother and I have made it to college because they can't stop us. Even now, my mother is unemployed and can't afford our education . . . but guess what? THAT WILL NOT STOP US! I am 19 and have been denied jobs because my name is Akuabba. I am the 99% looking for change. Until I am able to pay off my mother's piling medical bills, take care of my tuition bills and take my mother on a two week vacation, I will not stop occupying Chicago. (http://wearethe99percent.tumblr.com/post/14025883007/i-grew-up-in-a-single-parent-home-in-a-basement)

In Akuabba's story, we hear about her struggles. She voices the oppressive environment in which she grew up, with no government support for her family since 1995. She notes that her mother has been ill for the last two years, is currently unemployed, and therefore is unable to pay for Akuabba's education. It is in this backdrop of the fundamental lack of resources and the suffering that is caused amidst this absence of the bare minimum that Akuabba discusses her and her family's resilience, phrased in the statement "they can't stop us." She notes that she will not stop occupying Chicago until she is able to take care of her mother's medical bills, take care of her tuition bills, and take her mother on a two-week vacation. The metaphor of the occupation offers a frame for her articulation of social justice by disrupting the hegemony of neoliberalism through her personal narrative. The individual story of suffering experienced by Akuabba becomes the centerpiece of her struggle and her desire to occupy.

Occupation, therefore, emerges as a disruption of the structural violence embodied in the status quo. Here is a "We are the 99 percent" post from a man with dependents: "I am the father of two children. They have health insurance, but I can't afford insurance myself. I'm afraid of getting sick and losing my home. I am the 99%" (http://wearethe99percent.tumblr.com/). Here is another post from October 24, 2011:

> I am a 21 year old Army wife. $20,000 in debt for an education I can't use. I worked in College, but I just couldn't afford it. My husband was forced to join the army to make a future for us. I've been homeless for almost a year. I slept in a ghetto motel with prostitutes and drug addicts for 4 months. We've taken out several loans to fix the engine in our car. We just moved into an apartment and we're barely making it. My husband fights for your freedom . . . I fight for our *lives*. We ARE the 99%.

The image of the handwritten note on the website is accompanied by the following text:

> I was forced to dropout of college halfway through because I couldn't even afford the gas to get there and back. All of my loams have defaulted and there's nothing I can do. We've lived in this apartment for a month and we just got a bed a couple days ago. We don't have a tv, not even a can opener . . . but I guess that would only matter if we could afford food in the first place. I'm going job hunting this weekend . . . wish me luck. My husband fights for the freedom of the 1%, but where are they when we needed them? (http://wearethe99percent.tumblr.com/)

Evident in the voicing of the resistance of the participants who share their stories of suffering are the dramatic inequalities between the haves and have-nots in US society. The narratives rupture the assumptions of neoliberalism by bringing forth questions of justice and equity in the backdrop of the neoliberal rhetoric of trickle-down economics. In this instance, for the 21-year-old Army wife, the assumptions of the inequities find meanings amidst her everyday struggles to make a living and find a job. She notes that although her husband fights for the freedom of the 1%, the 1% don't offer safety nets and protection for her family. The voicing of inequalities and the unfair practices that relate to the inequities in distributions of power are also central to the following post:

> Since 6/15/2003. I am a striker at the Congress Hotel in Chicago. I've been on strike 8 years and 4 months where a millionaire stole my pay and benefits and those of my coworkers. We are the 99%. (http://wearethe99percent.tumblr.com/)

In another post, a Union striker notes:

> I am a striker, and until now I feel forgotten and that we are important to noone. Clearly the powerful help each other but to us poor they use us. I feel like the 99% and for the fault of the 1% I can't give a better life to my family. I don't have the luxury of good food, I barely have food and the guilty are the 1%. I want my job and insurance and dignified pay, for a better future, and I know that with Union Local 1 we will win it with hope and faith. (http://wearethe99percent.tumblr.com/)

Central to this narrative that foregrounds the inequities between the 99% and the 1% is the dialectical tension between the need for workers to require minimum resources to simply make a living and the need for the 1% to use/exploit the poor. In this narrative, the locus of the structural inequities and deprivations faced by the 99% are connected to the oppressive and exploitative practices of the richest 1%, thus creating a frame around the organizing for social justice.

This framework of inequities in material resources and in access to structures of decision making serves as the basis of the organizing for resistance in OWS. Videos posted throughout the OWS website as well as on sister websites document the everyday experiences of suffering by everyday Americans. For instance, the O4O website links to stories of people being evicted from their homes. Links are provided to other Occupy movements across the US that depict the structural violence experienced by average Americans and articulate possibilities of resistance. Here is one example from the Occupy Atlanta movement under the title "Occupy our Homes in Atlanta victory" (http://occupywallst.org/archive/Dec-20-2011/page-1/):

> On Tuesday December 20th State Senator Vincent Fort, Presidential Medal of Freedom recipient and Dean of the civil rights movement Rev. Dr. Joseph Lowery, civil rights leader Joe Beasley, and other members of the Occupy Atlanta family will be present at Brigitte Walker's house at 2607 South Hills Dr. Riverdale, GA at 11am to announce a major development not only for the local Atlanta Occupations, but for the "Occupy Our Homes" movement across the country.

> Brigitte Walker is a former Army Staff Sergeant and decorated Iraq War veteran. When she was medically discharged in 2007, her income was cut in half. Since then she has struggled not only with her wounds received in service to her country, but also with paying her mortgage. Occupy Atlanta finds this situation outrageous and hopes her story will bring light to the many other similar stories unfolding across America.

> Banks have been found, over and over again, to be breaking laws while they take our homes. We've got a new kind of bank robber— banks robbing our homes. Americans across the country are standing up. We're defending our homes. We've decided to stand up and fight for what's ours.

> More Background:

> . . . The sad reality is that countless families in Georgia have their homes auctioned off at county court houses every month. Many believe that homes auctioned on the court house steps are unoccupied. This is not true; Occupy Atlanta has seen multiple families begging auctioneers not to sell their homes. For many, this auction is the last nail in the coffin of their American dream, their home. Let's not get it twisted, the auctioning of occupied foreclosed homes in Georgia is nasty business.

In Georgia, the foreclosure process can begin after just one missed payment. The lender then sets a sale date for that home to be auctioned off, and publishes the sale notice in the county paper. They are only required to give the homeowner 30 days' notice, and there is no requirement that the homeowner receives the notice, only that it is sent. If the sale goes through, there is no right of redemption in Georgia, meaning there is no way for a homeowner to reclaim their home. Disrupting the auction of a home literally gives a family one more month of housing, and in some cases one more chance to save their home.

A six to nine month moratorium on evictions and foreclosures would allow time for bank inflated home values to be re-assessed to realistic payable levels. The banks' irresponsible practices played a huge role in our current crisis. In their time of need we bailed them out. Now it's their turn to do the right thing, to stop holding our economy hostage

After two press conferences on her lawn, a national call in day, and direct action on Chase Bank, Occupy Atlanta did what Brigitte Walker couldn't do in years, get a loan modification. If it weren't for Occupy Atlanta and Brigitte Walker's willingness to resist Chase Banks she would have had her American Dream auctioned off on the Fulton county court house steps. Instead Brigitte Walker and her family can breathe easy knowing they can continue to live the American dream of home ownership.

Winning Brigitte's home is a win for the people. It should be a call for Georgians to fight for their homes, and fight for their neighbors' homes. Let's not forget, we outnumber the bank executives.

Here's video of the original press conference at Brigitte Walker's home with Occupy Atlanta (linked to http://youtu.be/j_jz93CJ1Jo)

The story of Brigitte Walker's suffering is turned into a mobilizing call for social justice, pointing to the unjust practices of the banks, the inequitable communicative processes within which these practices are constituted, and the abuse of state-judiciary-banking power to evict everyday Americans

Figure 2.2. Uploaded by "OccupyAtlantaAction." http://youtu.be/j_jz93CJ1Jo

from their homes. Brigitte's story returns the gaze of the banking industry, responding specifically to Chase and more broadly to the banking industry as a whole. Through the narrative of Walker's suffering, the Occupation movement disrupts the hegemony of the banking sector in working through its powerful nexus with state and judiciary structures to carry out violence on average Americans. In demanding for six- to nine-month loan moratoriums, for reassessment of loans, and for loan modifications, the Occupy movement creates alternative rationalities for re-conceptualizing economies and economic principles of organizing (more on this later). These stories of suffering and the corresponding calls for resistance circulate in interconnected local-global linkages of resistance.

Local-Global Linkages

In articulating its resistance against neoliberal economic policies, the OWS movement defines its identity within the interpenetrating relationship between the local and the global. The local nature of the OWS movement in New York connects to a broader OWS agenda that is globally constituted, drawing its lessons from other global social justice movements as well as sharing its lessons with other movements worldwide. The interconnected web of resistance on a global scale is constituted around global economic injustices that manifest themselves in locally situated oppressive and exploitative effects. Under the title "Who We Are," the movement website offers the following narrative:

> On July 13, 2011, "Culture Jammers HQ" at Adbusters issued a call to action: Occupy Wall Street! The goal stated is to gather 20,000 people to Wall Street, in New York, NY on September 17, 2011, beginning a popular occupation of that space for two months and more. Inspired by the popular assemblies of Egypt, Spain, Oaxaca and worldwide, those gathered will work to find a common voice in one clear, unified demand. (http://occupywallst.org/article/who_we_are/)

The local call to action to gather 20,000 people to occupy Wall Street in New York City is juxtaposed in relationship with the popular assemblies of Egypt, Spain, Oaxaca, and worldwide. These local voices are interlinked in a global unity that seeks to work in solidarity, coming together to craft a unified voice raising a unified demand at Wall Street, the symbolic and material heart of global capital. Simultaneously, the OWS movement emerges as a mobilizing force for connecting other movements of social justice globally. On November 17, 2011, in response to Mayor Bloomberg's attempt to evict the OWS movement from Liberty Square, several protests across the globe and in the US organized solidarity actions (see http://occupywallst.org/article/world-us-occupy-lives/).

This network of solidarity at the global level is evident in the tagline "Occupy Wall Street: The revolution continues worldwide." The reference to worldwide revolution connects to the "Occupy Together" site (http://www.occupytogether.org/) that offers information and resources for globally dispersed local occupation movements across several regions and countries, strategies for planning solidarity actions in local areas, and regular updates from various Occupy movements that have started building across several local sites. The site also offers information and planning resources for "Mass Days of Action," and a link to recent Twitter activity. At the top of "Occupy Together," the following buttons are offered: "Occupy Wall St.," "Actions & Directory," "InterOccupy," "#HowToOccupy," "Posters," "Discuss," "FAQ," and "Contact." The "Actions & Directory" button leads to Occupy Together meet-ups in several cities across the globe (the number was at 1,465 at the time of the writing on December 25, 2011). The hyperlink to the name of each Occupy city connects to a meet-up link with a callout for action.

The "Actions & Directory" button also provides individual entries about each local Occupy movement including name, state/country, city, website address [website, blog, Facebook page, meet-up page], and Twitter account information. The 1,465 local Occupy movements cover the span of the globe from Spain to Moscow to local cities like Indianapolis, Seattle, Pittsburgh, and Hong Kong. The link to the meet-up site on the "Actions & Directory" page offers information on the several meet-up communities of the Occupy movement spread throughout the globe (on December 25, 2011, the number of Occupy links at the meet-up site was listed at 2,560 cities with 21,841 occupiers). The meet-up site for the Occupy movement (http://www.meetup.com/occupytogether/) opens with a world map with pushpin links for each of the local Occupy sites spread throughout the globe. The meet-up site serves as a planning and mobilizing tool for local Occupy meet-ups, giving individuals and groups the capacity to put together a local meet-up call. The representation of the various Occupy sites under one platform serves as an entry point for global solidarity building among local sites of resistance. Furthermore, the meet-up site serves as a repository for mobilizing local communities for Occupy actions and for planning local meet-ups.

The ""#HowToOccupy" link connects to the "How to Occupy: Grassroots practices for global change" website discussed earlier in this chapter, which in turn, offers a variety of resources under the broader subheadings of assemblies (how to conduct general assemblies), camping (setting up camps), civil disobedience (nonviolent resistance and strategies for conducting nonviolent resistance), Internet (strategic uses of Internet tools such as voice chats, Internet Relay Chats (IRCs), mailing lists, and List-servs), legal (legal strategies and legal infrastructures such as the American National Lawyers Guild Mass Defense), police (how to interact with the police during question and answer, how to stay legal while protesting, mobile tactics for peaceful protests), revolution (strategies of resistance and revolution), and building a new world (alternative modes of organizing knowledge and material resources, such as ourproject at http://ourproject. org, a cooperative effort for generating free knowledge and free software for a free society). Worth noting here is the circular pattern of networks and linkages on the different sites of the OWS movement, each pointing to the other and thus building a global network of connected resources on the different aspects of mobilizing for social change.

The thematic of interconnected networks also becomes evident under the "InterOccupy" button, which leads to a site that describes its mission in the following words:

> We at InterOccupy seek to foster communication between individuals, Working Groups and local General Assemblies, across the movement. We do this in the spirit of the Occupy Movement and general assemblies which use direct democratic and horizontal decision-making processes in service to the interests of the 99%.
>
> We are currently hosting weekly conference calls using the Maestro conference call technology that allows up to 500 people to interact productively on phones. Maestro allows for smaller group breakout sessions so people with shared interests can connect in the middle of a large call. Our Weekly General Call is every Monday night. (http://interoccupy.org/about-io-post/)

InterOccupy emerges as a network of networks, connecting the local networks of action into a global network. Using the Maestro conference call technology, the InterOccupy site becomes a space for sharing resources, building local capacities, and generating global knowledge foundations for action based on the local lessons learned in the movements. The site offers opportunities for Occupy members from different local sites to register themselves for the conference call, to add agenda items (which is a Google docs working document that is collectively created by participants), and also to add announcements from their local sites (which is another collaborative Google docs working document titled "Announcements from across the land"). Here is the call for announcements that opens up the Google doc:

> This page is for the myriad of announcements that occupations and work groups across the country would like to make), whether you also made them on one of the InterOccupy national calls or not. It is a way to reach the widest possible audience. Make your announcement immediately below the blue double dashed lines directly under this paragraph so the most recent entry is always on top. Begin with the date you enter the announcement. When finished, put 20 "equal" signs across the top of your announcement so the next entry can go above it. (https://docs.google.com/document/d/12E17Wi431siEYgh 7Kx1Epw5zagdwj1JmqMen87D94nQ/edit#)

Therefore, the document itself becomes a collaboration, one that is created together nationally/globally by various local group members participating in the Occupy movement, thus serving as a growing repository of information on Occupy movements from across various global sites. Similarly, the InterOccupy site becomes the collaborative space for conversations and collaborations among the various local Occupy movements on issues, actions, as well as specific communicative processes, decision-making processes, and processes of collaboration. In this sense, the InterOccupy space itself becomes a space that co-constructs the processes, structures, and procedures of communication and participation. What it takes to participate, the procedures and processes of participation, and the development of decision-making structures become subjects of open-ended participatory processes, articulated through open-ended and dynamic nodes of communication among participants from several local Occupy movements spread across the globe.

Take, for instance, the InterOccupy teamwork on developing collaborations on lessons learned from facilitating meetings. Here is a link to the meeting announcement that is titled as "IO Facilitation/GA Conference Call":

PURPOSE: This call is to better assist and support area's General Assemblies facilitators and to discuss everything involved with facilitating meetings. This group will have no decision making authority, and will only discuss all different proposal(s) and/or options, the results of which will be latter presented the area's General Assemblies. It is optional for any area Assemblies to participate. (https://docs.google.com/document/d/12E17Wi431siEYgh7Kx1Epw5zagdwj1JmqMen87D94nQ/edit#)

It is important to underscore here the goal of the meeting to discuss processes and issues involved in the facilitation of meetings. The discussion group is presented as an open-ended group with no decision-making authority but only with the goal of discussing different proposals and options, with the goal of bringing the results of the discussion back to the local general assemblies. Learning and resources related to learning, therefore, are themselves constituted within collaborative processes. The description is followed by links to a collaborative public pad where participants/facilitators collaborate in co-creating process-based descriptions of facilitation and participation processes in the general assemblies. Embedded within the public pad are additional open resources, such as the Google docs link to "Online Resources for People's Assemblies" (https://docs.google.com/document/d/1gM1bHAg_n7dpbx3nv4cJ-Dh3SXcH7CJXUQdqx0joWKs/edit?hl=en_US#). Also embedded within the resources shared regarding the facilitation of general assemblies are international links, such as "Global Assemblies" (http://www.generalassemblies.info/). Here is the description of the global assemblies:

The purpose a Global Assembly Meeting is to better assist and support local General Assemblies and communication at every level between them. This meeting will have no authority to make decisions, and only is here to facilitate communication and help build broader consensus on global proposals. It is completely optional for any local/regional/national Assemblies to participate. There may be multiple global meetings that get scheduled, we see no problem with that, but everyone who gives there contact information will receive notice of any Global Assembly Meeting we hear about, not just this one. So if you know of one, let us know. (ga(at)wc.tc) The language of this meeting will be Fluent English. You can always change your preference at anytime simply by filling out this form again. (http://www. generalassemblies.info)

The InterOccupy site provides information for call-ins with details about the specific steps to be taken by callers from international locations to join the meetings via Skype (http://interoccupy.org/international-call-in-info/). Carrying out the local-global network theme, the InterOccupy site also becomes a space for planning global mass actions, coordinating synchronized mass actions on specific global sites of protest. For example, at http://occupyglobal.net, an OWS working group seeks to coordinate events and mass media tools to create a unified, cohesive voice for the Global Occupy movement, with the First Global General Assembly held on December 31, 2011. In this sense, while on one hand, OWS seeks to learn from the local movements elsewhere in the globe that have raised voices against economic, political, and social injustices, on the other hand, it seeks to become the conduit for a unified global voice that brings to the forefront the issues of economic inequalities and injustices, serving as a network of these various local movements coordinated and organized around the issue of global economic justice.

To the above post on OWS on July 13, 2011, which called for global solidarity, one of the commenters named Wedemay posted the following:

> Because if we don't the entire planet will die. This is not about politics, this is about the survival of the country and the evolution of pan global culture of responsibility and accountability. Service to the community is either towards peace and equality or war and violence that drain our economy and further conflict around the world. We need our nations resources and troops lives used to save our own country, not the corporations assets. Change is difficult, challenging and without it we will die in billions under the blind heel of corporate totalitarianism. (http://occupywallst.org/article/who_we_are/)

The survival of the country and the evolution of the pan global culture of responsibility and accountability are juxtaposed beside each other, interlinked with the broader question of sustenance of the planet. The questions of national security and national allocation of resources are positioned in relationship to issues of global conflict and global sustainability; the urgency of change is positioned in terms of the global impact of corporate totalitarianism. Saving the country is positioned in opposition to protecting the assets of corporations through war. The interconnectedness of global issues is well captured in the following post under the heading "Boycott 'Black Friday!' Solidarity with Striking Chinese Workers!"

> This Black Friday, as millions of Americans scramble to find the "best deals" on consumer goods, thousands of Chinese manufacturing workers are striking to demand livable wages, job security, and other basic rights. In Huangjiang alone, 8,000 striking shoe factory workers took the streets Thursday, blocking roads and standing down lines of riot police. Their factory, owned Yue Yuen Industrial Holdings, is a major provider to the sportswear company New Balance.
>
> It seems fair to say these workers are striking for a "new balance" with their management, and the system of global exploitation that management serves. Facing police repression and media censorship, striking Chinese workers are standing up against the same unfair economic system we are fighting on Wall Street and across the world. Today, Occupiers everywhere are standing up to Boycott Black Friday in an effort to raise awareness about the exploitation and inequalities that produce the goods Americans purchase. (http://occupywallst.org/article/solidarity-striking-chinese-workers/)

The "Black Friday" culture of consumption in the US is placed alongside the struggles of workers in China who are demanding livable wages, job security, and other basic human rights to produce the goods that Americans purchase. The commodity culture of Black Friday is resisted through the depiction of an alternative frame that presents the stories of the workers. The resistance of Chinese manufacturing workers in the Huangjiang province of China offers a framework of resistance against unfair economic systems that are also the sites of resistance for the OWS movement. The post then further goes on to discuss a series of resistive acts on Black Friday across several Occupy sites in the US:

Meanwhile, Occupy Atlanta, including many former employees of large retailers, mic-checked crowds (VIDEO) [linked to http://youtu.be/43q4IAfj7SI] of Black Friday shoppers around midnight last night, while Occupy Portland and surrounding cities planned to Occupy a Wal-Mart (but not buy anything) [linked to http://occupywallst.org/article/occupy-seattle-occupies-wal-mart/] today. Occupy Boston, Occupy DC, and other cities are hosting "Really Really Free Markets" to share goods with whomever needs them, proving that another world—and an economy where we take care of one another's needs instead of corporate profits—is possible. Here in New York, there is a march leaving at 2pm from Liberty Square to Foley Square to mark Black Friday.

Workers in China, in the U.S., and everywhere deserve fair compensation and an equal share in the prosperity our labor produces. In a season defined by consumption and consumerism, we stand in soli-

Figure 2.3. Uploaded by "OccupyAtlantaAction." http://youtu.be/43q4IAfj7SI

November 24th, Minutes Before Midnight

OccupyAtlantaAction   Subscribe   41 videos ▼

1:18 / 4:50

darity with the workers of China, and with all those who rise up for the global 99%! (http://occupywallst.org/article/solidarity-striking-chinese-workers/)

Once again, worth noting here are the interconnected linkages between the conditions of the workers in China and the practices of resistance articulated throughout several occupy movements across the US. The cultures of consumption and consumerism are resisted through the local organizing of events, such as "Really Really Free Markets," where people share goods with whoever needs them based on the principle of caring (more on this in the next section). The post is accompanied by a picture of the protests of Chinese workers in the Huangjiang province and an image of local protestors with banners, creating an avenue for the enactment of solidarity in support of the workers in China who are resisting to secure access to their fundamental human rights as workers.

Also important in the local-global linkages of OWS are the networks of solidarity. As Occupy movements started developing all across the US, lessons for these movements were shared on the OWS website as well as multiple sister websites. The "Occupy Together" site has emerged as a repository that connects to other sites and provides news updates about Occupy movements globally. Simultaneously, several Occupy movements started growing globally at various sites, sharing stories and mobilizing support for each other through the cross-posting of messages. In this sense, the new media presence of the OWS movement created an entry point for building and coordinating global solidarity and for bringing forth in unison the voices of resistance across the globe.

Along these lines of global-local linkages, posts on the OWS website are continually written by participants from around the world. Consider for instance the following posting by Aarohini from India:

this is great news. as a sufferer of global financial hegemony in distant India and not being able to do much through organising in our country to counter the evil emanating from Wall Street, I have often wondered what the american public is doing given that it too is suffering tremendously from the greed of the Wall Street financiers. at last

> there is now going to be a massive mobilisation against Wall Street.
> i wish you all the best for your efforts and lets hope that this signals
> the beginning of the end for the kleptocracy that rules the USA and
> with its cronies elsewhere, the whole world. There should be enough
> preparation to tackle the state as it will invariably try to suppress this
> uprising. (http://occupywallst.org/article/who_we_are/)

In this instance, Aarohini commends the positive role of OWS in taking
up the issue of global economic justice right at the heart of perpetuation
of this economic injustice, Wall Street. She points out the difficulties in
organizing against Wall Street in India and therefore commends OWS for
its local resistance at the very site of global capitalist hegemony. She notes
her hope that OWS signals the beginning of the end of kleptocracy in the
US and globally. The OWS call for protests on Wall Street in New York
City is accompanied by calls for and reports of similar protests at various
other globally dispersed local sites:

> S17 occupations of financial districts are also being planned in Mi-
> lan, Madrid, Valencia, London, Lisbon, Athens, San Francisco and
> hopefully many other cities still to be announced. S17 could well be
> the catalyst that ushers in a new global economic order. (http://oc-
> cupywallst.org/archive/Sep-8-2011/page-1/)

In this post by OWS on September 7, 2011, commenters articulated specific strategies of occupation in relationship to what was learned from the
Arab Spring. Here is what Strengthinthenumbers posted:

> I don't know if this has been promoted before, I wrote a standard
> message and sent it to many of my friends on Facebook. One of the
> main reasons the Arab Spring in Egypt was successful was because of
> Facebook. (http://occupywallst.org/article/who_we_are/)

In this instance, the specific approach proposed is modelled after the strategy of using Facebook as an active model of participation and recruitment
in the Arab Spring in Egypt. Even as the Occupy movement developed
through the lessons learned from the Arab Spring to resist the neoliberal
policies in the US and globally, it also dynamically emerged into a site of
solidarity for movements elsewhere in the globe. For instance, in response

to the violence enacted on female protestors on Tahrir Square in Egypt, the OWS movement issued a call for solidarity, holding local protests across the US, marching on the Egyptian consulate, and performing Occupy events in front of Combined Systems International, the supplier of tear gas to the Egyptian military junta, in solidarity with the global call for resistance issued by the activists in Egypt (http://occupywallst.org/article/answering-egypts-call-solidarity/).

The Stories of Global Spaces and Alternative Rationalities

In foregrounding spaces of resistance to the global concentration of power in the hands of financial capital and transnational corporations (TNCs), OWS seeks to foster communicative spaces for the articulations of alternatives to the oppressive structures of neoliberalism that minimize the opportunities for grassroots participation. For instance, OWS calls for a general assembly of all those who have been marginalized, oppressed, and excluded by the current global health, housing, food, employment, and economic policies (see Figure 2.4).

What is foregrounded in this call for the "Health Action Assembly" is the invitation for the marginalized, oppressed, and excluded to find a voice within the discursive space. Disrupting the assumptions regarding what constitutes communication in neoliberal structures of policy making and decision making, the call urges those who have been placed at the margins by the neoliberal system to come out and share their stories of marginalization and articulate their imaginations for solutions of change. At the heart of the Occupy movement is the alternative meta-narrative of communication. Based on the notion that the marginalization of the 99% has been carried out through top-down decisions that have been made by the richest 1%, the alternative narrative of the Occupy movement is based on the articulation of a horizontal movement structure that is leaderless and is based on the principles of cooperation, consensus, mutual respect, and horizontal decision making. In describing the OWS movement, the websites that have emerged articulate the organic, dynamic, leaderless, and horizontal structure of the movement, highlighting the distributed and networked nature of collective organizing. Affinity support groups such

Figure 2.4. Poster issuing the call for the excluded, exploited, and dehumanized to participate (http://occupywallst.org/article/ows-health-action-assembly-tomorrow/).

as those found on occupywallst.org emerge as online and technical support resources for resistance movements across the globe. The depiction of OWS on occupywallst.org, for instance, discusses the empowerment of local people to create change from the bottom up.

Slogans such as "This is what democracy looks like," "Students united shall never be divided," "You can't evict an idea whose time has come," and "Whose street? Our street" offer alternative visions of organizing societies and cultures. The depiction of democracy, by referring to the participation of everyday people, stands in resistance to the political economy of decision making in neoliberal, democratic structures where political processes, structures, and decisions are deeply intertwined with the economic interests of the rich. Similarly, slogans such as "Whose street? Our street" re-occupies the idea of the street as a public site, thus re-narrating the privatization of public spaces to serve corporate interests under neoliberalism. Fighting the corrosive power of global banks and the oppressive practices of the richest 1% offer the foundations for the co-creation of the alternative narratives of solidarity. Specific actions such as "Occupy Walmart" and "Occupy Black Friday" are constituted around offering alternative logics to the broader narratives of consumption that have fed the inequitable structures of neoliberalism. The story of consumption of narratives is resisted with an alternative narrative of a "really, really free market" where goods are given out generously for those that are truly in need. The basic values of selfishness, personal property, and individualized consumption are resisted with alternative narratives of compassion, caring, and cooperation.

Alternative rationalities disrupt taken-for-granted notions about the US democracy within neoliberalism, pointing toward the role of the police and the military in maintaining the interests of the rich and the powerful within the US. Live videos, recordings, audio files, and written texts are utilized in order to bring forth the exercise of police violence on peaceful protestors, thus demonstrating the limits to the language of democracy under neoliberalism and laying bare the nexus of politics and economics in utilizing police force to subvert possibilities of resistance (see, for instance, http://youtu.be/FNsG1szQPqo). Video recordings of police violence and aggression return the gaze of the dominant structures of neoliberal violence by materially documenting the acts of aggression and circulating the images and videos in the public sphere. In response to the acts of police violence, occupiers chant "The whole world is watching" (http://occupywallst.org/article/nypd-swarming-liberty-square-bloody-assault-all-ex/). Posts such as "Police: Whom do you serve?" offer video captures of police attacks on peaceful Occupy protestors, and simultaneously raise questions about the role of the police in serving the interests of powerful

Figure 2.5. Uploaded by "austintool." http://youtu.be/FNsG1szQPqo

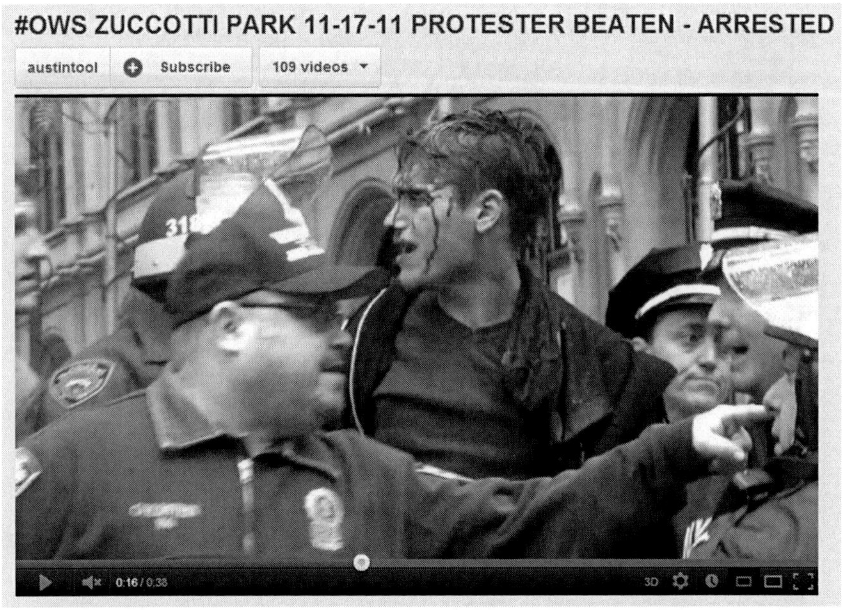
#OWS ZUCCOTTI PARK 11-17-11 PROTESTER BEATEN - ARRESTED
austintool
Subscribe
109 videos
0:16 / 0:38

political and economic actors, simultaneously minimizing the opportunities of resistance (http://occupywallst.org/article/whom-do-you-serve/). Here is an excerpt from the post:

> Such incidents are unfortunately common. Brutal repression has long been a daily reality for people of color, trans and queer people, criminalized drug users, sex workers, and other marginalized communities. But now that the 99% and the Occupy movement are standing up for social and economic justice, we all are subject to those same violent tactics of repression. How can the police protect and serve the public, when they repeatedly assault the public in the interest of the 1%? What exactly are the police defending—our right to free speech and peaceful assembly, or broken financial and government institutions?

In resistance to the police violence on Occupy protests across the US, occupywallst.org posted the following narrative of resistance on December 10, 2011:

Following last week's raid on Justin Herman Plaza, San Francisco police evicted Occupy SF from their last camp, in front of the Federal Reserve, at 4am this morning. 55 people were arrested. Occupy Pittsburgh is also facing an eviction deadline today, continuing an escalating trend of harassment and eviction of nonviolent protesters across the country and the world.

. . . Occupations across the country have found creative ways to persist, resist, and rebuild. We aren't giving up our public spaces. Last we checked, tents still stand in DC, Chicago, Boise, Oklahoma City, Buffalo, Miami, Chapel Hill, Cleveland, Providence, Baltimore, Orlando, Nashville, Pittsburgh, Pensacola, Lexington, Newark, Gainesville, Peoria, Eugene, Rochester, Orlando, Tacoma, Reno, Charlotte, Raleigh, New Haven, Houston, Austin, Tampa, Louisville, and elsewhere. In Anchorage, they even have igloos. On their two month anniversary, Occupy Minnesota will gather at The People's Plaza to reclaim their space and continue the fight for equality and justice.

. . . We are also disrupting business-as-usual from Wall Street to K Street. We have brought the festivity of Broadway into the streets. We mic check corrupt politicians and 1%ers everywhere they go. We have moved homeless families into empty foreclosed homes. We have spread our message by occupying the highway. In DC, Oakland, Santa Cruz, London, and Seattle we have liberated buildings from the banks and greedy corporations and begun to turn them into vibrant community centers.

While maintaining our nonpartisan focus on economic inequality and connecting a diversity of issues that impact the 99%, Occupations have begun to refine and hone our messaging around the big banks, foreclosures, evictions, and housing. Foreclosure auctions have been disrupted in Los Angeles, Atlanta, Bremerton, Reno, and New Orleans. Occupiers foreclosed on bank offices in Philadelphia, Los Angeles, San Francisco, San Jose, Buffalo and elsewhere. Today, a few weeks after Occupiers took over the Washington State Capital, Occupy Providence is marching on their State house to "ask this house for homes!" After the recent Day of Action to Occupy Our Homes, many cities continue to support families, especially in communities of color, as they fight back against unfair evictions. In Atlanta, Cleveland, Oakland, Chicago, Detroit, Philly, Rochester, New York, and Oakland, Occupiers are helping homeless families find shelter and resist eviction.

In solidarity with all oppressed communities, we are actively supporting the many social movements that comprise the global revolution. We have marched on U.S.-companies that supply teargas to the Egyptian government to support our comrades in Tahir Square; with immigrants rights activists against deportation, detention and wage-theft in Birmingham and New York; with seniors to advocate for social services; with students against tuition-hikes, with workers and unions for jobs, better working conditions, and fair wages; and with farmers fighting for food justice. Occupations in solidarity with OWS have arisen in Manila, Auckland, London, Amsterdam, South Africa and beyond. We've marched to draw attention to the connections between the corrupt banking system and issues like the prison industrial complex and climate change . . . (http://occupywallst.org/article/occupy-will-never-die-evict-us-we-multiply/)

Evident in the narrative presented above is the representation of the persistence of the Occupy movement in spite of top-down efforts at thwarting the undertaking through the use of force. The efforts of dominant political structures to evict the movement physically are resisted by the presentation of the Occupy movement as an idea, as a way of thought, and as a principle. The occupiers launched hunger strikes with the goal of liberating outdoor space and securing the right of people to protest (see, for instance, http://occupywallst.org/article/ows-hunger-strike-new-outdoor-occupation/). Similarly, the alternative rationality of OWS draws attention to the ironies in US government responses to the movement locally while rhetorically supporting other movements globally (see, for instance, http://youtu.be/S880UldxB1o). Irony also emerges consistently as a theme through the articulations of the incongruence between the rhetoric of democracy and the actual violence unleashed on peaceful protests. In a protest at Lincoln Center outside the final performance of Satyagraha, an opera on the life of

Gandhi, Occupy protestors drew attention to the hypocrisies in rhetoric that celebrates nonviolent resistance on one hand, and on the other hand, uses violence to silence nonviolent resistance locally. Here is an excerpt from a post on the protest:

> It's also a striking irony that Bloomberg L.P is one of the Lincoln Center's leading corporate sponsors. Mayor Michael Bloomberg has stifled free speech, free press, and freedom of assembly in an aggressive campaign against Occupy Wall Street protestors in New York City that has influenced a crackdown on the protests nationally. The juxtaposition is stark: while Bloomberg funds the representation of Gandhi's pioneering tactics of nonviolent civil disobedience in the Metropolitan Opera House, he simultaneously orders a paramilitary-style raid of the peaceful public occupation of Liberty Park, blacking out the media, while protestors are beaten, tear-gassed, and violently arrested. (http://occupywallst.org/article/occupy-museums-goes-lincoln-center/)

Figure 2.6. Uploaded by "scottmcfann." http://youtu.be/S880UldxB1o

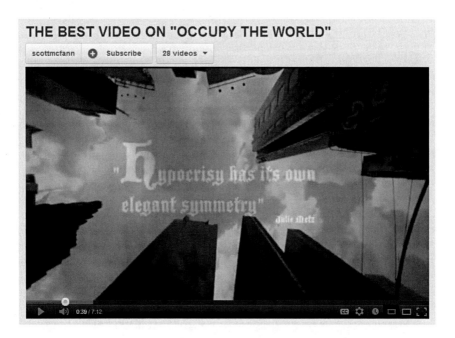

Alternative rationalities articulated through OWS also draw upon solidarity networks to point toward the injustices that are carried out through unfair housing policies. The mortgage-based housing industry that has been at the root of the foreclosures is interrogated through the framing of the issues of housing within the umbrella of the right of human beings to housing. OWS provides links to and organizes in relationship with the O4O movement, issuing calls that then connect with the O4O in seeking to take over foreclosed homes and fighting for the right of community members to their homes. Consider, for instance, the following post of the O4O movement under the title "Last O4O General Meeting of 2011 and Holiday Construction Drive":

> In the five months since our inaugural conference, O4O has blockaded an eviction, shut down a foreclosure auction, and mobilized for a national housing day of action. Our actions have succeed because of the work of our committed volunteers, and the support of so many of you.
>
> Now, as the temperature drops, the urgency of our actions is even greater. O4O is dedicating our energies to moving families off the cold winter streets and into vacant homes. We've identified a suitable home to occupy; we're working a family who is committed to O4O's mission; and we're prepared to defend their new home.
>
> *All we need are tools to make the house a livable home.*
>
> Help us build and occupy a home for the holidays! Our goal is to raise $2,000 by Christmas so we can purchase the construction tools and materials to get the job done. (http://www.o4onyc.org/2011/12/15/last-o4o-general-meeting-of-2011-holiday-construction-drive/)

Similarly, the broader occupying foreclosed homes movement interrogates the assumptions of neoliberalism that have treated home mortgages as commodities to be traded in the market. Instead, the narration of the right to a home as a basic human right re-frames the issue of home ownership into one of social justice. The logics of neoliberalism are resisted through the construction of resistance against the oppressive decisions of banks to foreclose homes, working in conjunction with the judiciary and police. The knowledge structures of neoliberalism are resisted by offering alternative knowledge structures that are rooted in alternative values.

Figure 2.7. General Assembly at Occupy Wall Street.

Alternative mediated sites such as the Global Revolution (http://www.livestream.com/globalrevolution) and WEvolution (http://www.wevolutiontv.org/) serve as the spaces for co-constructing these voices of resistance from the grassroots into global discursive sites. In doing so, the livestreaming of mediated depictions of localized resistance offer alternative narratives to the neoliberal agendas of mainstream media, re-narrating neoliberal agendas by occupying them and offering alternative discursive entry points. On the WEvolution site, for instance, individual stories of Americans disrupt the narratives of neoliberalism by interrogating the assumptions underlying the large-scale inequalities within the US and globally. Occupying, therefore, becomes the framework for offering alternative structures around issues and topics that have traditionally been narrated through the hegemonic interests of mainstream media. Local meanings emerging from the participation of individuals and communities at the local level weave together into alternative global narratives of resistance. Accompanying the livestreaming videos at the Occupy sites are parallel chat windows where community members participate online to discuss their views and ideas, offering another entry point into grassroots narratives. Livestreaming sites such as http://www.livestream.com/occupynyc and http://occupystreams.org/item/occupy-london-stock-exchange are interlinked under the broader umbrella of Occupy Streams at http://oc-cupystreams.org/. Ultimately, these alternative values narrated through the networks of solidarity across the Occupy movements offer the pathways of hope in resisting the global hegemony of neoliberal organizing of the economic sector.

Discussion

In summary, throughout this chapter we paid attention to the various aspects of discourses and discursive processes through which voices of resistance seek to bring about transformations in social, political, and economic structures that perpetuate global inequities under neoliberal hegemony. In order to depict the voices of resistance within the broader backdrop of economic justice, we read the case study of the Occupy Wall Street movement. The singular emphasis on OWS for the purposes of this chapter was meant to throw additional insights into the communicative processes and strategies through which local and global voices of resistance interrogate the assumptions and the hegemonic control of neoliberalism. OWS is an exemplar of a movement that connects local and global voices of resistance in global spheres of solidarity. The resistive voices narrated within the broader framework of the Occupy movements growing globally also point toward the interconnected spheres and issues of resistive politics, connecting several spheres of resistance within the broader umbrella of resistance against neoliberal policies and its hegemonic influence over various aspects of political, economic, social, and cultural life. The theme of neoliberalism and its economic effects emerge as key themes in the Arab Spring, with the protests in Tunisia and Egypt having strong undercurrents of resistance against economic policies that have generated large-scale unemployment and rising food prices.

Furthermore, as the neoliberal agendas are played out in several state responses across the US in passing "right to work" bills, localized forms of resistance, emerging in solidarity with national and global movements of economic justice, raise their voices in solidarity with the voices of workers seeking the legitimacy to organize through unions. The resistance against the "right to work" bill in Indiana is performed in solidary among workers and Occupy protestors (Bhattacharya, 2012). Consider, for instance, the following depiction of solidarity between the union movement and the Occupy movement, depicted in the backdrop of the organizing to "Occupy the Superbowl" in Indiana:

> In the coming days, it will be important to continue to build this fight in the streets. If we are to push the politicians into putting the right-to-work law on an upcoming ballot, then we need collective solidarity actions up and down the state, not just letter writing and call-in campaigns to representatives. Occupy activists in every town need to reach out to their local unions in order to plan and build actions, and unions need to encourage and support the Occupy activists.
>
> The 1 percent builds partnerships with corporations and political thugs to break our movements. As the 99 percent, we need to build our own solidarities. A strong alliance between organized labor and the Occupy movement is needed to stand up to this attack on workers' rights. (Bhattacharya, 2012)

The voices of resistance put forth in the context of the rights of unions are joined in solidarity with the voices of resistance in the Occupy movement. In Wisconsin, large-scale direct action and political resistance emerged in response to Governor Walker's proposal to pass a "budget repair" bill (see, for instance, http://www.huffingtonpost.com/news/wisconsin-protests/). Through direct action, the occupation of the state capitol, processions, protest marches, songs, and slogans, the protestors carry on their voices of resistance against the anti-union agendas of the Walker administration; images of the videos and protests are circulated on YouTube and on protest-mobilization sites on Facebook. Spoof performances, such as a phone call by a journalist to governor Scott Walker pretending to be David Koch, exposes the underlying agendas of neoliberalization carried on by the state; the video spread virally, mobilizing entry points of resistance at several sites across the US. The Wisconsin protests, in their solidarity with the protests in Tunisia and Egypt, also depict the frameworks of solidarity that connect local-global politics. Consider the following excerpt (Shapiro, 2011):

> On Friday, February 11, at the same hour that the world watched the former Egyptian president Hosni Mubarak resign his post, the newly appointed Republican Governor of Wisconsin quietly launched a ferocious attack on public sector unions—and the very notion of organized labor in America.
>
> For nearly fifty years unions have sought to safeguard and advance their rights through a process known as collective bargaining, which is the most powerful tool labor has for peacefully resolving disputes and ensuring workers a voice in negotiations on everything from fair wages to safety conditions and sick leave.
>
> The bill championed by Wisconsin's governor takes dead aim at this process by stripping most state workers of many of their collective bargaining rights. Union leaders have responded uproariously, claiming that the bill effectively guts public unions of their most critical asset in a state that pioneered many of the fundamental fights for worker's rights.

The voices of workers offer the narratives of resistance that challenge the constraining agendas of the policy:

> "We want to say loud and clear: it is not about those concessions," said Mary Bell, president of WEAC. "For my members, it's about retaining a voice in their professions."
>
> … "I think what people need to see in this is that it's not just an attack on public service unions. It's really a concerted attack by powerful interests that really want to see working class people be brought down," said Rick Badger, the executive director of AFSCME's Wisconsin 40 council. "Walker claims there's nothing to bargain with. The message

we need to get out there is that this could not be further from the truth." (Shapiro, 2011)

The depiction of the bill is situated in the backdrop of the wider global protests. The resignation of Hosni Mubarak is juxtaposed in the backdrop of the agendas of the state in minimizing the spaces for state workers to have a voice in discursive spaces. The voices of the union workers and union leaders in the discursive space highlight the attack of liberalization policies on the rights of workers to have a voice and to have a say in the realms of decision making.

As these issue-networks of resistance depict, matters of economic justice are intertwined with the consolidation of power in the hands of TNCs, thus shaping the communicative processes and logics of participation by concentrating political power in the hands of the few. As a result, although this chapter is organized specifically around questions of economic justice, what the narratives point toward are the interconnected spheres of political and economic decision making in agriculture, health, poverty, environment, and development that offer a broader framework of global organizing around neoliberalism. Therefore, as we move through the next chapters, we will specifically refer back to the OWS movement in examining nodes and linkages of global solidarity, especially as these entry points to solidarity offer both historical reference points as well as contemporary entry points for organizing resistance against neoliberalism.

Agriculture: Voices of Resistance

Introduction

In this chapter, we will listen to the voices of resistance that are constituted under the broader area of agriculture and the rights of local communities across the globe to grow food and secure access to it. In the context of agriculture, the tension constituting efforts of social change lies between the liberalization principles of national governments that have sought to turn agricultural lands into the hands of industrial projects, projects of mining, or large-scale agribusiness, and the rights of local communities at the global margins to grow their own food in sustainable and locally meaningful ways. The questions around which local agricultural communities organize relate to the capacities of communities to locally produce food and secure access to basic food resources. The question of local rights of farmers in the global South to grow food in their local communities and make a living on the basis of agriculture is also constituted amidst the inequitable agricultural policies at the global level that favor transnational agribusiness. Voicing the large-scale corporatization of agriculture and the consolidation

Chapter Three

of power in the hands of multinationals, the Gandhian activist Siddharaj Dhadda voices (2010, p. 247):

> the farmer used to preserve his own seeds, and this had been go-
> ing on for centuries. Now half a dozen multinational companies are
> striving to capture the seed markets of the whole world. All the seed
> that the world needs has to be brought from them. They are push-
> ing high-yielding seeds in the market, and government departments
> are helping them. These genetically engineered seeds are so struc-
> tured that seed from their crops would not bear fruit, or only very
> little. The farmer will thus have to buy seeds from corporations ev-
> ery year. The multinationals have patented their seeds and are forc-
> ing the government of India to amend our patent laws so that they
> are favorable to them.

Joining the voices of activists such as Dhadda, in chapter three, we review the processes through which global policies create the margins in the ag-ricultural sector, and the ways in which these global agricultural policies are resisted by farmers in local-global networks of solidarity. An overview of the political economy of food production and food consumption serves as the basis for exploring the (a) inequities in access to agricultural produc-tion and agro-markets in the different sectors of the globe, and (b) food in-securities that are created in the marginalized sectors of the globe through the deployment of neoliberal policies that are supportive of transnational hegemony. This chapter draws from specific case studies that discuss the experiences of marginalized communities in the agricultural sector, and brings forth the voices of farmers and farm workers in the co-construc-tion of the narratives of resistance constituted in the realm of agriculture. Of particular interest in this chapter are the discursive constructions and communicative processes through which voices of resistance articulate alternative frameworks for understanding and practicing agriculture in resistance to the structures of neoliberalism.

Connecting Local Resistance into Global Alliances
Voices of resistance around agriculture point to neoliberal policies globally that are played out in the local politics of agriculture experienced by peas-

ant communities. The voices of resistance of local farmers are articulated in the backdrop of neoliberal policies framed in the form of structural adjustment programs (SAPs) and development projects that are often antithetical to the interests of local farmers. For example, in organizing against the takeover of peasant lands, local and global activists came together in solidarity in Mali to voice a collective entry point to resistance. In a meeting held in Nyeleni on November 19, 2011, the global alliance against land-grabbing articulated the vision of the alliance in the following words:

> We, women and men peasants, pastoralists, indigenous peoples and their allies, who gathered together in Nyeleni from 17-19 November 2011, are determined to defend food sovereignty, the commons and the rights of small scale food providers to natural resources. We supported the Kolongo Appeal from peasant organizations in Mali, who have taken the lead in organising local resistance to the take-over of peasants' lands in Africa. We came to Nyeleni in response to the Dakar Appeal, which calls for a global alliance against land-grabbing. (http://ewwaunel.wordpress.com/2011/11/22/stop-land-grabbing-now/)

What becomes evident in the above voicing of the global alliance is the local-global interconnectedness of the alliance, crafting out a space for a collective voice that connects local issues with global stakeholders. The local organizations of peasant resistance paved the way for bringing together several peasant organizations from across the globe in a collective that offers a cohesive voice of resistance against neoliberal agricultural and development policies, layered on the local politics of resistance in Mali. The local-global linkage is defined on the basis of the articulation of the rights of small-scale local food providers to natural resources. The local resistance of the peasant organizations from Mali provides the impetus for the global network of peasant activists to come together under the framework of the global alliance.

In voicing their resistance, peasant activists in the global alliance question the issue of land rights within a local historical-cultural context that is situated globally:

> In Mali, the Government has committed to give away 800 thousand hectares of land to business investors. These are lands of communi-

ties that have belonged to them for generations, even centuries, while
the Malian State has only existed since the 1960-s. This situation is
mirrored in many other countries where customary rights are not
recognised. Taking away the lands of communities is a violation of
both their customary and historical rights. (http://ewwaunel.word-
press.com/2011/11/22/stop-land-grabbing-now/)

The historical depiction of the rights of peasants in the context of Mali is
utilized as a frame to offer a more global perspective on the non-recog-
nition of customary rights of subaltern communities on their lands. The
local experiences of Mali serve as the foundation for coalition building
that connects similar local experiences in the face of neoliberal policies
promoting land-grabbing. Here, discourse emerges as an entry point to
interrogating the politics of ownership. The right of the nation state to
land (and by extension, the right to give away this land to corporate investors) is contested in the backdrop of the narratives of ownership of land
by local communities that have owned the land through generations. The
interpenetration of the local and the global is furthermore evident in the
discourse as it takes up the language of global human rights to provide a
framework for interrogating the local oppressive practices of nation states:

Secure access to and control over land and natural resources are in-
extricably linked to the enjoyment of the rights enshrined in the Universal Declaration of Human Rights and several regional and international human rights conventions, such as the rights to an adequate
standard of living, housing, food, health, culture, property and participation. We note with grave concern that states are not meeting
their obligations in this regard and putting the interests of business
interests above the rights of peoples. (http://ewwaunel.wordpress.
com/2011/11/22/stop-land-grabbing-now/)

The reforms brought about locally under neoliberal frames of development
are resisted by appealing to a universal declaration of human rights, which
offers a framework for defining the rights of local communities to basic
standards of living, housing, food, culture, property, and participation.
The discourse of rights of the people to basic standards is foregrounded
to interrogate the privileging of the rights of global businesses.

The formation of the global alliance against land-grabbing came about through the *La Vía Campesina* movement, a movement born in 1993 involving farmers' representatives from four continents, which has paved the way for global organizing of farmers built on the leveraging of local organizing capacities at a global level. Involving over 150 local and national organizations from 70 countries in Asia, Africa, Europe, and the Americas, the international movement seeks to defend small-scale sustainable agriculture as a mechanism for promoting social justice and dignity by opposing corporate agriculture and transnational agro-corporations. In the description of the movement, the group's website spells out the local-global linkage in the following excerpt:

> La Vía Campesina is the international movement which brings together millions of peasants, small and medium-size farmers, landless people, women farmers, indigenous people, migrants and agricultural workers from around the world. It defends small-scale sustainable agriculture as a way to promote social justice and dignity. It strongly opposes corporate driven agriculture and transnational companies that are destroying people and nature. (http://viacampesina.org/en/index.php?option=com_content&view=category&layout=blog&id=27&Itemid=44)

By connecting a variety of local-global stakeholder groups, including peasants, farmers, landless people, indigenous communities, and migrants, the movement resists the neoliberal framework that promotes power and control of agriculture in the hands of transnational corporations (TNCs). The power consolidated in the hands of TNCs is resisted through the global networks of small- and medium-scale farmers from across the world. The promotion of global agribusiness under neoliberalism is resisted through these global linkages among farmers, represented through local and national organizations that are linked globally through *La Via Campesina*. Under the title "Globalizing hope, globalizing the struggle," the movement notes its global resistance to neoliberalism:

> La Vía Campesina is built on a strong sense of unity and solidarity between small and medium-scale agricultural producers from the North and South. The main goal of the movement is to realize food

sovereignty and stop the destructive neoliberal process. It is based on the conviction that small farmers, including peasant fisher-folk, pastoralists and indigenous people, who make up almost half the world›s people, are capable of producing food for their communities and feeding the world in a sustainable and healthy way. (http://viacampesina. org/en/index.php?option=com_content&view=category&layout=bl og&id=27&Itemid=44)

The excerpt spells out the linkage between the local and global stakeholders of the movement, pointing out that the global scale of neoliberal reforms needs to be resisted globally as well as locally at the specific sites where oppressions are enacted on farmers at local levels through structural adjustment programs. The foregrounding of the local capacity of farming, peasant, and indigenous communities to produce food is offered as an entry point to resisting the frames of neoliberalism that seek to constitute agriculture under corporate control of TNCs through top-down agendas of change. The local-global linkages of networks of solidarity are evident in the organizing structure of *La Via Campesina*, formed through the participation of farmer organizations at local and national levels. The movement is constituted on the basis of distributions of power into nine regions, with each region being represented by a man and a woman, which make up an International Coordinating Committee. The globally decentralized decision structure is connected through international conferences that emerge as sites of action as well as specific events of resistance. Examples of such events include International Women Day on March 8, International Day of Peasant's Struggle on April 17, and International Struggle Day against the WTO on September 10.

The need for developing and building a local-global linkage is seen as a resistive strategy for disrupting the global hegemony of TNCs that is exercised precisely through their mobility in globally dispersed markets. Therefore, *La Via Campesina* defines mobility in an alternative framework of networks of global solidarity:

We learned that we were not the only ones struggling. Globalization has meant the impoverishment of the majority of communities. All the communities of the world that have been deeply affected, over-

whelmed and crushed by this economic globalization—we are organizing ourselves. In other words, we need to globalize this struggle for
justice, for the survival of community, for the development of communities. We need to globalize this struggle in the poorest of communities everywhere just as the large capitalists have globalized the
economy. (Desmarais, 2007, p. 194)

The identification of a common platform for a global struggle is based on
the realization that the deleterious effects of globalization are faced across
communities all around the globe. That these effects experienced by communities are products of globalization serves as the fulcrum for organizing
global resistance of farmers and farming communities. The globalization of
the economy, therefore, needs to be countered by globalizing the struggles
of the poorest sectors, connecting them into broader networks of resistance. Resistance is also enacted in the linkages crafted out by the voices
of protest in the agro-sector with the voices of protest in other issue-based
contexts, creating collectives of resistance across issue frames.

   One instance of the interconnected linkages of resistance is articulated in the local struggles against neoliberalization of agriculture at the
core site of globalization of agriculture and consolidation of power in the
hands of the agro-industry, US. For instance, in its solidarity with the Occupy movement, the Occupy Monsanto movement in the US provides
a framework for resisting Monsanto in the US, at the very site of global
control that carries out the imperialist expansionist agendas of Monsanto
(http://occupymonsanto.wordpress.com/). The frame of occupation gets
taken up to disrupt the hegemony of Monsanto in the legal system, and to
offer a common framework for solidarity across issues. The Occupy Monsanto movement WordPress site is accompanied by an "Occupy Monsanto"
Facebook site. The website as well as the Facebook site emerge as avenues
for organizing protests and solidarity actions. For instance, the Facebook
site announced the details of the "Farmers vs. Monsanto solidarity rally!"
(https://www.facebook.com/events/157058514407689/):

   On January 31st, family farmers from across the county will take part
   in the first phase of the OSGATA et al. v. Monsanto court case filed to
   protect farmers from genetic trespass by Monsanto's genetically mod-

ified (GMO) seed, which can contaminate organic and non-GMO farmers' crops and open them up to abusive lawsuits.

As a result of aggressive lawsuits against farmers with contaminated crops, Monsanto has created an atmosphere of fear in rural America and driven dozens of farmers into bankruptcy.

But farmers are fighting back!

The Federal District Court judge has agreed to hear oral arguments in this landmark case to decide whether or not this case will move forward.

Occupy Wall Street Food Justice, Occupy Big Food and Food Democracy Now! will assemble in solidarity with farmers on the front lines of the struggle against corporate domination of our food system.

The resistance offered at the legal sites of neoliberalism that have traditionally been utilized to carry out the agendas of TNCs such as Monsanto to harass and abuse farmers through lawsuits disrupts the dominant logics of legal frameworks and institutional structures that are utilized to push Monsanto seeds on farmers and to harass farmers who don't grow Monsanto seeds. In offering a network of linkage with the Occupy movement, the legal action is complemented by direct action on the streets and at public sites, carrying out the discursive frame of occupation of political and juridical sites. The description of the protest and the invitation to participate in it is accompanied by the links to the three organizations, www.fooddemocracynow.org, www.osgata.org, and http://www.pubpat. org/monsanto-seed-patents.htmhttp://www.pubpat.org/monsanto-seed-patents.htmhttp://www.pubpat.org/monsanto-seed-patents.htm. Organic Seed Growers and Trade Association (OSGATA), filed a lawsuit against Monsanto in March 2011 as a pre-emptive strike to prevent Monsanto from its abusive practice of suing farmers and seed growers if their fields were contaminated by Monsanto's Roundup Ready seeds. Over the last several years, Monsanto had developed the practice of trespassing into the fields of farmers who had not purchased the Roundup Ready seeds from

Monsanto to investigate whether the farmers had Monsanto seeds growing on their land. In many instances, seeds blowing in from neighboring fields of farmers growing Monsanto seeds would contaminate the fields of farmers with non-Monsanto seeds; if these contaminations were detected by the Monsanto inspectors going into the fields, the farmer would then be sued by Monsanto and charged fines. The legal structures that provided Monsanto with its basis for harassing farmers are turned into the sites of resistance; the lawsuit frames Monsanto as the violator of the sovereignty of the farms. This point is well elucidated by the following statement by Jim Gerritsen, the President of OSGATA:

> "Today is Independence Day for America. Today we are seeking protection from the Court and putting Monsanto on notice. Monsanto's threats and abuse of family farmers stops here. Monsanto's genetic contamination of organic seed and organic crops ends now. Americans have the right to choice in the marketplace—to decide what kind of food they will feed their families—and we are taking this action on their behalf to protect that right to choose. Organic farmers have the right to raise our organic crops for our families and our customers on our farms without the threat of invasion by Monsanto's genetic contamination and without harassment by a reckless polluter. Beginning today, America asserts her right to justice and pure food." (http://www.osgata.org/judge-sides-with-monsanto-ridicules-farmers-right-to-grow-food-without-fear-contamination-and-economic-harm)

The threat of Monsanto to farmers is framed within a language of colonialism. Therefore, the lawsuit is constituted in a narrative of freedom, foregrounding the freedom of farmers to grow what they would like to grow without the colonial invasion of Monsanto. The seed monoculture of Monsanto is narrated as a form of imperialism, one that denies farmers their basic rights to choice in the marketplace and in determining what kinds of food they would feed their families. The frameworks of justice, access, and right to pure food offer an organizing framework for resisting the imperialism of Monsanto. The Facebook page of the Occupy Monsanto movement offers links to images, videos, and newsfeeds of protests organized across the US and globally against Monsanto. The website as well as the Facebook site also emerge as important resources for sharing information and for planning meetings. The solidarity among the farmers and between the farmers and other activists strengthen the structures of resistance from the grassroots. Similar to voices of resistance expressed in other contexts, networking within local spaces across various issue sites as well as networking across local-global spaces are important elements for building resistance to dominant structures of neoliberalism that shape agricultural policies.

Interrogating Power

The voices of resistance in the realm of agricultural policies interrogate the top-down nature of policy articulations and the ways in which these policy articulations under neoliberal governance have silenced the voices of local communities in the global South. For instance, in interrogating the policies of global land-grabbing that have been fostered by the neoliberal reforms imposed by international financial institutions (IFIs), the global alliance against land-grabbing notes the following:

> Land-grabbing is a global phenomenon led by local, national and transnational elites and investors, and governments with the aim of controlling the world's most precious resources. The global financial, food and climate crises have triggered a rush among investors and wealthy governments to acquire and capture land and natural resources, since these are the only "safe havens" left that guarantee secure financial returns. Pension and other investment funds have become powerful actors in land-grabbing, while wars continue to be waged to seize control over natural wealth. The World Bank and regional development banks are facilitating land grabs by promoting corporate-friendly policies and laws, facilitating capital and guarantees for corporate investors, and fostering an extractive, destructive economic development model. The World Bank, IFAD, FAO and UNCTAD have proposed seven principles that legitimise farmland grabbing by corporate and state investors. Led by some of the world's largest transnational corporations, the Alliance for a Green Revolution in Africa (AGRA) aims to transform smallhold agriculture into

industrial agriculture and integrate smallhold farmers to global value chains, greatly increasing their vulnerability to land-loss. (http://ew-waunel.wordpress.com/2011/11/22/stop-land-grabbing-now/)

The issue of land-grabbing here is framed in the context of discourses of power that point toward the roles of local, national, and transnational elites in garnering control over precious resources. In setting up a framework for understanding the politics behind land-grabbing, the excerpt points toward the role of the dominant power structures in justifying land-grabbing under the guise of economic development. Essential to the interrogation of neoliberalism in the global organizing of agriculture is the interruption of the logics of global economic development that facilitate corporate-friendly laws and policies, and simultaneously displace the global poor from their everyday forms of livelihood.

Pointing toward the role of global structures such as the World Band, IFAD, FAO, and UNCTAD, the articulations of resistance narrate the agendas of profiteering that are played out in desires to gain control over natural resources. The underlying motives of profiteering that are couched as development become the sites of resistance. The Alliance for a Green Revolution in Africa (AGRA) is brought up as an example of the interplay of power and control in the hands of TNCs that seek to transform local small-scale agriculture into industrial agriculture, thus increasing the vulnerability to land loss among smallhold farmers. At the heart of interrogating the paradoxes of neoliberalism is the questioning of the dominant logics that are circulated in neoliberal structures. For example, the language of agricultural prosperity that is taken for granted in the label of "green revolution" is disrupted by pointing out the vulnerability of smallhold farmers to land loss and, therefore, to food insecurity brought about by industrial agriculture that is propagated under the framework of the "green revolution."

In other instances, attention is drawn to the configurations of power to articulate the strategies for local-global solidarity. Pointing out the effectiveness of neoliberal reforms to carry out specific local-global linkages in generating profit, the following excerpt draws attention to the global positions of power that serve the agendas of the elite globally:

Land-grabbing goes beyond traditional North-South imperialist structures; transnational corporations can be based in the United States, Europe, Chile, Mexico, Brazil, Russia, India, China, South Africa, Thailand, Malaysia and South Korea, among others. It is also a crisis in both rural and urban areas. Land is being grabbed in Asia, Africa, the Americas and Europe for industrial agriculture, mining, infrastructure projects, dams, tourism, conservation parks, industry, urban expansion and military purposes. Indigenous peoples and ethnic minorities are being expelled from their territories by armed forces, increasing their vulnerability and in some cases even leading to slavery. Market based, false solutions to climate change are creating more ways to alienate local communities from their lands and natural resources. (http://www.grain.org/media/BAhbBlsHOgZmSSI6MjAx-MS8xMS8yNS8wNF8xMV8xMl80MjhfTnllbGVuaV9kZWNsYXJh-dGlvbl9GaW5hbC5wZGYGOgZFVA/Nyeleni%20declaration%20Final.pdf)

The global nature of land-grabbing remains the key point of resistance for the alliance. Therefore, whereas on one hand, the politics of the alliance operates on the basis of resisting the locally based land-grabbing in different regions of the globe for the purposes of industrial agriculture, mining, dams, tourism, and other projects that are carried out in the name of development, on the other hand, these local politics of land-grabbing are connected together in their broader underlying theme of serving the interests of transnational corporations. The emphasis of the alliance is in addressing the issue of land-grabbing at global sites because of the cross-border nature of this issue. In resisting the power of neoliberal structures of decision making, attention is drawn to the oppressive effects that are produced through projects that are carried out under the framework of development, dictated by the agendas of dominant political, economic, and social actors who shape the contours of global development.

Similar dynamic of interrogating the global power consolidated in the hands of TNCs is noted in the local activist networks of farmers that organize to question the policies and programs that are passed in order to facilitate the global exploitation of agricultural resources by transnational agribusiness. For instance, in India, based on the experiences with

Bt Cotton that is connected with the epidemic growth of farmer suicides, toxic effects, and effects on grazing animals as well as on local ecosystems, farmers across India mobilized to resist the country-wide adoption of Bt Brinjal (Institute of Science in Society, 2008). In the wake of the large-scale negative effects of Bt Cotton adoption in the country, farmers' unions, development scientists, environmental groups, consumer organizations, and other civil society groups came together to form the "Coalition for GM-[genetically modified] Free India." Including over 15 civil society groups represented from across the country, the coalition offered an umbrella for organizing against the large-scale adoption of GM crops. Its organizing activities are constituted under the tasks of generating awareness about GM crops; engaging media, civil society groups, and the general public; and creating an open climate for informed debate about GM crops. The coalition is constituted around the key goal of democratizing the framework of science and technology in the country, attending to the farmers' knowledge and local forms of livelihood and sustainability. Through local-level *jaiv panchayats* (living democracies), farmers organized into localized collectives that created discursive spaces for organizing protests against Bt Brinjal (Shiva, 2010).

On January 30 2010, more than one *lakh* Indians across the country went on a fast to hit home the message that the independence won by the country through the freedom struggle and through the leadership of nonviolent (*ahimsa*) noncooperation (*satyagraha*) offered by Gandhi cannot be lost to the imperialist practices of global agribusiness in the form of GM crops such as Bt Brinjal. Drawing on Gandhi's concept of *Hind Swaraj* (sovereign self-rule), the protestors noted that the agricultural economy cannot be turned into a source of exploitation in the hands of TNCs. With the slogan "Remember the Mahatma, Stop Bt Brinjal and Protect India's Seed & Food Sovereignty," the organizing of voices from the subaltern sectors across India was centered on fostering an alternative rationality for organizing agriculture that predominantly drew upon local, culturally based systems of knowledge that privileged traditional forms of knowledge. Consider, for instance, the following depiction of the fasts as forms of nonviolent resistance (http://aidindia.org/main/content/view/1207/442/):

Today we remember Gandhiji and Hind Swaraj. We fast in order to prevent profit-hungry corporations from taking control of our food and seed system through GM crops like Bt brinjal. We fast to stop insertion of genetic material that makes the brinjal plant produce Bt toxin. We fast because the Committee that cleared Bt Brinjal violated both science and ethics—based on inadequate tests, overlooking the deaths of animals grazing in Bt cotton fields and data that indicated harmful effects of Bt food on liver, kidney and other functions, and based on the votes of members closely associated with the industry. We fast because if we believe in the true meaning of Swaraj, we should not let India's farmers lose control over their seed and agriculture, and its citizens lose control over the food they eat. We fast because GM technology comes with many risks to environment and bio-safety, and it is fundamentally unwise to introduce this into the food chain of billions of people and into the environment on a large scale.

The meaning of *"Hind Swaraj,"* a concept that Gandhi drew upon from Indian philosophy to define the framework of the movement for independence, provides a space for organizing against the imperialism of GM technology. The concept of *"Hind Swaraj"* is presented as an entry point to draw attention to the violation of the self-sufficiency of India's farmers by turning the seeds and agricultural production processes over to the TNCs. The control of their agricultural processes and seeds is defined as the right of farmers, tied in to their sovereignty. Furthermore, process-based violations such as the violation of basic principles of science and ethics by the International Coordinating Committee that cleared Bt Brinjal also emerged as a key point of resistance. The tests that were done in constituting the approval process were noted as being inadequate, with omissions of key facts such as the effects of Bt on liver, kidney, and other functions as well as the deaths of animals grazing in Bt cotton fields. In essence, the questioning of the knowledge processes that constitute the logics of the dominant structures of science and technology in the agricultural sector are brought under scrutiny. The hidden logics of power underlying specific material outcomes are rendered visible and their taken-for-granted notions are interrogated.

The framework of an alternative rationality is further rendered visible in the following excerpt on the reason behind the National Day of Fast (http://aidindia.org/main/content/view/1177/442/):

In 2009 October, our country saw the making of the "worst disaster that can destroy India's self-reliance and sovereignty for ever". India's regulatory body for genetic engineering, the Genetic Engineering Approval Committee (GEAC) hastily approved Bt Brinjal for commercial cultivation—the first time in the world that such a poisonous genetically modified (GM) vegetable was given clearance by the unnatural insertion of foreign genes into brinjal.

100 years ago, in 1909 the Father of our Nation, Mohandas K. Gandhi produced his central work, his key-text, his seed-text, the *Hind Swaraj*. This small 91-page booklet today reads almost like a prophecy that predicted all of 21st century India's ailments. Gandhi clearly realised that the British continued in India as colonial masters not because of their superior military strength, etc., but simply because we Indians kept them "for our base self-interest." He concisely remarked: "We like their commerce; they please us by their subtle and get what they want from us . . ."

Gandhi was clear that "India is being ground down, not under the English heel, but under that of modern civilisation [that makes bodily welfare the object of life]." He repeated, in different ways how "(modern) civilisation's deadly effect is that people come under its scorching flames believing it to be all good."

The approval for commercial sale of Bt Brinjal seeds developed by Mahyco, the Indian partner of Monsanto, the world's most powerful and sinister agribusiness company, tragically reflects how they achieved this goal. The fact that the approval of a crop that will threaten life itself, cripple the environment and economy and decimate India's national biodiversity of brinjals was not based on hard, scientific grounds or vision for sustainable development for all vindicates this.

> In prophetic terms that warn us of the perils of globalisation the Ma-
> hatma said: "They wish to convert the whole world into a vast market
> for their goods ... They will leave no stone unturned to reach the goal."

The wisdom of Gandhi draws upon the historical-cultural narrative of
resistance against imperialism to hit home the point that the large-scale
adoption of GM crops amounts to a new form of imperialism. The logic
of the market is brought to interrogation, pointing out how that very same
logic of colonization remained at the root of British imperialism in India.
The reliance of the Indians on the British through the market retained the
hold of the British on their Indian colony; the analogy to Monsanto similarly notes how the market becomes the entry point to the colonial interests of the TNC. In offering a critique of the modernist desire to expand
and control, the narrative draws attention to the ways in which power is
exercised by the dominant capitalist structures under global politics to
turn the globe into a vast market for the capitalist goods. The call further
goes on to note the following:

> India is the Centre of Origin and Centre of Diversity of brinjal. We
> have around 2,500 varieties of brinjal in this country. In every state it
> is cultivated and consumed by all classes of people. Many of these va-
> rieties are pest tolerant, some are nutritious, medicinal and culturally
> important. One example is Udupi Gulla from Udupi region of Karna-
> taka. Farmers of this region cultivate Udupi Gulla as an offering to the
> temple there. This diversity is what keeps India going amidst various
> global crises. Once this is destroyed, then there is no India and there
> is no freedom. This is what Mahatma Gandhi always tried to tell us.
> But the scientists who are working on Bt Brinjal are least bothered
> about this. The sad part is that our policy makers tend to show more
> faith and commitment to these scientists and seed companies than to
> us. They have forgotten how we were enslaved by a British company
> for centuries and how we regained our freedom from them.

> Freedom is more important than *"Pranavayu"* for all of us. Hence we
> must protect our seeds and soil from multinational corporations and
> national seed companies who have joined hands with the MNCs. We
> have to reclaim our seeds from the hands of these seed companies. We

have to protect our seeds and ensure seed sovereignty and thus, food sovereignty. The seeds should be in our farmers' hands. The safety and sovereignty of food in this nation can no more be compromised. (http://aidindia.org/main/content/view/1177/442/)

The power of TNCs and national elite to shape the fabric of agricultural decision making is resisted through the privileging of local agricultural practices and local forms of knowledge production that foreground the sustainable nature of local technologies. The question of sustainability is brought to the forefront within the context of democratizing science and technology, creating greater access to forms of decision making by indigenous knowledge systems that have traditionally been undermined. The democratizing principles that seek to make discursive spaces of science and technology accessible offer resistance to the traditional forms of scientific and technological decision making that have consolidated power in the hands of TNCs.

For instance, the "Monsanto Quit India" day has been organized as a site of protesting the power of the global agribusiness in shaping the landscape of farming in India, corporatizing farming and simultaneously undermining the food sovereignty and food security of local grassroots farmers (Kuruganthi, 2011). On the day, protests are organized by farming communities all across India as well as in the state capital. On August 9, 2011, farmers voiced their resistance to the commoditization and privatization of agriculture, narrating their demands to the government in the form of four key claims: (a) no collaborative research projects and partnerships with Monsanto or other similar food corporations in state-owned agricultural universities or within the national agricultural research system; (b) no commissioned projects under GM crop trials in these institutions and no GM crop trials; (c) no public-private partnerships in the name of improving food productivity, particularly for crops such as rice and maize that pose serious questions of food security and food sovereignty; and (d) setting up sustainable grassroots systems of seed self-reliance that respect the local knowledge and technology of farmers, and simultaneously seek to support institution building and infrastructure around self-reliant systems. On one hand, the narrative of the "Monsanto Quit India" movement draws its cultural relevance from the "Quit India" movement that defines a key element of Indian history in the fight against agro-capitalism; on the other hand, it draws upon a historically rich cultural narrative to resist specific policies in oppressive structures of globalization that undermine the food sovereignty and security of local farmers.

Pada yatras (which are long marches that are intended to generate awareness and solidarity) and *palli sabhas* (which are local grassroots meetings with local communities) were organized across rural communities to engage in dialogue about GM seeds, the short-yield claims about these seeds made by the corporations, and the realities of the experiences in growing GM seeds. The *pada yatras* and *palli sabhas* are specifically organized in rural farming communities that have particularly been the targets of private-public partnerships in promoting the large-scale acceptance of hybrid maize, with the goal of generating local awareness about the false claims made by agro-corporations. *Beej yatra* (referring to the Gandhian salt march that played a key role in the Indian freedom struggle) is utilized as a frame to refer to a seed march seeking to take back the local ownership of the seed. In other forms of organizing protests, the narrative of the freedom struggle of India that was based on offering the alternative logic of local sovereignty to resist imperialism is brought back to resist agro-imperialism. The power of agro-imperialism is challenged through the invoking of locally empowering narratives of self-reliance, self-sustainability, and sovereignty. Several localized *Gram Sabhas* (local meetings) organized across the country emerged as sites of mobilizing, fostering alternative information systems that interrogated the top-down propositions of the state and the agro-industry. The power of the agribusiness sector played out through its economic strengths and public relations strategies is resisted through locally situated cultural rituals such as farmer meetings, dialogues, and marches that draw upon contextually embedded narratives of social change to give meaning to the localized forms of protest.

Meetings where farmers from the Vidarbha region narrated their experiences with the Bt cotton seeds and shared stories of the ongoing farmer suicides offered grassroots resistance to the GM rhetoric of yield and productivity that is utilized to persuade farmers to grow GM seeds.

Protest sit-ins at state agricultural offices were accompanied by demands that the government not allow GM crop trials. Local demands at various protest sites spread across India that were spearheaded by local farmers' organizations drew attention to India's Biological Diversity Act and the violation of farmers' intellectual property rights over seed resources by the processes through which the Bt Brinjal varieties were created. Farmers' groups went on one-day symbolic fast to deconstruct the hegemony of government-Monsanto partnerships and research on GM crops such as Golden Rice, hybrid rice, hybrid maize, and so forth. Memoranda submitted to ministers across separate states, meetings with ministers and policy makers were utilized as strategies for resisting the role of the state and state-based knowledge production systems such as state universities and research centers to carry out GM crop trials. Protestors utilized symbolic resources such as processions and posters, as well as innovative performances such as death processions of Monsanto and burial of Monsanto.

One of the core actors in India that plays a leadership role in the localized processes of organizing farmers and creating spaces for listening to the voices of farmers is the Alliance for Sustainable and Holistic Agriculture (ASHA), a loose network of over 400 diverse grassroots organizations across India that came together to organize a *Kisan Swaraj Yatra* (Farmer Sovereignty March) in 2010, organized with the agendas of drawing attention to the adverse effects of neoliberalism on local agricultural practices, the marginalization of farmers, and the exploitation of local farming communities in the hands of agricultural TNCs. The *Yatra* was seen by the participating actors as an avenue for raising awareness and generating greater participation in farmer-driven, pro-farmer, locally sustainable agriculture that served the needs of rural areas and simultaneously served the resource needs of urban communities, drawing upon and foregrounding the age-old practices of traditional agricultural knowledge. At the heart of the farmer sovereignty march was the idea of developing a discursive site of knowledge production that fostered alternative agricultural practices based on the principles of food sovereignty and sustainability, and the simultaneous articulation of the need to resist neo-colonial structures of knowledge production that pushed TNC-based agriculture through public relations practices, propaganda, and through the deployment of university-based research systems that facilitate the neocolonial expansion of industrialized agriculture. The national-level outreach and mobilization efforts of ASHA resulted in the articulation of the *Kisan Swaraj Neeti* (Farmer Sovereignty Policy) that is based on the four pillars of (a) fostering sustainable agriculture: (b) ensuring dignified livelihoods for all farmers, including the small and marginal farmers; (c) protecting the rights and control of farmers to seeds, land, and water; and (d) ensuring adequate and safe food for all. The *Yatra*, beginning symbolically from Gandhi's Sabarmati Ashram in Gujarat on October 2 (the day of Gandhi Jayanti), passes through 20 states to end up at Rajghat in New Delhi. The symbolic opening of the *Yatra* as the Sabarmati Ashram marks the framing of the *Yatra* as an effort at establishing sovereignty. Here is the announcement of the *Yatra*, along with the call to sign online petitions to the prime minister (http://www.kisanswaraj.in/kisan-swaraj-yatra/):

> The Kisan Swaraj Yatra is a nation-wide mobilization drawing fresh attention to the continuing agricultural crisis in India, and calling for a comprehensive new path for Indian agriculture—that will provide livelihood and food security for small farmers, keep our soils alive, and our food and water poison-free. The bus-Yatra will start at the Sabarmati Gandhi Ashram on Oct 2nd, and pass through 20 states to reach Rajghat, New Delhi on Dec 11th.
>
> Tell the Indian government to stop anti-farmer pro-corporatist policies, ensure dignified livelihoods for farming community, and promote sustainable agriculture. Send this petition to Smt.Sonia Gandhi, chairperson of UPA.

The continuing agricultural crisis in India is framed within the structural configurations of neoliberal agricultural reforms that have opened up Indian agricultural markets to TNCs and have simultaneously undermined the local productive capacities of farmers. In this backdrop, the *Kisan Swaraj Yatra* serves as a call for an alternative paradigm that is rooted in self-sufficiency. Images of the *Yatra* carried out all across India are shared on Flickr. Fostering a discursive site for the enunciation of an alternative framework of agriculture, the *Kisan Swaraj Neeti* is available for download on ASHA's website (http://www.kisanswaraj.in/wp-content/uploads/kisan-swaraj-neeti-dec.20111.pdf):

> The Kisan Swaraj Yatra, in its long journey through scores of villages, towns and cities of India, found that farmers are indeed struggling to have a viable livelihood and dignified living through farming and to hold on to their resources. We found that the ecological crisis in our agriculture is real and the damage is being experienced tangibly, whether it is related to land or water or seed. We also found that seed sovereignty is no longer an ideological or theoretical concept—choices related to Seed are indeed narrowing down for farmers, with seed monopolies of big corporations growing; issues around good quality, affordable, locally suitable diverse seeds in an accountable system throw up the need to look into seed self-reliance urgently.

The conceptual basis of the *Kisan Swaraj Neeti* is based on the real observations of the participants in the *Yatra* during their visits across agricultural sectors of India, noting the pauperization of farmers, the struggles faced by farmers in living a dignified life, and the narrowing down of seed choices for farmers, with the increasing dependence on agribusiness monopolies in India that seek to take over the seed market. Seed self-reliance is offered as an alternative to the imperialistic transnational seed monopolies and serves as the organizing point for the resistance.

Similarly, the localized context of struggles over intellectual property rights defines another domain of organizing in the agricultural sector, with efforts of local agricultural communities being directed at challenging the co-optive structures of knowledge profiteering at the global centers that seek to make profit by turning indigenous knowledge and resources into commodities to be sold in the market (Dutta, 2011; Dutta & Pal, 2011). Framed within the ambits of transnational capital, the agreement on Trade-Related Aspects of Intellectual Property Rights (TRIPS) serves neoliberal agendas by facilitating the hijacking of indigenous resources that belong to the subaltern sectors of the globe by TNCs. TRIPS and the processes written into it enable biopiracy by inherently privileging technologies of manipulation that modify local knowledge and resources and by simultaneously not recognizing already existing indigenous knowledge as "prior art" so as to prevent the exploitation of such indigenous knowledge by TNCs (Dutta, 2011). TRIPS does not take into account the local ownership of genetic resources and the knowledge that is inherently tied to the uses of these resources in the subaltern sectors, and instead privileges technologies developed by TNCs, often through the stealing of subaltern knowledge and resources (DeSouza, Basu, Kim, Basnyat, & Dutta, 2008). As DeSouza and colleagues (2008) point out, biopiracy is constituted and facilitated by TRIPS through its policies favoring transnational exploitation of subaltern resources, and operates with relative ease on the basis of differentials in power and control in the neo-colonial spaces of global organizing of knowledge and value, with the TNCs in the developed countries staking their claims on indigenous germplasm that were developed originally by farmers in the subaltern sectors of the globe. The ability of TNCs to stake claim on indigenous resources, steal indigenous knowledge, and patent such knowledge for purposes of profiteering is intrinsically tied to the privileges of communicative access that TNCs enjoy to political structures of decision making and public policy where ownership laws get arbitrated. With the case of Basmati, DeSouza and colleagues (2008) demonstrate that the foregrounding of indigenous knowledge claims and the indigenous ownership of knowledge create a resistive framework for disrupting the exploitation of the subaltern sectors, and for resisting new forms of colonialism under neoliberalism that are carried out through the robbery of local knowledge. Knowledge here is critical in carrying out the neocolonial interests of global corporations, and knowledge, therefore, is also the site of resistance. It is by participating in the sites where ownership of knowledge are debated that indigenous communities secure alternative claims of ownership that resist the expansive efforts of TNCs in the agro-sector.

In seeking to change the structures of knowledge claim then, access needs to be fostered to the processes through which the rules of these structures are determined. Because the claims of knowledge are often made at global structures of arbitration that are far removed from the indigenous sites at which these knowledge claims might have been generated, and because the languages, technologies, and tools utilized in these forms of knowledge claims are often impermeable to indigenous communities whose knowledge is being stolen or exploited, essential to efforts of resistance is the formation of local-global networks of opposition that create awareness at the grassroots level in indigenous communities as well as develop information infrastructures about the processes of participation at global sites of arbitration. For indigenous communities to talk back to the structures of domination that enable the stealing of their resources through the discursive processes and practices of domination, local-national-global solidarity networks offer crucial entry points. The political networking between subaltern and dominant institutional structures is crucial to the success of social change processes. For instance, the implementation of the Biodiversity Law in Costa Rica that protects the rights of indigenous people and peasant communities to the local knowledge that has been developed in these communities was made possible through the development of linkages with resource-based allies at national and global levels (Miller, 2006). These resource-based allies understood the technologies and techniques of neoliberal structures of policy making, and therefore, they collaborated with the subaltern sectors to build alternative infrastructures of resistance that ruptured the manipulative agendas of neoliberal expansion through the stealing of indigenous knowledge. In the face of the neoliberal agendas that seek to bring knowledge under the control of TNCs, the Biodiversity Law in Costa Rica sought to protect the intellectual property rights of the rural communities for the uses they have developed for the natural resources and the plants and animals they have bred (Miller, 2006). In the processes of organizing that sought to create spaces for discussion, debate, and creation of regulatory policies that would check the growing threats of bioprospecting, a coalition of legislators, lawyers, and scientists came together to work with the National Indigenous and Peasant Boards. Essential to the development of the policy was the collaboration between the indigenous communities and the experts who had access to the structures of neoliberalism and understood the language utilized by these structures. The experts in the coalition were organized under the broader framework of the Office for Mesoamerica of the World Conservation Union (IUCN) and the National University of Costa Rica. The power of neoliberalism that enables the expansion of TNCs was precisely resisted through localized power embodied in the solidarity between indigenous and peasant communities and expert communities, thus building regulatory structures in the form of the Biodiversity Law that put limits on biopiracy and bioprospecting.

The National Indigenous and Peasant Boards received outside support in the form of legislative involvement from among the political elite, legal and scientific advising from IUCN, and the support of the National University of Costa Rica through the Cambios Program that sought to train indigenous and peasant leaders about the biodiversity law debates and how to protect their indigenous forms of knowledge. Furthermore, international linkages were fairly crucial in developing the support structures for the processes of social change among the indigenous and peasant communities, with resources, information, training, and funding resulting from transnational linkages. Similarly, in the Philippines, the networks of scientific communities have worked collaboratively with legal experts and civil society to develop the biodiversity laws (Swiderska Dano, & Dubois, 2001). Similarly in India, NGOs working with indigenous communities have been actively involved in attempting to shape the biodiversity policies (Anuradha, Taneja, & Kothari, 2001). In the US, the filing of a lawsuit by OSGATA against Monsanto for contaminating the fields of farmers is another instance where resistance is articulated through the returning of the gaze. Consider the following excerpt from the voice of Bryce Stephens of Jennings, Kansas (http://archive.constantcontact.com/fs074/1104248386985/archive/1109089069494.html):

> I don't think it's fair that Monsanto should be able to sue my family for patent infringement because their transgenic seed trespasses onto our farm and contaminates and ruins our organic crop. We have had to abandon raising corn because we are afraid Monsanto wouldn't control their genetic pollution and then they would come after us for patent infringement. It's not right.

Here Monsanto is understood as the pollutant, the one that contaminates the fields of farmers and then carries out the oppression of farmers through charges of patent infringement. The co-optation of the very sites of meaning where oppression emerges becomes the strategy for resisting neoliberalism. The power of Monsanto to criminalize local farmers in the US is disrupted by turning the criminal frame onto Monsanto, defining its practices as trespassing and pollution of genetic resources.

Interrogating the Dominant Frames of Neoliberalism

Central to the voices of resistance in the backdrop of agriculture is the interrogation of the dominant frameworks of neoliberal agriculture that are circulated in the mainstream. For instance, in questioning the land-grabbing that has become widespread under neoliberal governance, the global alliance against land-grabbing directly questions the negative impacts of the economic models of neoliberalism and capitalism.

> The fight against land-grabbing is a fight against capitalism, neo-liberalism and a destructive economic model. Through testimonies from our sisters and brothers in Burkina Faso, Columbia, Guatemala, Democratic Republic of Congo, France, Ghana, Guinea Bissau, Honduras, India, Indonesia, Mali, Mauritania, Mozambique, Nepal, Niger, Senegal, South Africa, Thailand and Uganda, we learned how land-grabbing threatens small scale, family based farming, nature, the environment and food sovereignty. Land grabbing displaces and dislocates communities, destroys local economies and the social-cultural fabric, and jeopardizes the identities of communities, be they farmers, pastoralists, fisherfolk, workers, dalits or indigenous peoples. Those who stand up for their rights are beaten, jailed and killed. There is no way to mitigate the impacts of this economic model and the power structures that promote it. Our lands are not for sale or lease. (http://ewwaunel.wordpress.com/2011/11/22/stop-land-grabbing-now/)

What is evident in this framework is the framing of the goals of the alliance in terms of a fight against the destructive economic model of neoliberalism. The framing of the economic model of neoliberalism as destructive directly challenges the dominant frame imposed by IFIs that articulate neoliberalism in terms of development and economic growth.

Along similar lines, the *La Vía Campesina* movement challenges the dominant frames of neoliberalism that seek to globally corporatize agriculture and turn food production systems over to the hands of agribusinesses. It does so by offering an alternative framework of food sovereignty that highlights the local growing capacities of farmers. Here is an excerpt from the movement website under the title of "Defending Food Sovereignty":

> Vía Campesina launched the idea of "Food Sovereignty" at the World Food Summit in 1996. This idea has now grown into a global people›s movement carried by a large diversity of social sectors such as the urban poor, environmental and consumer groups, women associations, fisher-folks, pastoralists and many others. It is also recognized by several institutions and governments.
>
> Food sovereignty is the right of peoples to healthy and culturally appropriate food produced through sustainable methods and their right to define their own food and agriculture systems. It develops a model of small scale sustainable production benefiting communities and their environment. It puts the aspirations, needs and livelihoods of those who produce, distribute and consume food at the heart of food systems and policies rather than the demands of markets and corporations.
>
> Food sovereignty prioritizes local food production and consumption. It gives a country the right to protect its local producers from cheap imports and to control production. It ensures that the rights to use and manage lands, territories, water, seeds, livestock and biodiversity are in the hands of those who produce food and not of the corporate sector. Therefore the implementation of genuine agrarian reform is one of the top priorities of the farmer›s movement. (http://viacampesina.org/en/index.php?option=com_content&view=category&layout=blog&id=27&Itemid=44)

Food sovereignty now appears as one of the most powerful responses to the current food, poverty, and climate crises. In viewing food sovereignty as an alternative framework, the movement seeks to return the decision-making capacity regarding agricultural policies and practices in the hands of local agricultural communities.

The hegemony of TNCs to define, control, and manipulate food systems to serve their markets is contradicted by the definitions of agriculture in terms of sustainability, local meaningfulness, cultural appropriateness, and the rights of farmers. The conceptualization of food sovereignty as the broader discursive structure for understanding and approaching global agriculture resists the framework of market-based agricultural policies that turn agricultural systems into the hands of corporations. The right of local communities to produce, consume, and distribute their own food challenges the neoliberalization of agriculture, thus offering an entry point into the emphasis of the movement on agrarian reforms. As an alternative to market-based corporatized agriculture, *La Vía Campesina* offers the alternative model of peasant agriculture in a document titled "Sustainable Peasant and Family Farm Agriculture Can Feed the World":

> The contemporary food crisis is not really a crisis of our ability to produce. It is more due to factors like the food speculation and hoarding that transnational food corporations and investment funds engage in, the global injustices that mean some eat too much while many others don't have money to buy adequate food, and/or lack land on which to grow it, and misguided policies like the promotion agrofuels that devote farm land to feeding cars instead of feeding people. However, we cannot deny that our collective ability to grow enough food—including, crucially, how we grow it—is an important piece in the jigsaw puzzle of ending hunger. It is here where the corporate agribusiness model of large-scale industrial monocultures is failing us, and where peasant-based sustainable farming systems based on agroecology and Food Sovereignty offer so much hope. (http://viacampesina. org/downloads/pdf/en/paper6-EN-FINAL.pdf)

The food crisis and hunger are framed in terms of the control of food production and distribution systems, configured within structures of inequality. The promotion of agrofuels is offered as an example of misguided policies that serve neoliberal markets and simultaneously undermine the food security of communities. Peasant-based sustainable farming systems are offered as alternatives to agribusiness-based monoculture models of farming. The key tenets of peasant farming are the following agroecological principles: (a) enhance biomass recycling, optimize the availability of nutrients and balance their flow; (b) secure favorable plant growth conditions through enhancement of soil biotic activity and the management of organic matter and ground cover; (c) minimize loss of air, water, and solar energy through increased soil cover; (d) species and genetic diversification of the agroecosystem; and (e) enhance biological synergies among agrobiodiversity processes. The document spells out the basis of peasant farming in the following terms:

> The application of these principles in the complex and diverse realities of peasant agriculture requires the active appropriation of farming systems by peasants ourselves, using our local knowledge, ingenuity, and ability to innovate.

> We are talking about relatively small farms managed by peasant families and communities. Small farms permit the development of functional biodiversity with diversified production and the integration of crops, trees and livestock. In this type of agriculture, there is less or no need for external inputs, as everything can be produced on the farm itself. (http://viacampesina.org/downloads/pdf/en/paper6-EN-FINAL.pdf)

The dominant framework of neoliberal development in the agricultural sector that seeks to privatize agriculture in the hands of TNCs is resisted through the articulation of an alternative framework of peasant agriculture that foregrounds local knowledge, local participatory processes, and the capacity of local farmers to grow food to address local and global food needs. The sustainability of local agriculture where everything can be produced on the farm itself is contrasted with the external, input-heavy, dominant model of agriculture under neoliberal restructuring of agriculture globally. This juxtaposition becomes further evident in the following comparison:

> Despite the fact that agribusiness controls the majority of arable land and especially of good quality land–in almost every country in the world, it is due largely to peasants and family farmers that we have the food that is available today. In country after country, small farm-

ers control less than half of the farm land, yet produce the majority of the food that is consumed. (http://viacampesina.org/downloads/pdf/en/paper6-EN-FINAL.pdf)

The irony of the neoliberal logic serves as the foundation for the articulation of alternatives. The observation that in spite of the global control of arable land in the hands of global agribusiness, most of the food production in countries is done by small farmers at the local level, which offers openings for the articulation of peasant farming as an alternative to neoliberal structuring of agriculture. This contrast between neoliberal agriculture and peasant-based organizing of agriculture is evident in the following excerpt under the following subtitle "To Feed Future Populations, We Must Nurture the Land":

> Peasants feed people today, but how will we feed people tomorrow? If we follow the path of "business as usual," we will find even more land in the hands of the agribusiness that are failing to feed people well today, and that are destroying the productive capacity of the land for future generations. Corporations move their production around the world through global outsourcing, and they have no attachment to any given place. Rather they extract the most they can as fast as they can, in the search for quick profits, and abandon a given area once production passes its peak and begins to drop through soil degradation. They move on, outsource from somewhere else, and leave devastated agroecosystems and local economies in their wake.
>
> Peasant and small farm families, on the other hand, are rooted in the place where they and their ancestors have farmed for generations, and where their children and grandchildren will farm in the future. This gives them reasons to nurture the productive capacity of the land and surrounding environment. It is precisely in peasant and family agriculture where we see both traditional sustainable farming practices and the rapidly growing field of agroecology. (http://viacampesina.org/downloads/pdf/en/paper6-EN-FINAL.pdf)

The principles of corporate agriculture that focus on generating profits are contrasted with the principles of peasant agriculture that focus on sustainability and nurturing of land in order to pass along the land resources through generations. The rationale underlying the alternative logic of peasant agriculture is offered in resistance to the profit-driven principles of global agribusiness that is focused on global outsourcing with the goals of generating maximum output and profit. The short-term nature of profit-driven agribusiness that focuses on immediate productivity and yield is critiqued for its unsustainability, pointing out that the agribusiness moves out of the area once the production passes its peak, thus causing devastating effects on ecosystems. The local system of peasant agriculture in contrast is driven by principles of nurturing the productive capacity of the land, constituted within local relationships.

The interrogation of the dominant framework of neoliberalism also is continuously articulated across several local sites. Navdanya, an organization of farmers led by the feminist ecologist Vandana Shiva, resists the global framework of neoliberalism by interrogating the assumptions in trade-related intellectual property rights. Navdanya was started as a program of the Research Foundation for Science, Technology, and Ecology (RFSTE) in the form of a participatory research initiative to provide support and direction to environmental activism through support for local farmers. One of the successful campaigns organized by Navdanya was its campaign against the patenting of the properties of neem. The intellectual ownership of the fungicidal properties of neem was interrogated by the neem campaign by framing it as biopiracy, as the stealing of biological resources. Consider the excerpt below from Navdanya's description of the campaign for protecting the rights of indigenous communities to neem, a tree with medicinal properties:

> The new IPR laws embodied in the TRIPs agreement of WTO have unleashed an epidemic of the piracy of nature's creativity and millennia of indigenous innovation. RFSTE/ Navdanya started the campaign against biopiracy with the Neem Campaign in 1994 and mobilized 1,00,000 signatures against neem patents and filed a legal opposition against the USDA and WR Grace patent on the fungicidal properties of neem (no. 436257 B1) in the European Patent Office (EPO) at Munich, Germany.

Along with RFSTE, the International Federation of Organic Agriculture Movements (IFOAM) of Germany and Ms. Magda Alvoet,
former Green Member of the European Parliament were party to the
challenge. The patent on Neem was revoked in May 2000 and it was
reconfirmed on 8th March 2005 when the EPO revoked in entirety
the controversial patent, and adjudged that there was "no inventive
step" involved in the fungicide patent, thus confirming the "prior art"
of the use of Neem. (http://www.navdanya.org/campaigns/biopiracy)

The new intellectual property rights (IPRs) laws embodied in the TRIPS
agreement of the World Trade Organization are presented as an epidemic.
Trade-related intellectual property rights are framed in a narrative of piracy of nature's creativity and indigenous innovation. By framing intellectual property rights that are articulated in the dominant constructions
of TRIPS as protective of property as piracy, the neem campaign returns
the gaze of the dominant structures of neoliberalism and the assumptions
that underlie these structures. Furthermore, through the discursive move
of defining the use of neem as prior art, the campaign successfully worked
through local-global solidarity networks to interrogate the patenting of the
fungicidal properties of neem by the US-based corporation W. R. Grace.
The dominant frame of intellectual ownership crafted by a powerful pharmaceutical TNC was resisted through the articulation of an oppositional
frame that constructed the patenting of the fungicidal properties of neem
as stealing. This act of re-framing then was central to the challenge offered
by RFSTE to W. R. Grace within the legal structures of the EPO. Worth
noting in this instance is the co-optive potential of grassroots resistance
in challenging the exploitative practices of TNCs facilitated by neoliberal structures by circulating oppositional meaning frames within those
structures. The terrains of intellectual property and definitions of property
ownership are turned around in order to challenge the patenting of neem.

Similarly, in describing the processes involved in the development of
Costa Rica's Biodiversity Law, Silvia Rodriguez, chair of the Board of Di-
rectors of Genetic Resources Action International (http://www.grain.org/)
and one of the key participants in the drafting of the law, notes the resistance to neoliberal definition of intellectual property as individual owner-

ship by foregrounding the logics of indigenous communities (http://www.
inmotionmagazine.com/global/sr1.html#Anchor-Costa-3800):

> Speaking now in relation to intellectual property rights (IPRs), we
> could see that indigenous peoples don't want intellectual property
> rights on products they are selling. They believe that is not the way
> to really protect their resources.
>
> On the other hand, in the enterprises world, in the pharmaceutical
> companies world, and so on, they want IPRs as a mechanism, they say,
> to distribute benefits because without IPRs they won't have income to
> distribute to the people. But if you look at history, IPRs are a very new
> condition and you don't need to have them to commercialize these
> resources. Especially since communities think that in doing so, in
> granting intellectual property rights, the real control of the resource
> flies away from the communities and flies away from the country.
>
> And not only are communities the losers with IPRs. We have found
> that the idea of national sovereignty goes away when you lose that
> control, because the different companies, or whoever is accessing
> your resources, take control of it and in exchange they just give very
> little money.
>
> And it is not only a thing of money to pay for the samples taken. It is
> also that in the samples, adhered to those, is indigenous knowledge.

The very question of ownership that is tied to the depiction of intellectual property is interrogated in the knowledge articulations of indigenous
communities. The framing of knowledge within the structures of ownership is interrogated through the foregrounding of indigenous rationalities of ownership that predate intellectual property laws. The discourse of
resistance interrupts the basic framework of ownership by depicting how
intellectual property laws become mechanisms for stealing the resources
from communities and for undermining the sovereignty of communities
and nation states. Also worth noting are the notions of indigenous knowledge that are intrinsically tied to the samples, and as a result, the resistive
framing of bioprospecting as the stealing of indigenous knowledge.

. . . when you have indigenous knowledge. Indigenous people are not only giving you the material resource but also their knowledge. That knowledge is different from the knowledge that it is used in the so-called scientific world where it can be individually appropriated. Traditional knowledge grows out of sharing because if one person makes a step in the knowledge of a plant or whatever, to test its advantages he/she uses the trial and error system that can go over through generations, and little by little knowledge continues growing without being attributed to one single.

If isolated indigenous persons or even communities fall in the temptation to see this knowledge as individual property, that would kill their culture which is much more communally oriented and has its basis in sharing. They have an axiom that says "knowledge grows by sharing". IPRs are the contrary. With IPR's you just say that for 20 years nobody can use your innovation unless they pay for it. (http://www.inmotionmagazine.com/global/sr1.html#Anchor-Costa-3800)

The processes through which indigenous knowledge is produced are fundamentally different from the processes of knowledge production as defined under the parameters of modernist science and embodied in patents and concepts of IPRs. Whereas tradition knowledge grows through sharing and through the building of the knowledge through various iterations that are passed down through generations, continually being open to changes and modifications through collective processes of participation, knowledge in modernist science as embodied in IPRs is founded on the principles of individual ownership and through the demarcation of terms of use through models of economic exchange. IPRs, founded on the concept of private property and individualized notions of knowledge production, therefore, are mechanisms for erasing the local cultures of indigenous communities, and for erasing the fundamental knowledge systems of indigenous cultures through the top-down imposition of neocolonial configurations that privilege private property and establish mechanisms of valuing knowledge based on the privileging of private property. The interrogation of the fundamental notion of private property becomes the basis for putting forth the logic of community ownership of knowledge and genetic resources:

we call bio-prospecting biopiracy. And it's not only a matter of legality, it's also a matter of the taking of some of the last resources that communities have. And those resources have to do with health and food.

These big pharmaceutical companies, these big seed companies, are taking away the information of those resources. With the advance of biotechnology what they want is either a gene or the chemical information. And then, they start competing with the community.

In Costa Rica, the Biodiversity Law gives space to the communities to draft their own intellectual community rights. They don't call it property rights because they associate property with individual possessions. They call it intellectual community rights. They say we can share all that we have. We can share all that we own. We can sell certain resources, but we cannot grant intellectual property rights. (http://www.inmotionmagazine.com/global/sr1.html#Anchor-Costa-3800)

Resistance to neoliberalism is offered through the definition of rights in terms of community ownership. Rather than defining knowledge as an individual possession, knowledge is defined as a resource for sharing. The contestation of the logics of neoliberalism is carried out through several strategies of resistance that draw upon the interfaces between local systems of knowledge and global sites of knowledge circulation that carry out the top-down agendas of neoliberalism.

Strategies of Resistance

Essential to the global movements of resistance in the agricultural sector is the strategic utilization of resources in order to impact global policies and simultaneously impact local-level policies that influence the lives of farmers and the rural poor. For instance, the voices of resistance in the global alliance against land-grabbing point to the importance of creating pressure points by collaborating with international organizations and institutional structures. Also evident is the articulation of a framework of rights in order to frame the agenda of global resistance against land-grabbing. The broader framework of rights offers the rubric of meanings through which the narratives of resistance are constructed in global alliances of interconnected networks (http://ewwaunel.wordpress.com/2011/11/22/stop-land-grabbing-now/):

> Recalling the Dakar Appeal, we reiterate our commitment to resist land-grabbing by all means possible, to support all those who fight land-grabs, and to put pressure on national governments and international institutions to fulfill their obligations to defend and uphold the rights of peoples. Specifically, we commit to: *organise rural and urban communities against land-grabs in every form; strengthen the capacities of our communities and movements to reclaim and defend our rights, lands and resources; win and secure the rights of women in our communities to land and natural resources; create public awareness about how land grabbing is creating crises for all society; build alliances across different sectors, constituencies, regions, and mobilise our societies to stop land-grabbing; strengthen our movements to achieve and promote food sovereignty and genuine agrarian reform*

What is evident in the excerpt above is the local aspect of resistance in organizing for social change. Let's consider the specific sets of actions that are put forth by the global alliance against land-grabbing. Promoting food sovereignty and accomplishing genuine agrarian reform are two key objectives of the alliance, built through the partnerships. Specific actions outlined by the alliance as strategies of resistance include the following (collected verbatim from the Declaration at http://ewwaunel.wordpress.com/2011/11/22/stop-land-grabbing-now/):

- Report back to our communities the deliberations and commitments of this Conference.

- Institutionalise April 17 as the day of global mobilisation against land-grabbing; also identify additional appropriate dates that can be used for such mobilisations to defend land and the commons.

One of the key elements in the strategizing of resistance is the emphasis on carrying the messages back to the communities that are represented by the participants. Whereas on one hand, the alliance serves as a global platform for various representatives to come together and speak in a col-

lective voice, on the other hand, the participation of the representatives at
the alliance is also tied to their role in reporting back to their local communities, in taking back the lessons from the deliberations and commitments
of the conference to the localized sites of resistance. The physical meeting space at a global site becomes an organizing opportunity for deciding
on the strategy to mark April 17 as the global day of mobilization against
land-grabbing. The decision made at the global meeting then becomes an
entry point for action at local community levels.

Yet another strategy for political organizing is the development of specific arguments that disrupt the logics of neoliberalism. Essential, then, to
the building of arguments is the development of information infrastructures and information resources that offer entry points for engaging in key
debates, offering alternative arguments, and exposing the hypocrisies and
paradoxes that are embedded within neoliberal logics. Describing the active role of agricultural communities in India in voicing alternative rationalities of organizing agriculture, Shiva (2008, p. 279) offers the example
of the *Beeja Satyagraha* (also known as seed *satyahgraha*):

> According to Gandhi, no tyranny can enslave a people who consider
> it immoral to obey laws that are unjust. As he stated in *Hind Swaraj:*
> "As long as the superstition that people should obey unjust laws ex-
> ists, so long will slavery exist. And a passive resister alone can remove
> such a superstition."
>
> *Satyagraha* is the key to self-rule, or *swaraj*. The phrase that echoed
> most during India's freedom movement was "*Swaraj hamara janma-
> sidh adhikar hai*" ("self-rule is our birthright"). For self-rule did not
> imply governance by a centralized state but by decentralized com-
> munities . . .
>
> At a massive rally in Delhi in March 1993, a charter of farmers' right
> was developed. One of the rights is local sovereignty. Local resources
> have to be managed on the principles of local sovereignty, wherein
> the natural resources of the village belong to that village. A farmer's
> right to produce, exchange, modify, and sell seed is also an expres-
> sion of *swaraj*. Farmers' movements in India have declared they will

violate the GATT treaty, if it is implemented, since it violates their birthright. The positive assertion of local control over local resources has emerged as the *Jaiv Panchayat* (Living Democracy) Movement.

The depiction offered by Shiva of the concepts of *swaraj, satyagraha,* and *Jaiv Panchayat* create alternative rationalities for understanding the relationship of local communities with agriculture and agricultural resources, returning the scope of decision making into the hands of local communities, and drawing from cultural logics of agriculture that privilege the notion of sovereignty as birthright. As opposed to the neoliberal reforms being carried out across India that impose top-down privatization, industrialization and mining projects on communities without consulting them, and simultaneously shift the onus of responsibility at community and individual levels through programs of entrepreneurship, the alternative cultural logic that draws from the historical-political contexts of the freedom struggle articulates self-rule as a birthright and privileges the local decision-making capacity and sovereignty of a community in determining how best to allocate and utilize resources. The creation of an alternative narrative of relationship with seeds, food, and agriculture lies at the heart of the *Bija Vidyapeeth* (seed university) formed by Navdanya. The *vidyapeeth* offers education and training in community-based sustainable agricultural principles that draw upon local knowledge, and seeks to foster the principles of democracy, sustainability, participation, nonviolence, and self-sufficiency (Navdanya, 2009). The development of knowledge-based infrastructures for articulating and disseminating alternative ontologies and epistemologies lies at the heart of the *Bija Vidyapeeth*. This emphasis on building arguments is critical to organizing for social change. Consider, for instance, the following strategies that tie into the functions of information gathering in order to put forth effective arguments in policy platforms, public opinions platforms, as well as at juridical sites:

- Develop our political arguments to expose and discredit the economic model that spurs land-grabbing, and the various actors and initiatives that promote and legitimise it.

- Build our own databases about land-grabbing by documenting cases, and gathering the needed information and evidence about processes, actors, impacts, etc.

- Ensure that communities have the information they need about laws, rights, companies, contracts, etc., so that they can resist more effectively the business investors and governments who try to take their lands and natural resources.

- Set up early warning systems to alert communities to risks and threats.

- Establish a Peoples' Observatory on land-grabbing to facilitate and centralise data gathering, communications, planning actions, advocacy, research and analysis, etc.

- Strengthen our communities through political and technical training, and restore our pride in being food producers and providers.

- Secure land and resource rights for women by conscientising our communities and movements, targeted re-distribution of land for women, and other actions make laws and policies responsive to the particular needs of women. (http://ewwaunel.wordpress.com/2011/11/22/stop-land-grabbing-now/)

The organizing of change is built upon the concerted effort by the activist alliance to put together political arguments that expose the hypocrisies of land-grabbing that are framed under the language of development. Also critical to the efforts of resistance is the concerted attention paid to the actors, programs, and policies that promote land-grabbing. The gathering of evidence and information about specific cases of land-grabbing then becomes a key strategy for building a database about this subject. The information put together in the database serves as a key mechanism of resistance by attending to the evidence base that is needed regarding actors, impacts, and processes. Information emerges as a key strategy of resistance, and information about laws, rights, contracts, and companies are put together in order to build a global database of evidence that can be used in efforts of organizing against neoliberal policies that facilitate land-grabbing. Simultaneously, early warning systems and peoples' observatory provide mechanisms for monitoring. Local information capacity is strengthened through training programs. Gender-based conscientising offers a framework for organizing to make communities more aware of the rights of women to their land, and specifically targeting land redistribution programs. Therefore, information also lies at the heart of localized forms of gender-based, consciousness-raising efforts.

The information gathering, dissemination, and monitoring functions strengthen the strategies of resistance. These strategies of resistance that are focused on building information capacities are accompanied by communicative efforts that emphasize alliance-building. Alliance-building is the emphasis on fostering local-global relationships among key stakeholders to foster the politics of resistance within local and national structures, as well as exert influence through global structures (Dutta, 2011; Smith, 2004; Sperling, Ferree, & Risman, 2001):

- Build strong organisational networks and alliances at various levels–local, regional and international–building on the Dakar Appeal and with small-scale food producers/providers at the centre of these alliances.

- Build alliances with members of pension schemes in order to prevent pension fund managers from investing in projects that result in land grabbing. (http://ewwaunel.wordpress.com/2011/11/22/stop-land-grabbing-now/)

The building of alliances then plays out at several levels and across various social, political, and economic stakeholders. Building these alliances at local and global levels, simultaneously fostering awareness and relationships with various stakeholder groups such as members of pension schemes, creates entry points of resistance against land-grabbing.

Yet another strategy of organizing for resistance is focused on holding local political structures and leadership accountable. Building information capacity and awareness about rules becomes a key resource in holding the local leaders be accountable to the rights of local communities:

- Make our leaders abide by the rules set by our communities and compel them to be accountable to us, and our communities and organisations.

- Develop our own systems of legal aid and liaise with legal and human rights experts.

- Condemn all forms of violence and criminalisation of our struggles and our mobilizations in defense of our rights.

- Work for the immediate release of all those jailed as a result of their struggles for their lands and territories, and urgently develop campaigns of solidarity with all those facing conflicts. (http://ewwaunel.wordpress.com/2011/11/22/stop-land-grabbing-now/)

Developing legal infrastructures and capacities are essential to social change efforts that seek to disrupt the large-scale land-grabbing that is carried out globally to feed the expansionist agendas of TNCs. Developing localized legal infrastructures is critical to the struggles for defending the land rights of subaltern communities across the globe. It is also through the legal structures that systems of monitoring are established, accompanied by participation in systems of social change that challenge neoliberal reforms of land-grab that are carried out in the name of development. Access to legal structures also becomes critical in the fight for social justice, as points of solidarity for local protestors who are jailed, and to develop adequate tools to fight within the legal systems. Global solidarity of legal knowledge creates the expertise base for fighting cases in courts.

The building of alliances with legal infrastructures is accompanied by the building of relationships with media institutions and infrastructures:

- Build strategic alliances with press and media, so that they report accurately our messages and realities; counter the prejudices spread by the mainstream media about the land struggles in Zimbabwe.

- Develop and use local media to organise members of our and other communities, and share with them information about landgrabbing.

- Take our messages and demands to parliaments, governments and international institutions. (http://ewwaunel.wordpress. com/2011/11/22/stop-land-grabbing-now/)

The targeting of the media with specific campaign messages and the building of strategic alliances with the media is accompanied by various forms of performances and direct action at local, national, and international sites that disrupt the taken-for-granted notions of neoliberalism that inhabit these sites:

- Identify and target local, national and international spaces for actions, mobilizations and building broad-based societal resistance to land-grabbing.

- Plan actions that target corporations, (including financial corporations), the World Bank and other multilateral development banks that benefit from, drive and promote land and natural resource grabs.

- Expand and strengthen our actions to achieve and promote food sovereignty and agrarian reform.

- Support peoples' enclosures of their resources through land occupations, occupations of the offices of corporate investors, protests and other actions to reclaim their commons. (http://ewwaunel. wordpress.com/2011/11/22/stop-land-grabbing-now/)

Ultimately, the language of individualized rights that permeate global structures of neoliberal governance are co-opted within the framework of resistance to depict the violations of human rights that are carried out through land-grabs:

- Demands that our governments fulfill their human rights obligations, immediately stop land and natural resource transfers to business investors, cancel contracts already made, and protect rural and urban communities from ongoing and future land-grabs. (http://ewwaunel.wordpress.com/2011/11/22/stop-land-grabbing-now/)

The voices of resistance in the global alliance against land-grabbing out-line a series of strategies that simultaneously utilize the structures that are opened up through neoliberal governance to turn the logics of these structures on their head. The very language of neoliberalism, therefore, also becomes a tool for contesting the incongruences, paradoxes, and hy-pocrisies in neoliberal reforms.

Consider once again the organizing against Bt Brinjal that took place from 2008 to 2010, resulting in the landmark ruling that resulted in the ban on Bt Brinjal. In the call for the National Day of Fast on January 30, 2010, the "Save Brinjal" campaign drew upon the history of nonviolent resistance in India based on the Gandhian principles of *Hind Swaraj* (self-rule) and *satyagraha* (noncooperation). Here is an excerpt from the call that reflects this strategy of drawing upon culturally-based narratives to point toward specific structural inequities, to educate communities about the importance of resistance, and to mobilize concerted efforts of resis-tance (http://aidindia.org/main/content/view/1177/442/):

> many seed companies (national and multinational) along with ICAR institutions are going ahead with another kind of agriculture develop-ment which will take away any kind of self reliance left with the farm-ers. Genetic Engineering of seeds of different crops in the country is part of this faulty approach. The first seed of this kind was approved in the country in 2002 despite stiff opposition from farmers, social activists and many experts. This was Bt Cotton. In just seven years' time, the country has reached a stage where our cotton is owned by Monsanto, who by just franchising one gene—the Bt Gene—into all the Indian hybrids and varieties have subversively taken total control of the Cotton production in India.

> Cotton was at one time a political tool used by Mahatma Gandhi to fight with the British. But what has happened to that tool? It has gone into the hands of Monsanto- a sinister American MNC who wants to control the entire food in the world through genetic engineering of seeds and take control through patenting of such seeds.

> Now Monsanto-Mahyco and many Indian companies as well, fran-chised by them, are genetically engineering the Bt gene into brinjal,

rice, tomato and almost all other food crops. If Bt Brinjal is approved, then in another 2-3 years' time our brinjal seeds will also be in the hands of Monsanto. Eventually rice, tomato, cabbage, bhindi, . . . every seed will be lost to such multi-national corporates and we will have to stand in front of them with a begging bowl. They will dictate what we should grow and what we should eat. Our children will be at their mercy.

The voices of resistance presented here use the strategy of juxtaposition to draw out the imperialism that is embodied in the neoliberal principles of agricultural liberalization that opens up the local agriculture in farming communities to TNCs with their technologies of genetic engineering and patenting of seeds. The references to genetic engineering as tools of colonization draw out the eventual effects of such colonization that create food dependence and turn local communities into beggars that are dependent on the TNCs. The local ownership of agricultural communities of agricultural decisions are turned into imperial administrations of agriculture controlled by TNCs that dictate what the farmers should grow and what communities should eat. *Swaraj* becomes the basis for noncooperation (*satyagraha*), where locally based self-sustained agriculture disrupts the dependency-based colonial framework of GM seeds. The loss of local culture and local systems of production is narrated as the fundamental loss under colonialism, thus effectively erasing indigenous knowledge and simultaneously expanding the imperial control of TNCs through the expansion of markets and the fostering of dependency. The specific example of cotton is utilized to document how cotton served as a political tool in the independence movement in the fight against the British and now has been turned into a tool in the hands of Monsanto, which has taken over the production of cotton across India by franchising the Bt gene into all the Indian varieties and hybrids. The depiction of the reasons for the National Day of Fast then wraps up with the following call to action:

Towards achieving this, let us come together on January 30th, collectively remember Mahatma Gandhi, pray for his soul, understand what he told the nation during the freedom struggle and after independence, appreciate our diversity, culture and environment. Let us observe a one-day fast, to cleanse ourselves of wrong thoughts and doings, in order to begin a struggle to liberate our country and our soul from the profit-greedy corporations and their ways.

Remember, 'We are what we eat'. Let us resolve to keep our food free from genetic contamination. Let us take a pledge together to make this a reality. Let us observe this year's Martyrs' Day with a one-day fast and join thousands around the country doing so. (http://aidindia.org/main/content/view/1177/442/)

The remembering of Mahatma Gandhi, a symbolic icon of resistance, serves as the call for observing the one-day fast for cleansing and for participating in a struggle to liberate the country from the profit-centric agendas of transnational capitalism. Freedom and independence, along with preservation of cultural diversity and the environment, are positioned as resistive frames to neoliberal reforms of the agriculture sector that would turn the control of agriculture into the hands of transnational monopolies dictated by their narrowly constrained greed. The profit-oriented "greed" of corporatization is resisted by the spiritual and cultural values of freedom and diversity of local cultures. The observance of the day as a day to pledge to protect the freedom of the food system from genetic contamination seeks to mobilize participation in nationally in the politics of change, thus offering a counter-narrative to neoliberalism.

Conclusion

Through the various cases that we have explored in this chapter, we learn about the possibilities of social change in the domain of agriculture. These examples, drawing from specific localized struggles, also demonstrate the ways in which these struggles connect with each other, sharing resources, lessons, and strategies. Carrying the messages of social change across various global spaces, they offer a unified framework for mobilizing against the transnational mobility of global capitalism. The solidarity networks at the grassroots dispersed globally through webs of support find entry points into resisting global agribusiness at transnational sites. Ruptures are articulated not only at local and national sites, but also at global sites, thus bringing momentum to the processes of social change. These global processes of social change express the agency of local communities. They also foreground the voices from the global South that render impure the conceptual categories of the global North (Dutta & Pal, 2010, 2011), and through this rendering impure of discursive spaces and processes in the dominant structures of neoliberal hegemony, they put forth alternative rationalities for organizing the agricultural sector. Local cosmologies from the global South emerge into the discursive sites of knowledge production as legitimate sources of knowledge, redefining in the process the ways in which the agricultural sector is organized around neoliberalism. Alternative frameworks emerging from activist networks in the global North join in with the global sites of resistance against neoliberalization of agriculture. Organizations such as Food First in the US carry on the theme of democratizing food systems and creating discursive sites for the participation of local communities in realms of decision making. Consider for instance the depiction of Food First:

> Called one of the country's "most established food think tanks" by the New York Times, the Institute for Food and Development Policy, also known as Food First, is a "people's think-and-do tank." Our mission is to end the injustices that cause hunger, poverty and environmental degradation throughout the world. We believe a world free of hunger is possible if farmers and communities take back control of the food systems presently dominated by transnational agri-foods industries. We carry out research, analysis, advocacy and education with communities and social movements for informed citizen engagement with the institutions and policies that control production, distribution and access to food. Our work both informs and amplifies the voices of social movements fighting for food justice and food sovereignty. We are committed to dismantling racism in the food system and believe in people's right to healthy and culturally appropriate food produced through ecologically sound and sustainable methods, and their right to define their own food and agriculture systems— at home and abroad. (http://www.foodfirst.org/en/about/programs)

Essential to the organizing framework of Food First is the narrating of an alternative logic that challenges the dominant organizing discourses of agriculture in the US. Food justice and food sovereignty are defined in terms of the local rights of people to grow healthy and culturally appropriate food in sustainable ways and to have a say on how the agricultural system is organized. Concepts of food democracy, participation of farmers in agricultural systems and systems of decision making, and building local agricultural food systems emerge as the key strategies that are used by Food First; synergies across themes emerge in the narratives of Food First located in the global North and other organizations such as Navdanya *and La Vía Campesina* from the global South.

Pointing to the oppressive forces of neoliberalism that constrain the capacity of local farmers to grow food that they want to grow, the voices of resistance from the South and North draw attention to the hypocrisies of neoliberalism that deploy the narratives of freedom and liberty to rob local communities across the globe of their fundamental freedom and liberty to grow and eat food. Yet another key point articulated throughout the chapter is the interpenetration of the North and the South. The transnational flows of power have consolidated power in the hands of global elite dispersed across geographic spaces and have simultaneously created pockets of impoverishment and inaccess within the very sites of global capitalism in the North. In connecting voices across spaces, opportunities of global resistance are envisioned. Alternative forms of knowledge that interrogate the processes through which knowledge is produced, the methods of knowledge production, the evaluation of knowledge claims, the ownership of knowledge, and the attaching of value to specific forms of knowledge. In summary, the many voices we engage with in this chapter offer us openings for interrogating the structures within which we come to understand our relationship with agriculture and more specifically with food.

Resistance, Social Change, and the Environment

Introduction

Environment is one of the key sites of global social change, with environmental activist groups seeking to draw attention to the effects of specific practices on the environment, and subsequently seeking to impact policy making and practices that shape the environment (Castells, 1996, 1997, 1998; della Porta & Diani, 2006; Rootes, 2004; Sklair, 1995). In our discussion of the politics of resistance in this chapter, we will specifically focus on global social change movements that emphasize local participation and processes of change, situated amidst the broader backdrop of claims making and presentation of arguments that seek to impact the realms of policy making and programming. Drawing upon examples from the global North as well as from the South, we will particularly examine the ways in which social change processes are constituted amidst policy frameworks and articulations across various global spaces. We will attend to the discursive processes and strategies through which resistive efforts of transforming environmental policies are played out. The voices of resistance weaved together in this

Chapter
Four

137

chapter create opportunities for engaging in dialogue with alternative rationalities for organizing the environment and, more importantly, the knowledge about the environment.

In the voices of resistance to the global politics of the environment, entry points are created for disrupting the monolithic narratives of global policies that are dictated by the powerful influences of transnational corporations (TNCs) in shaping global, national, and local environmental policies (Pezzullo, 2004; Rootes, 2002a, 2002b; Sklair, 1995; Smith, 2002; Yearley, 1994, 1996; Yearley & Forrester, 2000). The nexus between transnational hegemonic actors and the realms of policy making is foregrounded into the discursive space, being interrogated for the linkages of influence that ultimately shape global environmental policies, what gets configured within these policies, what gets discussed, and ultimately the kinds of policies that get made. Therefore, central to the voices of resistance is the re-articulation of the realms of decision making, redrawing out the processes of decision making, suggesting alternatives, and seeking to bring the realms of decision making more into the hands of communities at the global peripheries (Dutta, 2011). Therefore, the very sites of policy making and arbitration by global hegemonic actors also emerge as the sites of protest. Consider, for instance, the voices of youth activists presented in a YouTube video organized at the very site of the United Nations Climate Meeting COP17 summit:

> Youth trying to buy back. Youth organizing bake sale at the Durban Climate Conference COP 17 to buy back the influence of everyday publics with policy makers. Noting the inequities in decision making structures and structures of policymaking in the context of environmental policies, the youth participants in the resistance movement note that the policy makers only seem to understand the language of money and therefore the bake sale is an attempt to engage policy makers in their own language. (http://youtu.be/-KhTSqsb6-w)

The notion of inequities in communicative opportunities for participation becomes the center point of various movements of resistance against neoliberalism (Dutta, 2011; Dutta & Pal, 2010). That the paradox of the neoliberal principles of freedom and liberty are essentially caught amidst

Figure 4.1. Uploaded by *"developmentreality." http://youtu.be/-KhTSqsb6-w*

the consolidation of communicative resources in the hands of powerful global actors motivates processes of organizing. That policy makers understand only the language of money becomes the entry point for organizing resistance, with the bake sale serving as a symbol of resistance by raising money to engage policy makers. Voices of resistance are narrated in the backdrop of the material constraints on the symbolic and discursive sites of articulation. The three examples of social change that we will specifically look at are 350.org, the campaign against the Keystone XL Tar Sands pipeline, and the International Campaign for Justice in Bhopal (ICJB).

350.org

The 350 movement is built on the framework of organizing to set the safe upper limit for CO_2 in the atmosphere to 350 parts per million (ppm), based on the findings of climate science. The website of the 350 movement opens up with the slogan: "We're building a global movement to solve the climate crisis." This teaser that articulates the voice of the movement within the broader context of social change then opens up into the question "Why?" which is hyperlinked into a new page that explains the broader goals and objectives of the movement. Offering the rationale for the movement, the website notes the following key points (http://www.350.org/):

1. The climate crisis is the biggest problem facing the world. Unchecked climate change means more natural disasters, more outbreaks of disease, more food shortages, and more sea level rise.

2. We need to make large-scale changes. The climate crisis is so big that we can't solve it with small, personal actions alone. We need to think bigger and bolder.

3. Large-scale change means changing policy. We need laws that rewire the way the world produces and consumes energy so that clean power is cheap, dirty power is expensive, and people everywhere can live sustainable lives.

4. Getting strong climate policy won't be easy. It means fighting the wealthiest and most powerful group on the planet: the fossil fuel industry.

5. We can win with a people-powered movement. We'll never have as much money as the fossil fuel industry, so we need to overpower them with our numbers and our determination instead. From the Civil Rights movement to women's suffrage, social movements have changed the course of history—so we're building a movement of people to solve the biggest problem in the world.

The problem of climate change is connected to other global problems such as food shortages, disease outbreaks, and rising sea levels. In connecting climate change to the broader domains of other global problems, the movement highlights the large-scale scope of change that needs to be made, and drives home the relevance of changes in the realms of policy making. It is in this backdrop of setting up the broader problem of climate change that the voices of resistance point toward the domains of policy making that are controlled in the hands of the wealthy. The concept of a people-powered movement is articulated in resistance to the top-down decisions and decision-making processes around climate change. This notion of people-powered politics of change seeks to dislocate the realms of decision making from the broader structures of power under neoliberal governance and instead place decision making in the hands of communities, foregrounding the role of people in shaping policies around climate control. The monetary power of influence of the fossil fuel industry is resisted by the empowerment, solidarity, and determination of the movement. In doing so, top-down power is dislocated by bottom-up power that emerges from the participation and voice of people who have been placed at the margins of communicative systems of decision making. Examples of the Civil Rights movement and women's suffrage are offered as examples of the influence of people-powered movements in achieving change and in solving some of the biggest problems of the globe.

Along the lines of the voicing of grassroots resistance, entry points are sought for building solidarities of resistance with other movements across the globe, both along issue lines as well as across issue lines. For instance, solidarity-building with the Occupy movement is envisioned under the umbrella of the "Occupy and the Climate Movement" hyperlink that asks readers to join the 99% (the Occupy movement is discussed in greater detail in chapter three). The hyperlink leads the reader to a page that notes the linkage between economic injustices and the politics of climate change. Note, for instance, the following explanation (http://www.350.org/occupy):

- Fossil fuels enable the current economic system to continue because it is global and requires a lot of fossil fuels for production and transportation. Multi-national corporations won't do well if we stop burning fossil fuels.

- Failure to act will result in catastrophic and runaway climate change that will dramatically undermine the systems that make earth livable. Therefore the reality of the climate science and the call for climate justice are critical filters through which all concerns for the economy, education, healthcare and democracy should be considered.

- We shouldn't build the revolution on a dirty energy economy. Those who are concerned about the economy and jobs today, shouldn't settle for short term economies based on fossil fuels which will undermine both the planet and economic opportunities and health for future generations.

Linkages are offered between the global economic injustices and the politics of climate control. The global economic system is connected to fossil fuels, pointing out how the use of fossil fuels supports the production and transportation systems of multinationals. The interconnectedness of issues is made salient when the effects on climate are interlinked with the effects on economies. The realms of education, health care, economy, and democracy are placed in the backdrop of the frame of climate science and climate justice. The articulation of an alternative economic system is interlinked with the articulation of an alternative energy economy. The sustainability of the planet is interwoven with the economic opportunities and health for future generations. The grassroots solidarity of resistance, therefore, creates the local space for the inter-linkages among issues, connecting climate justice with economic justice and the health for future generations. Local-level participation then creates an entry point for the narrativization of alternative rationalities, connecting several grassroots issues together under a broader frame that resists neoliberalism and its centralization of decision-making processes in the hands of those with economic power. This becomes further evident in the following excerpt about Occupy as a process:

> The occupations all over the world are bigger than a single issue, or a single campaign. Rather than a set of demands or a specific objective, it is a process that empowers communities to formulate and develop their own decisions. An occupation is space for all issues to be raised, discussed and put into action through a direct and consensus based process. An occupation turns a space into a forum for discussion and participatory democracy. By occupying a space, the physi-

cal structure of the camp reflects the goals of the people gathered—
to discuss and develop new participatory processes for democracy.
Those of us with in-depth knowledge on more specific subjects (like
tar sands, healthcare, or climate justice) can help draw the important
connections between our specific issues and the larger societal problems they embody. (http://www.350.org/occupy)

The empowerment of local communities to make their own decisions lies
at the heart of the processes of social change and social justice embodied
in 350.org and the Occupy movements. The linkages between these movements, therefore, offer a framework for connecting the issues to identify
and resist the broader domains of corporate control that influence decisions around a variety of issues. As embodied in the depiction above, occupations are envisioned as sites of local decision making based on consensus as opposed to top-down decision making embodied in dominant
structures of neoliberalism. The development of new participatory processes of democracy remains at the center of resistance, where participation becomes conceptualized as a process through which frameworks of
participatory decision making are articulated, debated, and configured.

The narrativization of the 350 movement discusses the grassroots efforts in 2007 that brought together communities across the US in raising
awareness and mobilizing politically to cut carbon 80% by 2050 under
the umbrella of the "Step It Up" campaign. What is pivotal to the voices
of resistance in the Step It Up campaign is the re-articulation of iconic
places in all 50 of the United States to share the story of climate change.
The networks of solidarity further built from the spaces within the US to
connect with other spaces globally to recruit participants in creative forms
of activism, bringing together activists from across the globe to organize
events on global days of action, to envision creative avenues from change
through participatory local action, to organize globally at the very sites
where climate policies are being arbitrated and decided upon. For instance,
the global day of action, October 24, 2009, brought together activists from
181 countries, who organized diverse resistive projects at various local
sites. Video narratives available on the website then wove together these
different stories of resistance that were constituted around the broader

theme of reducing carbon. On the website (http://www.350.org/en/story), YouTube videos document various messages of protest from around the world, coordinating messages for political leaders from various globally distributed local sites. Performances, street protests, and creative forms of action are mobilized to communicate the 350 movement message. The 350 movement's signage is displayed creatively at these various local sites. Also, events such as the Global Work Party hosted on October 10, 2010 across the globe bring about opportunities for local communities to develop alternative solutions to the carbon problem and to create platforms for voicing these solutions. Therefore, integral to the co-constructions of resistance among the various activist groups from around the globe is the emphasis on local solutions that are globally connected through the networks of solidarity.

The participatory frameworks of organizing in the 350 movement also emerge as creative sites of developing performative processes and messages that are creative and novel in nature. For instance, under the 350 Earth project, local communities across various global sites came up with novel messages of resistance communicating the key concept of carbon control (see, for instance, http://earth.350.org/). At the 350 Earth website, the purpose of the Earth project is described as using art to mobilize global climate movement. The description further discusses the ways in which art is creatively used to communicate the key messages of the movement:

> EARTH collaborates with creatives to transform the human rights and environmental issues connected to climate change into powerful art that gets people to stop, think and act.

> In 2010, 350.org launched EARTH, the world's first ever global satellite art project. In over 16 places around the world, the public collaborated with artists to create art so large it could be photographed from space.

> The art pieces highlighted a local climate change issue or solution. We found that art had the remarkable ability to bring thousands of people around the world including India, Egypt, South Africa, China, the

United States and more, to engage in the climate change movement for the first time. Many who participated and witnessed the pieces were transformed. Immediately after we heard in Spanish, Arabic, English, Hindi, "What can I do next . . ." And so EARTH was born. (http://earth.350.org/)

The principles of the 350 Earth project are defined in terms of utilizing locally created art to raise awareness and mobilize people around the issue of climate change. The global satellite component of the 350 Earth project, highlighted as the first of its kind, involved artistic installations co-created through the collaborations of people with artists into big formations that were so large in size that they could be photographed from space. The website offers links to the Earth art installations that were created in 2010, providing images of each of the installations. The local-global linkages in the 350 movement once again becomes salient here as the art pieces depicting local climate change issues or solutions across various sites around the globe including India, China, Egypt, South Africa, and the United States are interconnected under the 350 movement's broader message on climate change. Under the heading "Climate Street Art," links are provided to several art installations at numerous sites across the globe that take on specific local issues and seek to mobilize action around these local issues, interconnected around the broader umbrella of climate change and controlling the carbon content in the environment. Take, for example, the installation art titled "The Invisible Man," which was created by the artist Liu Bolin (see Figure 4.2).

The photograph of the art installation is accompanied by the following description on the website:

> Artist statement: China consumes more coal than any other country in the world, using it for everything from electricity and producing steel to deadly indoor heating and cooking in some rural areas. With their unregulated mines, China's coal mines are also fatal and thousands of people a year die due to explosions, cave-ins, and other disasters. Coal Pile is a conceptual commentary on the consequences of not only the dependence on coal, a limited resource, but the dan-

Figure 4.2. The "Invisible Man" art exhibit (http://earth.350.org/street-art/).

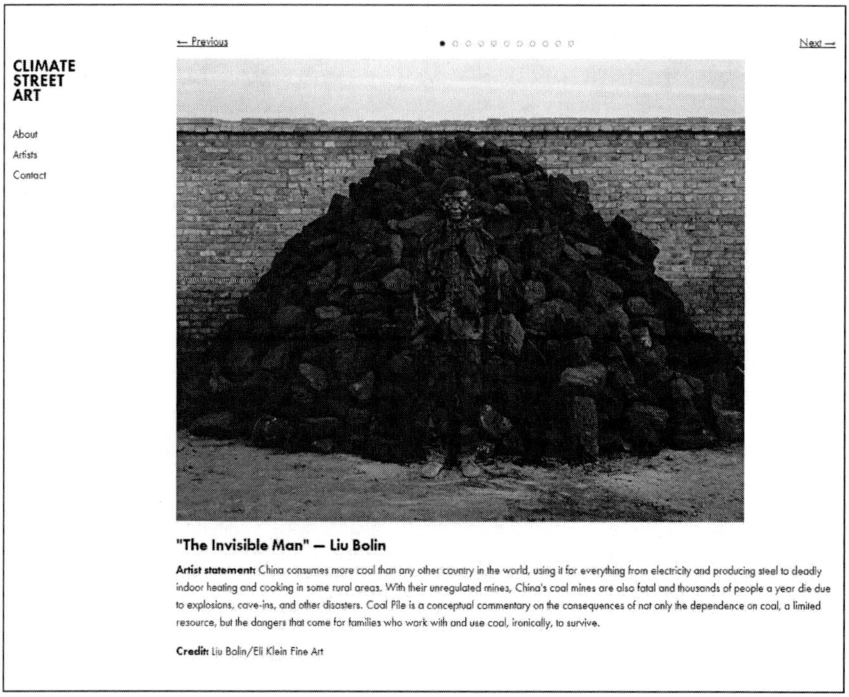

gers that come for families who work with and use coal, ironically, to survive. (http://earth.350.org/street-art/)

Worth noting here is the attention draw to the high usage of coal in China, the effects of coal use on the environment, and the conditions of the workers who toil in the Chinese coal mines. The depiction of the coal pile then draws attention to the dangerous consequences of coal use on the environment as well as the everyday risks that are posed for the individuals and families that work in the mines.

Similarly, another art installation titled "LA's Dirty Secret" depicts a yellow background with a black circle in the center. Below the black circle is the statement "Don't connect the dots." A link is offered to the site quit-coal.org/la. The illustration is accompanied by the following description on the Earth website:

Artist statement: Zelida collaborated with 350.org and Greenpeace to design this simple, provocative poster exposing Los Angeles's dirty secret. Los Angeles, the 15th largest economy in the world, receives over 40% of its energy from dirty coal. Globally, the burning of coal is the largest contributor to climate change. Los Angeles is based in the proverbial "Sunshine State" and could easily switch to solar. We hung these posters in the windows of Los Angeles businesses who want LA's City Council to drop coal and switch to renewable energy. The number of LA businesses opposed to coal is 400 and growing. See quitcoal.org/la for more. (http://earth.350.org/street-art/)

The description points to the large-scale consumption of coal in Los Angeles, seeking to expose this secret and create awareness about the role of burning coal in climate change. The poster serves as an entry point to mobilizing businesses and community members to pressure LA's city council to switch from coal to alternative energy sources. The link on the installation connects to the LA Quit Coal movement website, which is part of a broader US-wide Quit Coal movement hosted at quitcoal.org. What these installations depict are the ways in which local issues are connected to specific actionable steps, articulated within the broader framework of the 350 movement that seeks to reduce the carbon footprint globally.

The 350 movement utilizes other forms of performance, such as songs, in order to spread the message of the movement. For instance, the song "People Power," created by African musicians, became a vehicle for carrying the message of the movement. Here is a description of the song and the broader context within which it originated:

The United Nations climate talks have unfortunately been just that for 16 years—just talk and no real action, the most famous of these so far being the failed conference in Copenhagen in 2009. After the deep disappointment of Copenhagen, a South African anti-apartheid activist teasingly noted that the talks had failed because the climate movement didn't have a song!

For the 17th conference in Durban this December, we didn't want to make the same mistake twice! A group of leading musicians throughout Africa and other parts of the world to create a song that both tells the truth about how hard climate change is affecting Africa and that also inspires people to join together to create a brighter future for everyone.

Africa is the continent that is most vulnerable to climate change (according to the recent Maplecroft report, of the world's most highly vulnerable countries, approximately two-thirds are located in Africa). These impacts include more severe droughts, increasing deserts, worsening storms that damage people's croplands, and sea level rise affecting the coastal communities. People in the Eastern Horn of Africa are already being forced off their homelands due to the drought and famine made worse by climate change.

The African continent also has a rich history and recent past of fighting injustice, of creativity, of perseverance, of communal caring, and of traditional wisdom of living in harmony with nature. And it is the birthplace of humanity—all people, the world over, carry memories of Africa in their cells.

By filling the airwaves around the globe with the power of song and story, maybe we can reignite some of these memories and remind people of the power we have when we stand together. Together we can overcome climate change. Together we can create a brighter future! (http://radiowave.350.org/share-the-song/about-the-song/)

The story of the history of the "People Power" song positions itself in resistance to the empty conversations of United Nations climate talks. The UN climate talks are positioned in the backdrop of the power of songs to achieve social change and social justice. "People Power" seeks to tell the truth about the politics of climate change, drawing attention to the real impacts of climate change in the form of severe draughts, increasing deserts, worsening storms, and rising sea levels, also noting that Africa as a continent is most vulnerable to these effects of climate change. The local context of the issue, then, is organized as a framework for delivering a call for collective solidarity-building.

In the backdrop of the articulation of the materiality of climate change (narrated in terms of its impact, based upon linkages offered to evidence), the rich history and creativity of the African continent are foregrounded to put forth alternative rationalities of communal caring. The traditional wisdom of Africa is celebrated, foregrounding the richness and wealth of knowledge that the continent has to offer and locating Africa as the birthplace of humanity. It is from its origins in local spaces of Africa that the "People Power" song becomes the conduit for connecting global voices, songs, and stories of resistance. The song becomes an avenue for filling up the radio airwaves with songs and stories of resistance to climate change, mobilizing people globally by reigniting their memories of the power of people to bring change through collective solidarity. The local-global interplay of the movement is also visible in the lyrics of the song, with multiple artistes collaborating together in their own native languages. Here is a short excerpt of "People Power," sung by Zolani Mahola of Freshly Ground in isiXhosa and isiZulu:

> The sun was at its brightest
>
> the seasons coming in their own time
>
> flowers blossoming
>
> the rain bringing freshness to mother earth
>
> the rain releasing a smell of wonder
>
> the birds with their singing
>
> every season came in its right time
>
> Fix this mess you have created/this mess before us (http://radio-wave.350.org/share-the-song/song-lyrics/)

Similarly, on the website describing the song, a quotation from Archbishop Emeritus Desmond Tutu, a member of The Elders, notes:

> Africans have this thing called "ubuntu". It is about the essence of being human, it is part of the gift that Africa will give the world. We believe that a person is a person through another person, that my humanity is bound up, inextricably, with yours. When I dehumanise you, I inexorably dehumanise myself. The solitary human being is a

contradiction in terms and therefore you seek to work for the common good because your humanity comes into its own in belonging. (http://radiowave.350.org/share-the-song/about-the-song/)

The concept of "ubuntu" is noted as the essence of being human, and is celebrated as a gift of Africa to the world. Resisting the notion of individualism that lies at the heart of neoliberal formulations of global policies, Ubuntu puts forth the notion of relationship as the defining feature of humanity. Humanity is constituted in belonging, and this becomes the framework for storying a narrative of resistance. "People Power" also serves as a catalyst for the 350.org campaign that attempts to confront the issue of climate change by leveraging the power of radio:

Since it began 3 years ago, the 350.org network has developed a reputation for bold grassroots action—action that's powered by the web and new forms of media. The campaign we're about to invite you to embark on falls somewhere within that description, but it also reconnects us with two much older forms of media: our voices and the radio.

For two weeks starting on the 21st of November we will unleash a wave of radio broadcasts around the world (we're calling it "350 Radio Wave") all on the topic of the climate crisis and the growing movement to solve it. We want the voices of local climate activists—that would be you—to be the stars of these broadcasts. (http://radiowave.350.org/)

The call highlights the role of radio in spreading the message of the movement, voiced through the participation of local activists across the globe. In preparation for the 2011 UN Climate Change Summit, the radio campaign sought to build global awareness about the science and impact of climate change, and simultaneously narrate the power of people in creating avenues for change through locally narrated solutions.

The radio component of the campaign also provides access to resources, such as public service announcements, interview guides, tips on setting up interviews, pre-recorded interviews, and local podcasts, to be used by activists as well as by local radio stations. As of January 2011, reports of radio waves were noted from over 60 countries from across the globe. The radio campaign catalyzed several localized narratives of social change in the context of climate justice. Additionally, songs such as "Climate Justice #Occupy," created by local musicians in Durban, South Africa at the site of COP17, further leverage the intersections of the 350 movement with the Occupy movement, sharing the "occupy" metaphor to displace the power imbalance in climate talks held by transnational capital (http://radiowave.350.org/occupy-with-music/). Here is a Radio Wave update on the global uptake of the song:

> 350's amazing global grassroots network spread People Power, a new climate change song, to the airwaves in over 60 countries! Together, we harnessed the power of music to educate the public about climate change. Some organisers managed to get their personal stories onto radio stations with huge audiences; others were smaller stations that the local community listened to. From stations in Texas to Cape Town, uplifting messages from the movement's frontlines reached thousands of people's hearts and minds.
>
> The story of the song, People Power, continues to unfold. It was in regular rotation on South African radio stations during the UN climate talks, and now DJs are creating amazing remixes. iTunes recently featured it as the "Free iTunes Song of the Week"—the first time a climate song has ever made this coveted spot. Already, we're at 100,000 downloads and still counting!
>
> This wonderful energy of people power—rippling out in story and song—has been so important in recent months. At this moment in history, politics and our media seem to be dominated by corporate polluters. Hope for climate action can seem dim, and we all worry that our message isn't getting through.
>
> But, over the past few weeks, 350 Radio Wave helped inspire people around the world to create a new wave of climate action, and I couldn't be more grateful to be part of the movement that made it happen.
>
> Let's keep turning it around. (http://radiowave.350.org/)

The hegemonic narrative of climate change as depicted in the mainstream media is sought to be resisted through the grassroots-level political action of local communities across the globe that are using the radio to draw attention to the issue of climate change. 350.org provides links to additional resources that could be used by local groups working with the 350 movement's message. For instance, the events FAQ resource offers links to local activist groups interested in organizing an event for the 350 movement. The FAQ walks the reader through steps outlining methods for organizing local community members into 350 action, putting together posters and signage for 350, as well as specific steps for involving local community members, taking photos, submitting photos, and engaging with the media. Here is a section that outlines suggestions for a 350 action video:

> The truth is that a banner is often the simplest, surest way to get a big 350 into your image. Click here to check out a good banner-making guide. But not every action needs a banner, and even banners can involve more creativity than just a big number. Here is a good place for a creative friend or volunteer to lend a hand.
>
> Think about banners that say "Beirut for 350!" (in Arabic) or "Vamos 350!" (in Buenos Aires). Or think about forming a huge 350 out of the people attending the action, or for bicycle actions consider forming a 350 out of bicycles, or for trash clean-ups maybe form a 350 out of the trash collected from your site.
>
> Be creative and have fun with it—and be sure to plan in advance and designate a friend or photographer to make sure you get the digital photo image you need to submit to 350.org afterwards. (http://www.350.org/en/node/3191)

The idea of the banner, for instance, spells out specific tactics for putting up banners in different languages, or for forming attention-drawing configurations, such as forming "350" with people attending the event, or forming "350" with bicycles or trash cans. Other resources include logos, the 350 badge, pre-made banners, fact sheets, organizing guides on how to hold first meetings, blogger and social networking tools, guidelines for creating collaborative art projects, multimedia guides, and guides on creating videos (http://www.350.org/resources). In seeking to create transformative spaces for climate justice, 350.org also provides a variety of information resources on topics such as "Climate Science Factsheet," "Climate Policy Factsheet," and "Agriculture and Climate Change Factsheet." Also, through animations and videos placed on 350.org, the science of climate change and global warming is presented, serving as the framework for introducing the goals and objectives of the 350 movement.

Campaign Against the Keystone XL Tar Sands Pipeline

One of the recent environmental movements in North America that is directed at environmental justice is the campaign against the Keystone XL Tar Sands pipeline. The pipeline system was proposed in 2005 by TransCanada Corporation to carry synthetic crude oil and diluted bitumen from Athabasca Oil Sands in Canada to multiple locations in the US in Oklahoma, Texas, Illinois, and Montana. The plans for building the pipeline are divided into phases, with phase 1 and phase 2 developing the basic transportation infrastructure of the pipeline, and then with subsequent extension segments.

Early resistance in Canada against the pipeline is situated amidst a long history of indigenous protests against projects in the Tar Sands, bringing to the forefront questions related to the effects of the pipeline on the environment and on indigenous cultural resources (see the Indigenous Environmental Network site at http://www.ienearth.org/). In September 2008, two blockades by First Nation communities in the Saskatchewan Province halted construction for a few days by shutting down the Trans-Canada Highway (Treaty One First Nations, 2008). In the narrative of indigenous resistance against the project, questions are raised regarding the exploitation of resources that are owned by indigenous communities without compensating them, set alongside questions related to the impact on the environment (Doha, 2008). During the protests organized by First Nations, Red Pheasant First Nation Chief Sheldon Wuttunee noted the following: "We want to put out a message that we've had enough, that we're going to stand together as Indian people to make sure we get our fair share of the resources that come from our traditional lands" (http://

www.canada.com/saskatoonstarphoenix/news/story.html?id=31d87e83-d18a-4d91-b1cf-62600e3ed05e). The articulation of the indigenous claim to the collective ownership of the resources disrupts the oil profiteering motivations of projects in the Tar Sands.

The Federation of Saskatchewan Indian Nations Vice Chief Morley Watson noted:

> We believe that the governments have failed; they have failed the First Nation people by not consulting us. They have a duty to consult and accommodate us. They haven't and again our communities are frustrated. We want what everybody else has, that's jobs and opportunity and profitability and, unfortunately, the governments have bypassed us. (http://firstnationsdrum.com/2008/10/saskatchewan-first-nations-protest-pipeline/)

Evident in the narrative of resistance is the overall erasure of indigenous communities from the realms of decision making, and the simultaneous erasure of indigenous voices and interests from the material spaces of oil profiteering. Foregrounded in the articulation is the logic that the people whose collective resources are being exploited ought to be consulted and their needs accommodated. The voices of resistance, organized under the broad umbrella of the Canadian Indigenous Tar Sands Campaign, point out the material marginalization of the indigenous communities in the backdrop of the highly profitable oil industry that gain from the exploitation of the resources.

On January 7, 2009, the Indigenous Environmental Network along with the Rainforest Action Network produced a statement written to President Obama, requesting him to stop all processes related to the approval of the Tar Sands development and expansion (Indigenous Environmental Network, 2009). This statement was issued in conjunction with the meeting held by the One Chiefs of Manitoba, Canada, with President Obama regarding the Enbridge Alberta Canada and Keystone XL project (Treaty One First Nations, 2008). In the written statement, the indigenous leaders cite multiple arguments regarding the violation of indigenous rights and the degradation of environmental and cultural resources in indigenous communities. Consider the following excerpt (Indigenous Environmental Network, 2009):

> Beaver Lake Cree Nation of Treaty 6 (BCFN) launched a massive civil lawsuit against the federal and Alberta governments, claiming unbridled oil and gas development in its traditional territory renders its treaty rights meaningless. BCFN claims the developments have forced band members out of traditional areas, degraded the environment and reduced wildlife populations, making it impossible for them to meaningfully exercise their Treaty 6 rights to hunt, trap and fish.

The specific effects of oil and gas development on indigenous life and lifestyle are discussed, noting the displacement of band members from their traditional areas, degradation of the environment and wildlife populations, and the impact on indigenous ways of living. The life and culture of indigenous communities is discussed in the context of the deleterious effects of the industry on wildlife populations. References to Treaty 6 rights of Indian communities offer the basis for the legal challenge offered to the federal and Alberta governments; it is on this articulation of indigenous rights that legal opposition is offered to the Tar Sands project and expansion. The violation of treaty rights serves as the basis of resistance enunciated through juridical structures. The statement further goes on to note the following:

> When considering energy production and resource extraction, the incoming administration must take into account the disproportionate impacts of climate change and energy development on the first inhabitants of this Turtle Island—North America. When considering energy and climate change policy, it is important that the White House and federal agencies consider the history of energy and mineral exploitation and Indigenous Nations, and the potential to create a dramatic change with innovative policies. Too often tribes are presented with a false choice: either develop polluting energy resources or remain in dire poverty. Economic development need not come at the cost of maintaining cultural identity and thriving ecosystems. The Indigenous Environmental Network, the First Nations of northern Alberta and all Indigenous Nations want to work with President Elect

> Barack Obama and his administration for catalyzing green reserva-
> tion economies—not the continuation of an unsustainable fossil fuel
> economy. (Indigenous Environmental Network, 2009)

The history of exploitation of Indigenous Nations is foregrounded, documenting the ways in which the exploitation of indigenous resources has
constituted the backdrop of the energy economy. Energy production
and resource mistreatment have taken place through the exploitation of
indigenous land. The frames of energy resource development are interrogated by paying attention to the underlying dichotomies between poverty in indigenous communities and the harnessing of polluting energy
resources. Green reservation economies are presented as alternatives to
the unsustainable fuel economy. Subsequently, a blueprint for a green energy economy is presented:

> A just nation-to-nation relationship means breaking the cycle of ask-
> ing First Nations of Canada or American Indians and Alaska Natives
> to choose between economic development and preservation of its
> cultures and lands. Renewable energy and efficiency improvements
> provide opportunity to do both simultaneously. A green, carbon-
> reduced energy policy has major national and international human
> rights, environmental and financial consequences, and we believe
> that this administration can provide groundbreaking leadership on
> this policy. The reality is that the most efficient, green economy will
> need the vast wind and solar resources that lie on Indigenous lands
> in the U.S. and Canada. This provides the foundation of not only a
> green low carbon economy but also catalyzes development of tremen-
> dous human and economic potential in the poorest community in
> the United States and Canada–Turtle Island. (Indigenous Environ-
> mental Network, 2009)

The advantages of a green, carbon-reduced energy economy are articulated
in the voices of resistance. Renewable energy is positioned as a solution
that fulfills both energy needs as well as protects indigenous rights. The
resistance against the development and expansion of the Tar Sands project
offers a space for proposing alternative energy economies that respect hu-

man rights and protect indigenous culture, lifestyle, and simultaneously develop human and economic potential.

The resistance against the pipeline is established in the backdrop of the articulations of the communicative processes of decision making through which indigenous voices are silenced and erased, accompanied by the manipulative strategies deployed by the dominant structures to mislead indigenous communities (http://www.ienearth.org/what-are-tar-sands.html):

> The government of Canada has legally been forced by First Nations to consult with Indigenous communities about development projects. But consultation is just that, telling a community a project is being proposed that may or may not have impacts to a First Nation and the recognition of its Treaty rights. As of yet, there is no legal framework within the Constitution of Canada that recognizes the principles of Free, Prior and Informed Consent (FPIC) for the right of First Nations to say "No" to a proposed development. In 2010, Canada signed the UN Declaration on the Rights of Indigenous Peoples (UNDRIP), however with qualification, objecting to the FPIC principles, as central tenets of the Declaration.

What we hear in these voices of resistance is the systematic erasure of indigenous communities from platforms of decision making. References are made to façades of dialogue that serve as mechanisms for manipulating and co-opting indigenous participation, or simply as avenues for informing indigenous communities of top-down decisions that have already been taken. The resistance to Tar Sands project, then, is based on raising foundational questions regarding the manipulation in the communicative processes and claims made by the dominant structures (http://www.ienearth.org/what-are-tar-sands.html):

> Government and industry spend vast amounts of money on public relations campaigns with promises of jobs, environmental cleanup and carbon offset markets to create the illusion of an 'ethical, clean oil sands' industry.

> Decades ago, the Alberta government enticed impoverished First Nations band council's to lease treaty reserve lands to the tar sands in-

dustry as a means for economic development and jobs. This allowed the first experiments with tar sands operations in the 1960's and 1970's on lands inhabited mostly by Dene, Cree and Métis people. Companies such as Exxon, Shell, Syncrude Canada, BP/Husky, CNRL and Suncor Energy moved into the area with well funded public relations campaigns targeting First Nation communities, schools, and senior citizens on how tar sand expansion would be good for its Indigenous neighbors. However, after decades, First Nation communities in Northern Alberta continue to suffer chronic unemployment. Many of the existing jobs for First Nations in the tar sands industry tend to be menial labor, not management level positions or monitoring positions. But with a rapidly growing population (80, 000 Aboriginal people today as compared to 1,200 in 1960's), many communities are forced to choose between a paycheck and their health.

Resistance to the Tar Sands project is enacted through the identification of the communicative strategies and practices embodied in the public relations campaigns run by the industry and the government to generate perceptions of employment generation, environmental cleanup, and carbon offset markets. Resistance is framed in the form of interrogating the false promises of employment generation and economic development that were utilized in order to establish projects in treaty reserve lands. The reality of the continued impoverishment and unemployment of First Nations people is juxtaposed against the promises of development and employment generation that served as the cornerstone of the public relations campaigns starting in the 1960s and the 1970s, which sought to buy public opinion through well-funded campaigns targeting First Nation communities, schools, and senior citizens. In Alberta, several First Nations groups have filed lawsuits to challenge Tar Sands development and have simultaneously launched local organizing campaigns connecting various First Nations. The Beaver Lake Cree First Nation filed a lawsuit against the government of Alberta for infringing on First Nation treaty rights related to the Tar Sands development. Similarly, the Prairie Chipewyan First Nation filed a lawsuit against the government of Alberta for not appropriately consulting the First Nation community for building a Tar Sands project on their traditional territory. Several local activist groups organized resistance to

Tar Sands operations through education, awareness creation, lawsuits filed in local courts, civil disobedience, direct action, and social networking. "Aboriginal title," a term that refers to aboriginal legal rights to land, is framed as the basis for constructing issues of land rights under the structure of nation-to-nation political and legal relations with Canada. Drawing on these collective experiences of resistance at several local sites and organized through various First Nations, the Indigenous Action Network is a collective solidarity network of indigenous organizations and indigenous leaders that organizes its protests through blockades, street protests, sit-ins, participation in civil disobedience, signing petitions, developing letter writing campaigns, visiting key political stakeholders, using judicial processes through lawsuits, and so forth.

In spite of early resistance against Tar Sands projects and the building of the pipeline, the Canadian Energy Board approved the construction of the Canadian portion of the pipeline, and in 2008, the US Department of State issues a presidential permit allowing the construction, maintenance, and operation of facilities at the US-Canada border. The pipeline has been criticized by the environmental community for delivering "dirty fuel" at high costs, and has come under the scrutiny for the very high impact that it would have on the environment. The pipeline received strong criticisms from 50 Democrats in Congress in June, 2010; in July 2010, the House Energy and Commerce Committee urged the Department of State to block the pipeline proposal because of the potential impact on the environment and health hazards attached to the project. In the same month, the Environmental Protection Agency ordered a revised draft report of the environmental impact study for Keystone XL. The report was released in August 2011 stating that the effects of the pipeline on the environment would be minimal if adequate environmental protection plans were to be followed, although the likelihood of impact on specific cultural resources was high. It is in this backdrop of the politics of seeking to secure approval for the building of the Keystone XL Tar Sands pipeline that the resistance against the pipeline is constituted.

Tar Sands Action, the network of resistance efforts in the US against the pipeline proposal, describes its goals in terms of sustained civil dis-

Figure 4.3. Keystone pipeline protestors demonstrate at dusk (iStockphoto, contributed by sharply_done).

obedience directed at stopping the expansion of the pipeline. Through direct action, nonviolent resistance, sit-ins, blockades, speeches, processions, and innovative performances, the activist network draws the attention of the public, policy makers, and the media. The on-the-ground strategies of Tar Sands Action are accompanied by organizing on the web (www.tarsandsaction.org), Facebook, YouTube, and other social media sites. Images and video are shared on these social media sites to garner awareness as well as to initiate action and to mobilize support. E-mail communication strategies are utilized to converse with key stakeholders. The direct action protests organized across North America by several loosely constituted Tar Sands Action groups also find entry into mainstream media networks, thus generating avenues for publicity. The effectiveness of communication strategies by the Tar Sands Action network is positioned in the backdrop of the large budget media campaigns that are run by the oil industry. "Putting bodies in the line" became the strategy of civil disobedience for getting the message of resistance across to the political decision-making structures.

The Tar Sands Action website served as the centerpiece of the activist movement, as well as a way to share stories that pointed toward the hypocrisy and incongruence of processes. For instance, during the Department of State hearings, the Tar Sands Action website opened up a space for participants at the hearings to share their experiences at the meetings directly at the website or through a hotline. Several incongruences in the processes undertaken at the hearings were made evident by the attend-

ees. Note, for instance, the following post written by one of the participants, Kathy DeSilva (http://www.tarsandsaction.org/state-department-
hearings/#more-1548):

> I attended and spoke at the Port Arthur State Dept. meeting last
> night. I left with the feeling of being scammed. We arrived 45 min-
> utes early to sign up, & found hundreds of oil field workers already
> in line (having been bused in) wearing navy blue or orange match-
> ing t-shirts, bold lettering: BUILD KEYSTONE XL NOW! GOOD
> JOBS! U.S. SECURITY! Once we were allowed to sign up to speak
> (at a table staffed by Cardno Entrix, according to their name tags)
> we entered the room to find the first 8-10 rows, (left side:suits, right
> side: oil field workers), filled by these individuals and their slogans.
> This after being told we could not bring any signs into the meeting?
> The 2 microphones were set up in the middle, just behind the last
> rows of bright shirts. When one stood up to speak, these were the
> only people in the field of vision. The first 40 or so speakers were for
> the pipeline (having been bused in & stood in line to sign up first).
> They were told their time limit was 3 minutes, but it was not strictly
> enforced. Once people started speaking in opposition, we were told
> it was getting so late, the time was now 2 minutes (strictly enforced).
> On the sign up table, there was a stack of papers entitled, "Fact Sheet,
> Keystone XL Pipeline". No where in this publication is tar sands oil
> referred to, just "crude oil". The paper ends with these words: ABOVE
> ALL ELSE, THE DEPARTMENT IS COMMITTED TO MAINTAIN-
> ING THE INTEGRITY OF A TRANSPARENT, IMPARTIAL, AND
> RIGOROUS PROCESS. After driving 4 hours to attend and speak
> at this meeting, I feel like it was a scam and in no way transparent,
> impartial and rigorous.

What becomes evident in the description of the process is the deployment
of communicative strategies to close off the possibilities of resistance. The
communicative structures of the hearings are constituted in ways that
minimize the opportunities for listening to resistive voices. In this context,
then, the activists raise question about the very nature of the process in the
hearings, noting that the hearing process is not transparent, impartial, and
rigorous. Another comment from a participant who attended the hearings

notes, "These hearings are a scam." Posts refer to arrests that were made and threats made at the Austin hearings where participants questioned the processes. Here is an excerpt from another report on Texas Vox of the hearings and the inherent conflict of interest in the processes that were set up (http://texasvox.org/2011/09/29/austin-tar-sands-hearing-a-farce/):

> According to Karen Hadden, the Executive Director of the Sustainable and Economic Development (SEED) Coalition, "This was not a hearing, this was a farce." Ms. Hadden arrived and had been waiting for a couple of hours to give comments when they cut the hearing off. Later, when she was attempting to find out what her options were for providing comments to the State Department given she was unable to do so at the hearing, she was told she must leave the premises or she would be arrested.
>
> According to Brad Johnson of ThinkProgress
>
> In a stunning conflict of interest, public hearings on federal approval for a proposed tar sands pipeline are being run by a contractor for the pipeline company itself. The U.S. Department of State's public hearings [link to http://www.keystonepipeline-xl.state.gov/clientsite/ keystonexl.nsf/e327883380befe0b862571f60062011e/4f437629026 83eef062575390056f38b?OpenDocument&AutoFramed] along the proposed route of the TransCanada Keystone XL tar sands pipeline this week are under the purview of Cardno Entrix, a "professional environmental consulting company" that specializes in "permitting and compliance."
>
> Cardno is not only running the State Department hearings, but also manages the department's Keystone XL website [link to http://www. keystonepipeline-xl.state.gov/clientsite/keystonexl.nsf?Open] and drafted the department's environmental impact statement [link to http://thinkprogress.org/green/2011/08/26/305374/tar-sands-action-day-seven-this-is-our-environmental-impact-statement/]. Comments from the public about the pipeline go not to the government, but to a cardno.com email address.

Cardno Entrix was contracted by TransCanada Keystone XL LP ("Keystone") to do the work for the Department of State, to assist DOS in preparing the EIS and to conduct the Section 106 consultation process.

Throughout the history of the DOS review of the Keystone pipeline, the work has been conducted not by civil servants but by representatives of the pipeline company. During the Bush administration, the Department of State appointed TransCanada "and its subcontractors to act as its designated non-federal representatives" [link to http://www.cardnoentrix.com/keystone/xl/feis/FEIS01_Biological-Assessment.pdf] to assess the potential impact of the Keystone pipeline on endangered species.

Cardno Entrix contractors are running the public hearings from Port Arthur, Texas, to Glendive, Montana. It is not clear from media reports whether the State Department "representatives" at the hearing were in fact Entrix employees. ThinkProgress Green is awaiting information from the State Department.

"All of this adds up to the old saying, the fox is guarding the hen house," says Jane Kleeb, the Nebraska activist leading the fight to protect her state from the risks of the Keystone XL project.

The voices of activists points toward the inequities of the communicative processes and communicative structures that are manipulated to carry out the strategic agendas of the pipeline: that Cardno Entrix is a contractor for Keystone XL and also in charge of the public hearings on the pipeline; that the entire process of the Department of State management of the Keystone case starting from the reports to the management of the process is handled by Keystone and its contractors points toward the manipulation of the process.

As the campaign continued, it sought to expose deeper underlying structures of decision making and the corruption that is built into the processes of political decision making, drawing attention to the role of oil money in shaping the political landscape. For instance, the action network brought to attendance the hiring of the Keystone lobbyist Broderick

Johnson as a new senior advisor to the president's re-election campaign (Tar Sands Action, 2011a). Similarly, under the title "State Department Political Scandal," the Tar Sands Action website documents the revolving door between Keystone lobbyists and powerful public officials. Consider, for instance, the following post on the Tar Sands Action (2011b) website:

> The scandal began when it was revealed that a top Clinton campaign operative, Paul Elliot, was working illegally as a foreign agent to lobby the Department to approve Keystone XL, and gained new steam when released emails showed the same lobbyist in a too-cozy relationship with State Department staff, who offered special favors and treatment to Elliot as he lobbied for Keystone XL's approval. Later it was discovered that the State Department had used a major TransCanada subcontractor to conduct its environmental review process. In sum, the scandal shows that the oil industry is calling far too many shots in the State Department, making them incapable of fulfilling their mission of protecting the US national interest when it comes to Keystone XL.

The post specifically draws attention to the role Paul Elliot, a top Clinton operative, played as a lobbyist for Keystone XL. The involvement of Elliot in shaping the political process to secure approval for the Keystone XL project by utilizing his political influence within the Department of State drew attention of activists who questioned the biases that are inherent in this governmental organization's decision-making processes, including the decision to utilize a TransCanada subcontractor to conduct the environmental review of the Keystone XL project. A link in the story to Friends of the Earth (http://www.foe.org/keystone-xl-pipeline-influence-scandal) provides additional details, and Tar Sands Action urges readers and activists to Tweet to *Meet the Press,* CNN's *State of the Union,* and ABC's *This Week* to ask them to query Clinton about the Keystone XL scandal.

Specific content of the Keystone XL campaign is challenged through the articulations raised by the activists. For instance, one of the primary frames that is utilized by Keystone XL to justify the building of the pipeline is the promise of the jobs that will be created by the pipeline construction projects. Public relations strategies of TransCanada largely focus on disseminating and manipulating the language of job creation to generate public opinion and public policy support. The key strategy of Tar Sands Action emphasized the disruption of the narrative of job creation by interrogating the underlying empirical evidence and by systematically documenting the actual number of jobs that would be created as opposed to the rhetoric of job creation that is widely circulated by Keystone XL to generate support for the pipeline project (see, for instance, http://www.tarsandsaction.org/cornell-global-labor-institute-study-finds-keystone-xl-pipeline-create-jobs/). This link leads to the Cornell Global Labor Institute study titled "Pipe Dreams? Jobs Gained, Jobs Lost by the Construction of Keystone XL," documenting evidence that describes the actual possibility of reduction in employment opportunities because of the building of the pipeline. Here is an excerpt from Lara Skinner, associate director of research at the Cornell Global Labor Institute: "The company's claim that Keystone XL will create 20,000 direct construction and manufacturing jobs in the U.S. is unsubstantiated. There is strong evidence to suggest that a large portion of the primary material input for KXL—steel pipe—will not even be produced in the U.S." The Facebook page of the campaign provides access to additional information that questions the job creation numbers offered by Keystone XL.

Personal appeals made to the president from supporters became an organizing point for the crusade, drawing attention to the promises that were made by Obama in his presidential campaign, and drawing upon a personal narrative of political involvement to urge the president to develop policies and programs in line with his campaign rhetoric. Protestors organized visits to Obama 2012 campaign offices with signs and banners to protest. Protestors also disrupted Obama's speeches with protest signs and with questions asking the president about why he had not yet stopped the Keystone XL project. Images and videos of these innovative forms of direct action were circulated through social media and through the Tar Sands Action website. Many of the protestors who had earlier worked on the Obama campaign declared on the Tar Sands Action website that they would not support the president in the future if the Keystone XL project was approved. Here is an example:

In 2008 I worked for President Obama in Cincinnati Ohio as a Canvass Coordinator. Fresh out of college, my idealism and energy ran high. I managed over one hundred paid canvassers who knocked on tens of thousands of doors throughout the fall. After eight years of a Bush presidency marked by environmental devastation, oil-centered energy policy, and oil-driven foreign military action, I was absolutely enthused at the possibility of a progressive president. I remember running door to door until the very last minute the polls were open on election night. No amount of effort was unnecessary when it came to electing Obama. Like so many other staffers, I lived and breathed the 2008 election. The dedication of hundreds of volunteers and inspired workers paid off: Hamilton County (home of Cincinnati) went blue for the first time since 1964 and we successfully unseated a 14-year incumbent Republican congressman. I cried tears of joy on election night. I knew it was a hard road ahead but I finally felt we had an ally in the White House and the nation was on the right track.

Nearly three years later my idealism of 2008 is but a distant memory. I've grown disillusioned watching Obama cave in to pressure from big oil and big coal. We've all watched cap and trade legislation be sidelined, offshore drilling continue, and clean air standards die at the hands of big business. Mountaintop removal has not been stopped, and Fracking continues unregulated throughout the nation. Obama won't even fulfill his promise to put Solar panels back on the White House. I often wonder if my time and dedication in 2008 was wasted. Yet rather than despair, we must be driven to action. (http://www.tar-sandsaction.org/obama-i-worked-for-you-your-turn/)

The promises made by the president in his election campaign are foregrounded to then draw attention to the gap between the rhetoric embodied in those promises and the actual actions taken by Obama. Here the narrative of a campaign worker and his disappointment with the actions of the president on energy-related policies is invoked to urge Obama to act. Images from the presidential campaign that talked about building an energy-friendly US economy are circulated as markers of reminder.

Starting in August 2011, Tar Sands Action organized civil disobedience protests at the White House as a mark of communicating to the president directly the resistance against the pipeline construction, and as an avenue for directly communicating the protests against the pipeline projects. The website and Facebook emerged as avenues for organizing the protests, and for drawing participation into the protests. Images of the protests were posted on YouTube, Facebook, blogs, and the Tar Sands Action website. Video images of protests accompanied by songs and protests, speeches by activists, and speeches by policy makers circulated around the Internet. Consider, for instance, the following video of the resistance movement that documents several forms of direct action, including the protests at the White House with many activists peacefully expressing their dissent against the pipeline project (http://youtu.be/ozmOQqRw0j4). Along with several other activist groups that gathered outside the White House, the Indigenous Environmental Network participated in civil disobedience in Washington, DC, from August 20 to September 3, 2011 (Indigenous Environmental Network, 2011). On the Indigenous Day of Action on Sep-

Figure 4.4. Uploaded by "StopKeystoneXL." *http://youtu.be/ozmOQqRw0j4*

tember 2, 2011, indigenous groups from across North America gathered together in front of the White House to voice their protest against the pipeline project. In November 2011, the Tar Sands activists were back at the White House, encircling the building with demands to the president to stop the pipeline.

Figure 4.5. Uploaded by "FriendsofEarthScot." http://youtu.be/V26AyA8ZKGI

Essential to the Tar Sands Action network is the inter-linkage with other activist sites and movements both within the US and across several other regions of the globe. For instance, tracking the financial trail of Tar Sands-related business deals, Friends of the Earth Scotland take the message of resistance directly to the Royal Bank of Scotland (RBS), one of the key investors in Tar Sands deals. Through performances that are hosted on YouTube and on the Tar Sands Action website, the Friends of the Earth Scotland activist group interrogates the green image and the pro-environment public relations strategy of RBS, pointing to the hypocrisy in the greenwashing strategies of the bank. The video of the song is posted on You-Tube (http://youtu.be/V26AyA8ZKGI) and wraps up with the message "If RBS are serious about investing in low carbon technologies, it must come with hand in an immediate end to providing finance to companies: operating in the tar sands, exploring new oil and gas, and developing new coal." The concerted campaign of various stakeholder groups achieved its moment of success when President Obama sent the proposal back to the table, with request for redoing the entire reporting process because of its procedural flaws.

The International Campaign for Justice in Bhopal (ICJB)

Gas leakage in the Union Carbide plant of Bhopal, India, in 1984 severely affected a large portion of people living in the city, killing many, injuring many others, and adversely affecting the health of the community for generations to come. ICJB is an activist network that was formed to fight for the appropriate compensation for the half million of people in Bhopal who were exposed to the poison gas caused by the leak in the Union Carbide plant in 1984, and to secure appropriate justice for the gas-affected people. The localized struggle of ICJB is situated amid a global landscape of policymaking and policy implementation, negotiating environmental laws at national levels of multiple countries that emerged as the sites of the struggle. One of the earliest movements of social change constituted around environmental justice, ICJB embodies the struggles of a community in the global South seeking to hold a TNC (Union Carbide, which later came to be owned by the Dow Chemical Company) accountable in local, national, and international courts. In this sense, ICJB returns the gaze of the dominant social structures and the logics that are written into such structures. The erasure of the global South from spaces of representation is resisted through the participation of those very sectors of the globe in mainstream juridical and civil society processes that serve as sites of erasure by turning subaltern populations as passive aggregates to be worked on by global and national policies and programs. As a social change movement that originates from the global South and that seeks to hold accountable the practices of a TNC headquartered in the global North, ICJB demonstrates the role of localized activism from the South in resisting the corporate control of juridical systems in the hands of transnational hegemony. The ICJB is both a material struggle as well as a struggle for recognition and representation in the dominant structures of transnational hegemony, depicting the intertwined relationship between symbolic and material struggles.

Drawing on a local-global network of solidarity, the ICJB is a coalition of people's organizations, nonprofit groups, and individuals who have joined forces to campaign for justice for the survivors of the Union Carbide disaster in Bhopal. Three organizations of survivors from Bhopal play a leading role in the international network, depicting the role of local agency, local participation and decision-making capacity, and collective participation in processes of change in order to seek transformations in inequitable global structures; the resistive voices emerging from these local networks are accompanied by voices of resistance from global sites that carry the messages of resistance into international structures of decision making. Local voices from the South find their way into global sites of power through these local-global solidarity networks. The politics of change also becomes the politics of representation, seeking to carve out spaces for representation. Because the effectiveness of TNCs such as the Dow Chemical Company depends upon their ability to manipulate local, national, and global juridical systems by using their locational ambiguity and mobility to evade accountability, the resistance of ICJB is constituted in the formations of local-global networks of solidarity that take the messages of accountability and justice to courts and spaces of public opinion located locally, nationally, and globally. Resistance in ICJB takes on a mobile presence in order to counter the mobility of transnational capital. The intervention of ICJB is constituted in mainstream public spheres that typically emerge as the sites of violence on subaltern communities by disenfranchising them. In a nutshell, the formation of the ICJB as a network is constituted in resistance to the networks of corporate power with influences in executive, legislative, and judiciary structures within nation states, across nation states, and at global platforms. This local global link is well narrated in the following depiction of ICJB (http://studentsforb-hopal.org/about):

> The International Campaign for Justice for Bhopal (ICJB) is a coali-tion of disaster survivors and environmental, social justice, progres-sive Indian, and human rights groups that have joined forces to hold the Indian Government and Dow Chemical Corporation account-able for the ongoing chemical disaster in Bhopal, India. It was set up to address the grave injustices suffered by the half million Bhopal Gas Disaster survivors.
>
> In North America, Students for Bhopal and ICJB is a network of stu-dents, professionals, activists, and partners working in solidarity with the survivors of the Bhopal disaster in their struggle for justice. We use education, grassroots organizing and non-violent direct action to pressure Dow Chemical and the Indian Government to uphold the Bhopalis' demand for justice, and their fundamental human right to live free of chemical poison. SfB/ICJB work directly to improve the condition of Bhopal's survivors. Our role is to empower and train lead-ers in the worldwide movement to end this crime against humanity.
>
> We all live in Bhopal and we will not rest without justice in Bhopal!

The global network structure of ICJB is directed by the voices of resistance that emerge locally, seeking justice in Bhopal through adequate compensa-tion, by holding Union Carbide (and its parent company Dow) account-able in the national and international courts, and by pressuring for the chemical clean-up of the toxic poisons in Bhopal. The fundamental hu-man right of the people of Bhopal to live free of chemical poison emerges as the key framework for the politics of resistance (for more information on frames of resistance, see Snow & Benford, 1992, 1998; Snow, Rochford, Worden, & Benford, 1986), drawing in the global networks of support to impact international, national, and local policies and rulings that would secure justice for the survivors in Bhopal. The international reach of ICJB serves as a conduit for carrying the messages of the Bhopal survivors to global platforms, seeking out justice in these global platforms, and holding Dow accountable in global platforms. An excellent example of this global impact of ICJB is evident in the local-national-global organizing that was directed at stopping the sponsorship of the 2012 London Olympics by the Dow Chemical Company, resulting in awareness campaigns, direct action, signing of online petitions, and ongoing dialogues with various political actors (see http://studentsforbhopal.org/get-dow-out-of-the-olympics). The online campaign offers the following introduction to the issue, also setting up the relevance of the issue:

> Dow Chemical acquired Union Carbide as a wholly owned subsidiary in 2001. They are therefore responsible for the clean up of the former Union Carbide Factory site in Bhopal, India. The area around the factory is densely populated and continues to be heavily contaminated by chemicals and toxins produced by the factory which Dow, despite their evident responsibility, have thus far refused to clean up.
>
> The situation in Bhopal is a humanitarian and environmental catastrophe that continues to affect tens of thousands of people today.
>
> The organizers of the Olympic Games claim that they are commited to organising a sustainable and environmentally friendly event. It is therefore completely unacceptable for Dow Chemical to be partnered with the London Olympic Games, and the wider International Olympic Organisation.

The environmental façade of the Olympic organizing committee is brought into question and is juxtaposed against the backdrop of the decision of the committee to partner with the Dow Chemical Company. The international event is utilized as a setting to hold the Dow Chemical Company accountable and to draw attention to the role of this company in cleaning up the oil spill. Direct action in London and in the US carry the voices of resistance to the key sites of decision making regarding the Olympic Games sponsorship.

Through their networks of solidarity, the members of ICJB continue to pressure Union Carbide's current owner, the Dow Chemical Company, and the US and Indian governments to ensure adequate health care, safe environment, and proper rehabilitation for the survivors of the disaster and their children. Essential, therefore, to the politics of activism in the ICJB movement is the articulation of a framework of justice that is directed at the three key stakeholders that were involved in the crisis, seeking to hold these stakeholders accountable. Exemplary punishment of the corporation and its guilty officials is one of the key demands of ICJB (http://www.bhopal.net/oldsite/icjb.html), and a key component of the voices of resistance is the emphasis placed on grassroots organizing seeking entry points into the legal structure in order to hold the Dow Chemical Company accountable (http://studentsforbhopal.org/taxonomy/term/46):

> A curative petition for compensation for disaster victims is pending in the Supreme Court of India. A curative petition recognizes the grave miscarriage of justice in the previous compensation judgement, which resulted in appallingly inadequate support for a fraction of the affected population. *We're talking 7 U.S. cents a day for a lifetime of unimaginable suffering.* In the current civil case, figures of death reported is 5,295, while the Indian Council of Medical Research (ironically, a Government agency!) shows the number to be closer to 25,000. Bhopalis in India, after failing with several measures to urge the Government of India to change the figures for the death and injured of the disaster, organized a "rail roko" (stop the trains) on the 27th anniversary. With such a drastic measure taken, the Government is now willing to come to the table with activists.

Discursive engagement with the legal structures, processes, and discourses creates a framework for pointing out the injustice carried out in the insufficient compensation provided to the survivors and their families. References to numbers and estimates of death, and the contestations of the numbers used for judgment are utilized as frameworks for resistance. Legal action within court systems are complemented by direct actions such as "stop the trains" on the street.

The ICJB website provides a list of international members within the network of solidarity that include the Association for India's Development (US), Bhopal Information Network (Japan), Corpwatch (US), and Greenpeace International and Pesticide Action Network (US and UK). The campaign against the Dow Chemical Company, therefore, is constituted on the basis of local-global network structures that connect in solidarity to fight for the justice of the people in Bhopal. Worth noting here is the interconnectedness of the local and global networks, and the leveraging capacity of these networks to exert pressure on key stakeholders through various local, national, and global sites of influence. The local-global solidarity networks of the ICJB become evident in the Occupy Bhopal protests that were enacted across the world on December 3, 2011, on the 27th anniversary of the Bhopal disaster, enacted in Occupy protests in Boston, die-in actions in San Francisco, documentary screenings in Toronto, and Bhopalis in India laying their bodies on railway tracks. The website of the ICJB offers a link to the images of the protests, witnessing the acts of resistance performed across various sites around the globe (http://www.flickr.com/photos/72877823@N07/sets/72157628579196095/). Linkages across issue frames were instrumental in putting forth a structure of solidarity. Consider, for instance, the following depiction of the Bhopal protests at Occupy Boston (http://studentsforbhopal.org/taxonomy/term/46):

> Members of the Boston chapter for the International Campaign for Justice in Bhopal (ICJB) spoke about the disaster at Occupy Boston, drawing parallels between the struggle of the Bhopalis against Dow's corporate power manipulating governments and the struggle of the 99% against unregulated corporate practices. They also screened the award-winning documentary "*Bhopali*" (2010), which describes the events leading to the disaster as well as its aftermath. Sanjay Verma, an activist and survivor from Bhopal, was present during both the events to discuss questions with people, urging people to continue to pressure the Olympic Committee to drop Dow as a partner.

The local-global network of solidarity in resistance is strengthened in the voices of participants in Occupy Boston who draw out the similarities between issue frames, noting how the resistance in Bhopal is also similar to the resistance voiced in the Occupy movement, seeking to counter the manipulation of legislative, juridical, and executive systems by TNCs.

One of the key aspects in the localized voices of resistance is the collection of information in order to counter the public relations strategies that are utilized by the Dow Chemical Company; the public relations spin offered by the company is countered by the truth offered by the activists.

Truth emerges as the key site of contestation, as activists engage their politics of change on the articulation of truth, which then becomes the very basis for seeking social justice. As demonstrated in chapters two and three of this book, information plays a key role in the public relations functions of TNCs, both in the arguments made by TNCs in legal structures as well as the information presented by TNCs in public discursive spaces with the goal of strategically shaping public opinion. This information function becomes a key component of the ICJB website, with the website offering information resources that provide a detailed description of what happened on the deadly night, thus accounting for the events and offering an entry point into the claims of truth, set in opposition to the public relations practices and message claims made by the Dow Chemical Company. Creating access to information and to truthful accounts of the events become the framework of organizing for social justice and for contesting the public relations frames offered by Union Carbide and the Indian and US governments. Contestation of truth based on evidence and based on live accounts of witnesses of the events offer alternative frameworks for challenging the public relations messages and information claims that are put forth by those responsible. Therefore, the voices of the victims are foregrounded in constituting the truthful accounts of the events. Authenticity of the accounts of what happened on that fateful night becomes the site of claims making.

According to the website, on December 3, 1984, poison gas leaked from a Union Carbide factory, killing thousands. Reports have differed on the number of victims. Whereas Union Carbide states that 3,800 victims were killed, municipal workers who picked up bodies with their own hands, loading them onto trucks for burial in mass graves or to be burned on mass pyres, reckon they shifted at least 15,000 bodies. Here, the claims of Union Carbide are contested by the claims of the municipal workers who actually worked at the sites, loading and burying bodies. Survivors, basing their estimates on the number of shrouds sold in the city, conservatively claim about 8,000 died in the first week. The contestation of the death counts becomes a site of resistance, and is framed in the backdrop of the statement, "such body counts become meaningless when you know that the dying has never stopped, (http://www.bhopal.org/what-happened/), noting the ongoing deaths that continue to happen because of the chemical poisoning.

What happened on that fateful night and the account of the events is yet another domain of truth claims where the resistive voices of the ICJB counter the claims of Union Carbide. Countering the accounting of the events is a key strategy for organizing, as it is this very accounting that lies at the heart of the judgments and justice that are offered to the victims and the voices of resistance organized in this backdrop. Providing the analysis of what went wrong, the ICJB website writes:

> The Union Carbide factory in Bhopal seemed doomed almost from the start. The company built the pesticide factory there in the 1970s, thinking that India represented a huge untapped market for its pest control products. However sales never met the company's expectations; Indian farmers, struggling to cope with droughts and floods, didn't have the money to buy Union Carbide's pesticides. The plant, which never reached its full capacity, proved to be a losing venture and ceased active production in the early 1980s. (http://www.bhopal.org)

The setting up of the context by providing historic information also creates a broader framework for understanding the negligence of the plant by the Union Carbide company, drawing attention to the unethical practices of the company and putting it under the scrutiny of the juridical structures. The website explains that due to the Indian venture turning into a loss-making proposition for the company, vast quantities of dangerous chemicals remained in the plant; three tanks continued to hold over 60 tons of methyl isocyanate (MIC) without appropriate storage measures. Although MIC is a particularly reactive and deadly gas, the Union Carbide plant's elaborate safety system was allowed to fall into disrepair. The offering of step-by-step evidence regarding the role of Union Carbide in not following preventive measures and in neglecting to properly monitor the plant offer the basis for claims of justice and appropriate punishment of the involved stakeholders in juridical platforms. It is this claim of negligence that becomes the basis for activist organizing that seeks to hold the key leaders of Union Carbide accountable. The claim of negligence also emerges as the material basis for subaltern organizing that seeks to hold accountable the dominant structures of decision making and arbitration within the neo-liberal configuration. The website argues that the management's reasoning seemed to be that since the plant had ceased all production, no threat remained. Every safety system that had been installed to prevent a leak of MIC—at least six in all—ultimately proved inoperative. Challenging the dominant narrative of Carbide, ICJB provides the diagram of the plant and gives a blow-by-blow account of how the accident happened. It also documents testimonies of several victims, who narrate their experiences of the fateful night and their experiences of pain and suffering in years thereafter. Subaltern voices emerge into the discursive space as sites of contestation. They resist the efforts of erasure, manipulation, and co-optation by Union Carbide through their presence at the discursive sites in the mainstream. In an account of the events, survivor Aziza Sultan notes:

> At about 12.30 am I woke to the sound of my baby coughing badly. In the half light I saw that the room was filled with a white cloud. I heard a lot of people shouting. They were shouting "run, run". Then I started coughing with each breath seeming as if I was breathing in fire. My eyes were burning. (http://bhopal.net/the-1984-gas-leak/)

ICJB offers the information that since the disaster, survivors have been plagued with an epidemic of cancers, menstrual disorders, and what one doctor described as "monstrous births." Remarking upon the effects of the poisoning, the site notes that the gas-affected people of Bhopal continue to succumb to injuries sustained during the disaster, dying at the rate of one each day. Treatment protocols are affected by the company's refusal to provide information it holds on the toxic effects of MIC. Both Union Carbide and its new owner the Dow Chemical Company claim the data is a "trade secret," frustrating the efforts of doctors to treat gas-affected victims. Once again, the company and its unethical practices emerge as spaces of interrogation. The site itself has never been cleaned up, and a new generation of victims is being poisoned by the chemicals that Union Carbide left behind (http://www.bhopal.org/what-happened/).

On its website, ICJB has made available Union Carbide's version of the tragedy, which has changed several times. The blame of the gas leak was attributed to an extremist attack, followed by sabotage by a disgruntled employee. These public relations practices of Carbide are interrogated by ICJB and are opened up to refutation, providing evidence to demonstrate the negligence of the corporation that led to the accident. In mobilizing collective resistance, the ICJB website fundamentally ruptures the hegemonic constructions of truth by Union Carbide and the Dow Chemical Company, establishing itself as a repository of alternative information that challenges Union Carbide's version of the truth, and privileging the voices of the victims and survivors as the authentic sites for the production of truth. The experiences of the victims of the tragedy are constituted in the narratives presented on the website. These narratives move beyond the realm of simply contesting the number of victims to articulating the experiences of the tragedy by the victims. In doing so, the website reconfigures what constitutes knowledge—legitimizing the individual stories of pain and suffering through which the collective plight of the victims of Bhopal come to life.

In resisting the dominant framings of the tragedy, the ICJB website covers a variety of issues related to medical consequences, engineering, and management shortcomings, Union Carbide's and Dow's use of public relations to avoid taking responsibility, the role of Indian politics at central and state levels, and the environmental consequences of the contaminated factory. In presenting the dominant arguments and subsequently refuting them, the site communicates the struggles over power and control of the framing of the issue at different levels, highlighting the relevance of contesting the hegemonic versions of "what happened in Bhopal."

In the backdrop of the documentations of the unethical practices of the dominant actors embodied in the actions of the Union Carbide, the website presents the struggles of the survivors in their fight for justice. Here is an excerpt that depicts the resilience and courage of the victims:

> Yet the victims haven't given up. Their struggle for justice and dignity is one of the most valiant anywhere. They have unbelievable energy and hope . . . the fight has not ended. It won't, so long as our collective conscience stirs. (http://www.bhopal.org/ways-to-help/international-campaign-for-justice/)

Through stories of protest marches, processions, picketing, effigy-burning, and so forth, the website draws attention to the everyday forms of local resistance among the survivors and invites participation in resisting the oppressive practices of the dominant actors in transnational hegemony. The hopes of the victims are presented as markers of the movement, and it is articulated that resistance will continue as long as the dominant social and political structures continue to marginalize the victims of the tragedy. The spirit of the fight is embodied in the collective will and consciousness of the victims at the local level, and this is articulated on the site through the narratives of the victims who discuss the various avenues in which they participate in processes seeking to change the structures around the tragedy.

The website serves as a location for communicating to global publics about the various ways in which local activists continue to enact their agency in challenging the dominant structures and in seeking to transform these structures, sharing information about the movement as well as calling for participation from various global stakeholder groups. The information about ICJB's fight demonstrates the principles and practices of its offline struggle; the offline struggle finds voice through narratives that are shared and circulated in various online platforms. For instance, a video posted on the website captures the attempts of the activists to clean up a contaminated site, and subsequently shows them being beaten up and arrested by the police. This video is accompanied by an article titled "Which side is the government on?" The article provides another instantiation of celebrating agency by confronting the complicitous relationship among corporations, governments, and law enforcement officials within neoliberal structures of governance:

> the violence of the police, unprovoked and over-the-top as it was, can't be ignored. The world has seen the video footage and it's about time people knew what the survivors struggling for justice are up against: not just an immoral corporation and its allies in the US establishment; not just a succession of Indian administrations so eager to cultivate rich multinationals that they betrayed their duty to their own poorest people; but a Madhya Pradesh state government, various officials

of which have over the years demonstrated themselves to be spine-
less, incompetent and corrupt. It was the state government that sent
in the goons, but it is Union Carbide (now hiding like a toxic Jonah
within the Dow whale) that is responsible for the problem. (http://
www.bhopal.net/oldsite/peoplevpoison.html)

Stories of resistance are circulated through the various platforms of
the site. The pictures of an indefinite hunger strike and an 800-kilometer
march (*padayatra*) by the Bhopal victims depict their agency in collective resistance. Stories of resistance offer hope and encouragement. For
instance, the website presents information about the march and hunger
strike of April 2006, which culminated in a meeting with the prime minister of India, who granted four demands of the activists. The four demands
assured by the Indian government are action on clean water, clean-up of
toxic waste sites, setting up a coordinating committee on medical and
economic rehabilitation, and are reflective of the activist group's ability
in securing justice.

The celebration of local agency is presented as an exemplar for global
action against dominant neoliberal structures. Through the sharing of the
narratives of resistance at local level, the site becomes a discursive space
for promoting global resistance against other forms of structural oppression. The case of Bhopal is linked with other instances of corporate crimes
at a global level, and the local issue is connected with the global politics of
transnational hegemony. The broader resistance of ICJB against neoliberalism is reflected in the following paragraph posted on the site:

Bhopal isn't only about charred lungs, poisoned kidneys and de-
formed foetuses. It's also about corporate crime, multinational skull-
duggery, injustice, dirty deals, medical malpractice, corruption, cal-
lousness and contempt for the poor. Nothing else explains why the
victims' average compensation was just $500—for a lifetime of misery
. . . (http://www.bhopal.org/ways-to-help/international-campaign-
for-justice/)

Through these stories, the site invites global involvement in action directed
at impacting international, national, and local policies that would influ-

ence the Bhopal case. Opportunities for online participation and mobilization complement forms of direct action, performances, protests, and blockades. It opens up the discursive space for globally dispersed online publics to join protests through several means. For instance, petitions and letters to authorities demanding "justice and dignity" for the victims in Bhopal are made available to online readers. The letters and petitions are drafted with clear articulations of the injustices inflicted on the people of Bhopal and specify the demands that are being sought. With a click on the "signature" key for each of these letters and petitions, anyone with Internet access can become part of this global fabric of struggle by being one of the voices that resists the dominant structure in this fight. For instance, this is what the petition to the Dow Chemical Company demands (http://www.petitiononline.com/bhopal/):

> I support the struggle for justice of the people of Bhopal. More than 20,000 innocent people have already died and 120,000 are suffering today from health effects (see www.bhopal.org) related to their gas exposure. It was Union Carbide's cost-cutting that turned Bhopal into a gas chamber (see www.bhopal.net/oldsite/poisonpapers.html) and it's the responsibility of Carbide's new owner, Dow Chemical, to resolve the outstanding legal and moral obligations it has in Bhopal (see www.studentsforbhopal.org/DowIsLiable.htm)

The petition puts forth a narrative that questions the TNC, and in doing so, brings to the fore the structural conflicts authorized by global capitalism, simultaneously reversing the dominant configurations of power. The solidarity with the subaltern communities at the margins fosters the entry point for global action that is directed at structural transformation through various forms of participation. The petition highlights the negligences by the Dow Chemical Company that contributed to the gas tragedy—absence of a siren, disfunctioning of all safety systems, under-investment in an inherently hazardous plant located in a crowded neighborhood, use of unproven designs, storing lethal MIC in reckless quantities, and cutting down on safety staff and training in an effort to cut costs. It elucidates these negligences by the Dow Chemical Company and makes the following demands on one of the biggest global corporations: face trial, provide long-term health care and social support, and remove the contamination of the ground water and soil in and around the abandoned Union Carbide factory to ensure safe drinking water.

Organizing for justice in Bhopal becomes embodied in a broader struggle against corporate control of juridical processes and infrastructures. The dominant structure is a hirerarchical structure that does not question the Dow Chemical Company, while the victims of its corporate crime continue to fight for moral and social support. As ICJB states on the website:

> Bhopal is about what kind of a world we will all live in. If India can stand up to the biggest chemical company in the world and say "you can't do business here until you repair the damage you have done to our country and people," that precedent could fundamentally challenge the reign of profits over people globally. It could become a building block for all the movements for social justice and for a non-toxic future that have piled up behind it for twenty-one years. (http://legacy.bhopal.net/march/archives/2006/04/striking_it_or.html/)

In its articulation of India's position with respect to the Dow Chemical Company, ICJB locates the struggle in the backdrop of the legislative and juridical power exercised by corporate interests. In its letter to the Indian Prime Minister Manmohan Singh, which is also available for its online supporters to sign, ICJB urges (http://www.studentsforbhopal.org/FaxAction/fax_action.php):

> we are disappointed that you refused to take action against the criminal corporations responsible for the disaster. Instead of prosecuting them, your Government has openly made moves to facilitate the business of Union Carbide's new owner, Dow Chemical Corporation. Carbide is at-large, even while it and its owner Dow continue to profit from doing business in India. Why does India seem so concerned with appeasing a corporation—Dow Chemical—which continues to flout and scorn Indian law by sheltering its fugitive subsidiary Union Carbide from appearing for trial in India?

It is a discourse that resists the uneven social order. Urging India not to "appease Dow Chemical," ICJB invokes a counter-hegemonic discourse that resists unequal power relations and situates ICJB's resistance within the politics of transnational relations. For instance, urging the Indian authorities to prosecute Union Carbide and blacklist all the products of the company in India, ICJB is constructing a narrative that envisions the principles of true democratic governance.

The website also brings forth many alternative forms of communication that are being used by its different stakeholders for planning and carrying out actions such as vigils, demonstrations, street plays, and art (music, theatre, movies, art exhibition). But these diverse communicative actions converge on the web space and discursively construct a vision—that of supporting a section of marginalized people, who have been abandoned to their suffering without adequate medical, financial, or social help. Involvement in supporting the victims means partaking in ICJB's resistance to uncover the dominant capitalist interest and champion human rights through a variety of strategies, such as registering to participate in hunger strike, sending a free fax to the prime minister of India, signing an online petition to the Dow Chemical Company, making a donation to aid the Bhopalis' justice struggle, making a donation to help open a free medical clinic in Bhopal, and joining the student campaign.

The collective resistance gets carried to non-local terrains as the website urges its supporters from all over the world to join them in a global rolling hunger strike by registering online. People from local and diverse non-local territories establish their presence in the collective resistance by posting their blogs and pictures, creating a global solidarity network for Bhopal activists. The march and hunger strike of April 2006 culminated in a meeting with the prime minister of India, who granted four demands but said he has no power over Dow. Bhopal activists called off their indefinite fast on April 17, 2006, the seventh day of the fast, based on the assurances from the government. As the website articulates the whole process as a victory for the people, it establishes ICJB as a resistance movement that works toward and has the potential to impact dominant practices. But it juxtaposes the information on victory with the following question: "Why did it take an 800 kilometer march and an indefinite hunger strike to win a victory we should never have had to fight for?" (http://www.bhopal.net/delhi-march.html). What manifests in the question is continuation of its resistance to challenge the systemic knowledge construction that privileges the dominant ideologies of corporations at the cost of human interests. ICJB's question attempts to alter the hegemonic discourse by granting agency to the subaltern as the knowing subject and as a site of knowledge production in the global economic order. Along these lines of localized resistance in the global South, the people's tribunals in the global South (http://www.guardian.co.uk/global-development/poverty-matters/2010/nov/12/dhaka-climate-court-criminals) are one example of the shifts in the locus of accountability from the traditionally powerful sites in the global North to the impoverished sectors of the South. Other similar protest movements carrying themes of the environment such as "Save Niyamgiri," "Narmada Bachao Andolan," and "Cochabamba" are organized under other subheadings in the book because of the multi-topical nature of these social change efforts.

Conclusion

In conclusion, the case studies presented in this chapter document the various innovative strategies and tactics through which voices of resistance seek to transform local, global, and international environmental policies. Specifically worth attending to is the deployment of innovative communicative strategies that, on one hand, disrupt the expectations of the status quo and, on the other hand, reach out to a large audience to build a framework of solidarity. The creativity of communication lies at the heart of these efforts of social change and structural transformation that seek to resist the mediated dominance of corporate elites through their public relations and advertising campaigns by the deployment of innovative grassroots strategies of social change that seek to foster spaces of recognition and representation in dominant public spheres.

Social Change and Politics

Introduction

The dominant narratives of political structures are resisted through the interrogation of the logics of these structures, seeking to displace the top-down power from the sites of decision making that minimize the opportunities for political participation among communities that have been placed at the margins. Social change movements that seek to rupture the inherent logics of political structures do so in order to challenge the inherent logics that justify the erasure of subaltern communities from the realms of policy making, representation, and participation. The marginalization of communities is tied to the systematic erasure of these communities from political processes and from dominant systems of governance. Therefore, political processes of change are directed at transforming the oppressions that are written into the organizing of political structures, which minimize the opportunities for public participation, and simultaneously, justify the violence (both structural as well as physical) carried out on the margins through the depiction of the margins as backward, primitive, and in need of interventions.

Chapter Five

185

At the core of the voices of resistance that are directed at bringing about transformations in political structures is the desire to transform the politics of silencing and erasure that are tied to the configurations of these structures, and the logics of organizing within which these structures are formed and reproduced. The political marginalization of specific groups is tied to the mobilization of these groups to seek to transform the basic modes of organizing of these dominant structures that marginalize. In this chapter, we will discuss the efforts of social change seeking to transform political structures in the Zapatista Army of National Liberation (*Ejército Zapatista de Liberación Nacional, EZLN*), the Arab Spring, and the political movement of the indigenous communities in Bolivia that led to the election of President Evo Morales.

EZLN

One of the earliest examples of subaltern resistance against neoliberal governance complementarily organized, networked, and articulated through the Internet is the Zapatista movement, an indigenous crusade in the Chiapas region of Mexico that sought to resist the neoliberal reforms that were being carried out in Mexico under the rhetoric of development (Cleaver, 1998; Dellacioppa, 2009). The Zapatista movement stood as one of the earliest voices of resistance from the global South that sought to resist the oppressive material effects produced by neoliberal policies imposed by the nation state; formulated within the terrains of the movement was the story of oppression carried out on indigenous communities through projects of neoliberalism that further perpetuated the marginalization of indigenous communities through their displacement. In response to the implementation of neoliberal policies in Mexico and the marginalization of the indigenous population in the Chiapas region of Mexico, the EZLN emerged as an indigenous movement that challenged neoliberal policies of the state and demanded indigenous autonomy, and in doing so, drew upon a transnational solidarity network to articulate a resistive politics against neoliberalism (Dellacioppa, 2009; Garrido & Halavais, 2003; Muñoz Ramírez, 2008).

The EZLN was founded in 1983 in the jungles of the Chiapas region to resist the antidemocratic nature of neoliberal projects sponsored by the Mexican government that imposed oppressive top-down policies on the indigenous people of the region, the selling of collective indigenous lands to transnational capital, and the historic exploitation of indigenous people. Drawing upon a locally grounded participatory framework of decision making that is culturally based, the EZLN recruited local villagers, starting conversations in the communities about the problems such as health and access to land, and building health clinics in the villages. The locally driven processes of decision making were intrinsically tied to local cultural logics of consensus and policy formulation as opposed to the top-down forms of decision making embodied in the neoliberal reforms that were being carried out across Mexico. As the villages in Chiapas started participating in the EZLN, each village had a representative that would report to the insurgents and meet with each other to discuss the antidemocratic policies of the government and the strategies needed to resist these policies; through this process, participation became a key decision-making tool of the movement. Participation here was directed toward respecting the local commitment and agendas of community members. Of particular concern to the EZLN were the continued marginalization of the indigenous population in the face of structural adjustment policies and the continued erasure of the indigenous population from the state policies that exerted control on indigenous land. In the early 1990s, the revision of Article 27 of the Mexican constitution that opened up collective indigenous lands to foreign investment under structural adjustment programs (SAPs) catalyzed the EZLN to take up arms against the government, embodying the building frustrations among indigenous communities about the disenfranchisement of these communities from symbolic and material spaces.

The North American Free Trade Agreement (NAFTA) provided the backdrop for the expression of resistance, which in turn opened up a sustainable and long-term space for resistance against neoliberalism initiated from the global South. Resisting the signing of NAFTA in 1994 (that involved Mexico as one of the participants), the EZLN took control over five municipalities in Chiapas, demanding work, land, food, housing,

health, education, independence, freedom, democracy, justice, and peace
in their first communiqué issued from the main balcony in each of the
municipalities they had taken over (Dellacioppa, 2009; Muñoz Ramírez,
2008). Particularly salient in the demands of the EZLN are the resistive
concepts of liberty, freedom, and democracy, concepts that are rhetorically positioned as the underlying principles of neoliberalism (see Dutta,
2011). Here is an excerpt from the first communiqué, termed as the "First
Declaration of the Lacandon Jungle" that specifically plays on this act of
redefining neoliberal definitions of liberty and democracy (http://www.
struggle.ws/mexico/ezln/ezlnwa.html):

> We are a product of 500 years of struggle: first against slavery, then
> during the War of Independence against Spain led by insurgents,
> then to avoid being absorbed by North American imperialism, then
> to promulgate our constitution and expel the French empire from
> our soil, and later the dictatorship of Porfirio Diaz denied us the just
> application of the Reform laws and the people rebelled and leaders
> like Villa and Zapata emerged, poor men just like us. We have been
> denied the most elemental preparation so they can use us as cannon
> fodder and pillage the wealth of our country. They don't care that we
> have nothing, absolutely nothing, not even a roof over our heads, no
> land, no work, no health care, no food nor education. Nor are we able
> to freely and democratically elect our political representatives, nor
> is there independence from foreigners, nor is there peace nor justice
> for ourselves and our children.
>
> But today, we say ENOUGH IS ENOUGH.
>
> We are the inheritors of the true builders of our nation. The dispos-
> sessed, we are millions and we thereby call upon our brothers and
> sisters to join this struggle as the only path, so that we will not die of
> hunger due to the insatiable ambition of a 70 year dictatorship led by
> a clique of traitors that represent the most conservative and sell-out
> groups. . . . To prevent the continuation of the above and as our last
> hope, after having tried to utilize all legal means based on our Con-
> stitution, we go to our Constitution, to apply Article 39 which says:

"National Sovereignty essentially and originally resides in the people. All political power emanates from the people and its purpose is to help the people. The people have, at all times, the inalienable right to alter or modify their form of government."

Therefore, according to our constitution, we declare the following to the Mexican federal army, the pillar of the Mexican dictatorship that we suffer from, monopolized by a one-party system and led by Carlos Salinas de Gortari, the maximum and illegitimate federal executive that today holds power.

According to this Declaration of War, we ask that other powers of the nation advocate to restore the legitimacy and the stability of the nation by overthrowing the dictator.

We also ask that international organizations and the International Red Cross watch over and regulate our battles, so that our efforts are carried out while still protecting our civilian population. We declare now and always that we are subject to the Geneva Accord, forming the EZLN as our fighting arm of our liberation struggle. We have the Mexican people on our side, we have the beloved tri-colored flag highly respected by our insurgent fighters. We use black and red in our uniform as our symbol of our working people on strike. Our flag carries the following letters, "EZLN," Zapatista National Liberation Army, and we always carry our flag into combat.

Beforehand, we refuse any effort to disgrace our just cause by accusing us of being drug traffickers, drug guerrillas, thieves, or other names that might by used by our enemies. Our struggle follows the constitution which is held high by its call for justice and equality.

Therefore, according to this declaration of war, we give our military forces, the EZLN, the following orders:

First: Advance to the capital of the country, overcoming the Mexican federal army, protecting in our advance the civilian population and permitting the people in the liberated area the right to freely and democratically elect their own administrative authorities.

Second: Respect the lives of our prisoners and turn over all wounded to the International Red Cross.

Third: Initiate summary judgments against all soldiers of the Mexican federal army and the political police that have received training or have been paid by foreigners, accused of being traitors to our country, and against all those that have repressed and treated badly the civil population and robbed or stolen from or attempted crimes against the good of the people.

Fourth: Form new troops with all those Mexicans that show their interest in joining our struggle, including those that, being enemy soldiers, turn themselves in without having fought against us, and promise to take orders from the General Command of the Zapatista National Liberation Army.

Fifth: We ask for the unconditional surrender of the enemy's headquarters before we begin any combat to avoid any loss of lives.

Sixth: Suspend the robbery of our natural resources in the areas controlled by the EZLN.

To the People of Mexico: We, the men and women, full and free, are conscious that the war that we have declared is our last resort, but also a just one. The dictators are applying an undeclared genocidal war against our people for many years. Therefore we ask for your participation, your decision to support this plan that struggles for work, land, housing, food, health care, education, independence, freedom, democracy, justice and peace. We declare that we will not stop fighting until the basic demands of our people have been met by forming a government of our country that is free and democratic.

JOIN THE INSURGENT FORCES OF THE ZAPATISTA NATIONAL LIBERATION ARMY.

The declaration resists the neoliberal reforms in Mexico by putting forth a bottom-up process that foregrounds local participation as a way of representing the community's voices in decision making. Local participation becomes an avenue for impacting state-level policies, specifically those policies that have key ramifications for local populations. It engages with the language of the structure (liberty, democracy, freedom) to resist the structure, redefining these terms in order to point out the oppressions that are tolerated by the reforms written into neoliberalism. The oppression carried out on the dispossessed serves as the basis of the social change movement, connecting the voices of resistance to the long history of oppression and articulating an urgency for action. The hunger and the everyday economic struggles of the poor for resources are placed in the backdrop of the neoliberal greed of state actors who have sold out the economy to imperial forces. The narrative of disenfranchisement outlining the specific forms of marginalization in health care, education, employment, and food insecurity experienced by the poor serves as the basis for the organizing of resistance. Also salient in the story of resistance is the framing of the oppressive communicative context where the participatory and democratic decision-making capacity of the people has been fundamentally denied; this denial sets up the context for the armed struggle. Worth noting here is the returning of the gaze at the structures of neoliberalism that utilize the narratives of freedom and democracy to impose top-down forms of structural violence that deprive the poor from access to basic material and communicative resources.

Reference to Article 39 of the Mexican constitution substantiates the legitimacy of the movement as operating within the country's constitutional framework. The declaration forges out a local-global linkage by connecting the appeal of the EZLN to specific audiences that include the people of Mexico as well as to international organizations. References to the Geneva Accord provide the framework for constructing the armed struggle as a liberation struggle. It is within this framework then that the articulations of human rights and social justice draw upon a global reference framework to create legitimacy for the movement as well as to create a global constitutive base of support for the movement and its demands (Garrido & Halavais, 2003). Note in the declaration the argument related to the right of the people to natural resources, serving as the basis for identifying and resisting what is termed as the robbery of natural resources.

Drawing upon a locally based conceptual system of decision making rooted in the local culture, the EZLN utilized consensual decision making that operated at the level of the local communities, and this quickly emerged as a global model for organizing against neoliberalism, simultaneously drawing upon global support from transnational actors to resist the neoliberal policies of the Mexican state. The participatory processes of community organizing among the EZLN quickly emerged as a model for the development of a transcultural community activist network against neoliberalism (Dellacioppa, 2009; Schulz, 1998). The EZLN rapidly emerged on the global stage as an exemplar of resistive politics against neoliberalism, demonstrating the intersection between the local and the global in the politics of locally driven social change. The local cultural politics of the EZLN demonstrates the interplay between structure and agency in challenging global structures of neoliberalism.

As demonstrated with the example of the EZLN, it is in the realm of the control enacted by dominant global actors that resistive strategies are deployed by activist publics and communities dispersed around the globe; just as globalization expands the geographic and material scopes of transnational corporations (TNCs), it also opens up new spaces and methods of global organizing directed at social transformation at the global level. Global resistance is at once both modern and postmodern; it explores the material roots of global inequities and simultaneously foregrounds the temporality of discourse that is continuously shifting and open to reinterpretations in complexly layered global structures. The "complex interplay of economic and cultural dynamics" (Appadurai, 1990, p. 201) played out in the realm of transnational activism necessitates an understanding of its implications for communication research. For instance, the concept of the "scapes" articulated by Appadurai (1990) demonstrates that public consciousness no longer stretches across national spaces, but "ignites the micro-politics of a nation-state" (Robins, 2000, p. 236). Hence, what are the challenges for communication research in view of these complex global shifts, especially as it enters into conversations about communicative processes of social change?

In the realm of the materiality of global resistance spaces, there are multiple sites through which activists are organizing in response to global economic restructuring (Dellacioppa, 2009). While working in a community-based setting, grassroots organizers are increasingly networking with transnational activists to effect changes in specific communities, thereby connecting the local and the global (Naples & Desai, 2002). With the growing presence of locally rooted networks structured around global issues, we see complex interaction between local and supranational activism. Though these groups occasionally participate in transnational protest events, their activities remain strongly rooted in the local. Agency is expressed through the continued used of cultural symbols in transformative politics of social change. For example, Zapatismo emerges as a global concept for activist organizing that offers an alternative consensus-based participatory approach to decision making in communication for social change (Dellacioppa, 2009). Diani (2005) writes that in the North as well as in the South, there has been a reemergence of social movements on a scale unprecedented since the 1960s. These are largely collective actions against neoliberal approaches, promoting a different model of globalization. Several other factors give an impetus to the growing activist interests: growth of voluntary or political organizations mobilizing on transnational issues, the density of inter-organizational collaborations between them, participation in major "no global" gatherings such as Genoa 2001 or Florence 2002, and the consolidation of a transnational community of professional activists and campaigners. Locally situated cultural articulations and interpretive frames offer avenues for the enactment of agency that challenges local, national, and global structures.

Contemporary forms of resistance such as the EZLN open up opportunities to further explore the communicative practices by which local struggles connect with global politics with a potential to contribute to policy formulations. Let's once again consider the transcultural element in the resistive politics of the EZLN. In 1996, the Zapatistas issued a call for an "Intercontinental Encounter Against Neoliberalism and for Humanity," holding a global platform for bringing together activists and intellectuals from around the globe to discuss and construct a global alternative to neoliberalization (Dellacioppa, 2009). Termed as the "First Declaration of La Realidad for Humanity and against Neoliberalism," the declaration notes (http://www.struggle.ws/mexico/ezln/ccri_1st_dec_real.html):

> "I have arrived, I am here present, I the singer.
> Enjoy in good time, come here to present yourselves those
> who have a hurting heart.
> I raise my song".
> Nahuatl Poetry.

To the people of the world:

Brothers and Sisters:

During the last years, the power of money has presented a new mask over its criminal face. Above borders, no matter race or color, the Power of money humiliates dignities, insults honesties and assassinates hopes. Re-named as "Neoliberalism", the historic crime in the concentration of privileges, wealth and impunities, democratizes misery and hopelessness.

A new world war is waged, but now against the entire humanity. As in all world wars, what is being sought is a new distribution of the world.

By the name of "globalization" they call this modern war which assassinates and forgets. The new distribution of the world consists in concentrating power in power and misery in misery.

The new distribution of the world excludes "minorities". The indigenous, youth, women, homosexuals, lesbians, people of color, immigrants, workers, peasants; the majority who make up the world basements are presented, for power, as disposable. The new distribution of the world excludes the majorities.

The modern army of financial capital and corrupt governments advance conquering in the only way it is capable of: destroying. The new distribution of the world destroys humanity.

The new distribution of the world only has one place for money and its servants. Men, women and machines become equal in servitude and in being disposable. The lie governs and it multiplies itself in means and methods.

A new lie is sold to us as history. The lie about the defeat of hope, the lie about the defeat of dignity, the lie about the defeat of humanity. The mirror of power offers us an equilibrium in the balance scale: the lie about the victory of cynicism, the lie about the victory of servitude, the lie about the victory of neoliberalism.

Instead of humanity, it offers us stock market value indexes, instead of dignity it offers us globalization of misery, instead of hope it offers us an emptiness, instead of life it offers us the international of terror.

Against the international of terror representing neoliberalism, we must raise the international of hope.

Hope, above borders, languages, colors, cultures, sexes, strategies, and thoughts, of all those who prefer humanity alive.

The international of hope. Not the bureaucracy of hope, not the opposite image and, thus, the same as that which annihilates us. Not the power with a new sign or new clothing. A breath like this, the breath of dignity. A flower yes, the flower of hope. A song yes, the song of life.

Dignity is that nation without nationality, that rainbow that is also a bridge, that murmur of the heart no matter what blood lives it, that rebel irreverence that mocks borders, customs and wars.

Hope is that rejection of conformity and defeat.

Life is what they owe us: the right to govern and to govern ourselves, to think and act with a freedom that is not exercised over the slavery of others, the right to give and receive what is just.

For all this, along with those who, above borders, races and colors, share the song of life, the struggle against death, the flower of hope and the breath of dignity . . .

The Zapatista Army of National Liberation Speaks . . .

To all who struggle for human values of democracy, liberty and justice.

To all who force themselves to resist the world crime known as "Neo-liberalism" and aim for humanity and hope to be better, be synonymous of future.

To all individuals, groups, collectives, movements, social, civic and political organizations, neighborhood associations, cooperatives, all the lefts known and to be known; non-governmental organizations, groups in solidarity with struggles of the world people, bands, tribes, intellectuals, indigenous people, students, musicians, workers, artists, teachers, peasants, cultural groups, youth movements, alternative communication media, ecologists, tenants, lesbians, homosexuals, feminists, pacifists.

To all human beings without a home, without land, without work, without food, without health, without education, without freedom, without justice, without independence, without democracy, without peace, without tomorrow.

To all who, with no matter to colors, race or borders, make of hope a weapon and a shield.

And calls together to the First Intercontinental Gathering for Humanity and Against Neoliberalism.

To be celebrated between the months of April and August of 1996 in the five continents, according the following program of activities:

First: Continental preparation assemblies in the month of April of 1996 in the following sights:

1.- European Continent: Sight in Berlin, Germany

2.- American Continent: Sight in La Realidad, Mexico

3.- Asian Continent: Sight in Tokyo, Japan

4.- African Continent: Sight to be defined

5.- Oceanic Continent: Sight in Sidney, Australia.

Note: The continental sights can change if the organizing groups decide to do so.

Second: The Intercontinental Gathering for Humanity and Against Neoliberalism, from July 27th to August 3rd of 1996, in the Zapatista "Aguascalientes", Chiapas, Mexico.

With the following Bases:

Agenda:

Table 1.- Economic aspects of how one lives under neoliberalism, how one resists, how one struggles and proposals of struggle against it and for humanity.

Table 2.- Political aspects of how one lives under neoliberalism, how one resists, how one struggles and proposals of struggle against it and for humanity.

Table 3.- Social aspects of how one lives under neoliberalism, how one resists, how one struggles and proposals of struggle against it and for humanity.

Table 4.- Cultural aspects of how one lives under neoliberalism, how one resists, how one struggles and proposals of struggle against it and for humanity.

Organization: The preparation meetings in Europe, Asia, Africa and Oceania will be organized by the Committees in Solidarity with the Zapatista Rebellion, related organisms, and citizenship groups interested in the struggle against neoliberalism and for humanity. We call upon groups of all countries so that they work united in the organization and achievement of the preparation assemblies.

The intercontinental gathering for humanity and against neoliberalism, to be celebrated from July 27th to August 3rd of 1996 in Chiapas, Mexico, will be organized by the EZLN and by citizens and Mexican non-governmental organizations that will be made known in opportune time.

Accreditation: The accreditation for the preparation assemblies in the 5 continents will be made by the organizing committees formed in Europe, Asia, Africa, Oceania, and America, respectively.

The accreditations for the gathering in Chiapas, Mexico, will be done by the committees in solidarity with the Zapatista rebellion, with the people of Chiapas, and with the people of Mexico, in their respective countries; and in Mexico, by the organizing commission, which will be known in opportune time.

General and Intercontinental Note: All which has not been completed by this convocation will be resolved by the respective organizing committees regarding the continental preparation assemblies, and by the intercontinental organizing committees regarding the gathering in Chiapas, Mexico.

Brothers and Sisters: Humanity lives in the chest of us all and, like the heart, it prefers to be on the left side. We must find it, we must find ourselves.

It is not necessary to conquer the world. It is sufficient with making it new. Us. Today.

Democracy!
Liberty!
Justice!

Neoliberalism is taken to task in the first call for global resistance. The call identifies neoliberalism as a criminal face of wealth concentration activities that contribute to the perpetuation of global inequities and to the concentration of wealth in the hands of few.

The movement utilized the Internet not only to distribute information about local oppressions and struggles in the Zapatista communities, but also to create networks of solidarity across the globe with other indigenous actors as well as actors in the environmental and feminist sectors (Cleaver, 1998; Garrido & Halavias, 2003; Schulz, 1998). In doing so, it developed a model of solidarity among indigenous communities for resisting the dominant global-national-local structures that perpetrated their exploitation and erasure, and connected these indigenous struggles with issues of environmental activism and women's rights.

The success of the movement was attributed to its capacity to utilize the Internet to globally situate a grassroots struggle of resistance in a marginalized community, to build linkages with struggles that bypassed and often resisted national policies of structural adjustment, to create a global base of support and public opinion for the local Zapatista struggle, and to place into the mainstream public spheres of globalization local models of alternative rationality, participatory processes, and organizing that stood in opposition to the values and organizing principles of neoliberalism. Noting the revolutionizing role of the EZLN in creating a global network of grassroots solidarity utilizing the Internet, a network analysis conducted by Garrido and Halavias (2003) demonstrated that Zapatista-related sites are central to the global network of non-governmental organizations (NGOs) and play a pivotal role in binding them together.

Along similar lines, the Internet emerged as a key site of mobilization, information dissemination, public opinion formation, and expression in resistance to the Multilateral Agreement on Investment (MAI) in 1998. Mobilization by NGOs across the globe connected through the Internet and protesting the MAI ultimately led to its failure (Ayres, 1999, 2001). Similarly, the Association for the Taxation of Financial Transactions for the Aid of Citizens (ATTAC) was created in 1998, mobilizing activist communities throughout the globe using the Internet to create a people's education movement seeking to generate awareness and transparency of the economic policies of neoliberalism and the economic procedures of decision making in neoliberal governance (della Porta, Kreisi, & Rucht, 1999; Grignou & Patou, 2004). Having started in France with approximately 250 local communities that were represented, ATTAC gained international support, with over 35 separate movements that were created all across the world including Brazil, Japan, and Senegal, among others (Grignou & Patou, 2004). At the top of ATTAC's organizational chart is a scientific community of approximately 20 academics and researchers who publish key concepts in ATTAC books and provide intellectual and conceptual fodder for ATTAC campaigns. These ideas offer counter-expertise to dominant narratives of neoliberalism and provide entry points for targeted action for local activist movements that seek structural transformations.

The Arab Spring

The Arab Spring offers insights into the processes of resistance through which political structures are sought to be transformed, particularly as it relates to collective-based efforts of transforming authoritarian structures of rule that limit the possibilities of participation and voice. Although several localized movements were continually mobilizing throughout the 1990s across the Middle East, the years 2010 and 2011 marked the emergence of rebellions in Tunisia and Egypt that soon spread to other parts of the region, framed as the Arab Spring and narrating the story of solidarity in youth resistance throughout the Arab world. Worth noting in the Arab Spring is the highly localized resistance to contextually constituted structures, and the simultaneous threads of connectivity that linked these localized movement networks into broader processes of social change. The cultural narratives of the movement construct a highly localized contextually situated storyline; simultaneously, they bring forth the articulations of structural constraints that highlight the economic injustices, unemployment, poverty, rising food prices, and so forth that are located within the broader backdrop of neoliberal reforms and globalization processes.

The movement in Tunisia was spearheaded by localized forms of protests offline accompanied by the online infrastructure of resistance set up by the organization Takriz, a Tunisian think tank that was formed in 1998, and that describes itself as a street resistance network (http://www.facebook.com/takrizo?sk=wall#!/takrizo?sk=info). The online infrastruc-

Figure 5.1. A rally in Tahrir Square on February 25, 2011 (iStockphoto, contributed by jcarillet).

ture emerged as the mobilizing space for the movement. In its objective statement, the Takriz Facebook page proclaims, "We make revolutions!" It goes on to set up the following objectives: "Tunisia release of the dictatorship. Defend our freedom. Fight against tyranny and the censorship of the Internet in Tunisia." Building alliances with trade unionists, students, teachers, human rights activists, online dissidents, street youth, and soccer fans, Takriz played a key role in constituting offline and online strategies of resistance against the dictator Zine El Abidin Ben Ali. Takriz uses serious political analyses and persuasive strategies of resistance to reach out to these different stakeholder groups. The core values of Takriz are described here:

First Article : Freedom

TAKRIZ is freedom. It has the power to act according to its will, contingent on the means which it has, without being hindered by the power of whoever.

Second Article : Truth

TAKRIZ is truth. Our definition of this word is most closer to that of Spinoza. It is the adequacy of the idea with the object. Certainly, as the light makes itself known and reveals the darkness, the truth is standard of itself and the forgery. TAKRIZ is standard of itself and the government lies circulating in Tunisia, it makes itself known and reveals the infringements on the liberties in Tunisia which after all affect it, being Free like defined in the 1st article. Yet it is censored.

Third Article : Anonymity

TAKRIZ is strictly anonymous. The anonymity protects TAKRIZ and its members (TAKRIZIANS) in pursuing their quest for Freedom and Truth.

TAKRIZO ERGO SUM

TAKRIZ is anonymous for many reasons. Censored after 2 years of existence, from 2000, it became the target of a relentless repression by the Tunisian government. On top of providing a safe home to the members of TAKRIZ and their respective families, the anonymity is here to address all selfishness and egocentrism safeguarding this way the core values of TAKRIZ. "TAKRIZO ERGO SUM" can not be true without this condition. (http://www.facebook.com/takrizo?sk=wall#!/takrizo?sk=info)

The values of freedom, truth, and anonymity set up the backdrop for the politics of resistance. Anonymity is seen as a strategic resistive response that counters government oppression and simultaneously opposes the values of selfishness and egocentrism. Truth emerges into the discursive space as a site of struggle and as an articulation of resistance. It is through the lens of truth that Takriz seeks to expose government lies. This search for the truth and the desire to expose the corruptions carried out by the Ben Ali government lie at the heart of the Tunisian movement, also referred to as the Jasmine Revolution.

Shaped within their initial aims of fostering accessible Internet access and promoting freedom of speech, the network of Takriz activists, also known as Takrizards or Taks, organize their resistance and articulate their voices in anonymity online, thus resisting state repression. Takriz came under government surveillance in 2000 and was blocked by the government in Tunisia (Pollock, 2011). This led to the formation of several other Tunisian resistance websites. A social networking site called SuXydylik was launched by a Tak who had the online name "SuX." Another Tak who had the online name "Ettounsi" started a political humor-based webzine called TuneZine. He was later imprisoned and tortured, which led to his death. The online resistive strategies of Takriz worked in solidarity with several offline protests that were taking shape in Tunisia in 2000. For example, in 2008, protests against corruption and poor working conditions erupted in the mining town of Gafsa, and this became a site for continuous demonstrations and corresponding attacks by security forces; Takriz sent members to the region to start building bases for solidarity. Reports of Gafsa on Facebook led the Ben Ali regime to block Facebook. Takriz created an online community that built the momentum of resistance, fostered spaces of organizing, and offered the infrastructure for the movement once it took off. The growth in online social media sites that fostered resistive narratives was accompanied by the large-scale growth in Internet use in Tunisia from 2000 to 2009, with approximately 39% of the population being Internet users in 2009 (Wagner, 2011).

However, as noted earlier, the online context of the protests in Tunisia served as a complement to what was happening offline. With the global economic crisis, as food prices increased dramatically along with the rising unemployment in Tunisia, more and more voices of dissidence started being expressed in discursive spaces. In the town of Sidi Bouzid, on December 17, 2010, a poor fruit seller named Mohammed Bouazizi set himself on fire after having been humiliated by local police and after his scale was confiscated. When he wanted to see the government officials, Bouazizi was not allowed in. He went to a nearby gas station, filled up a canister and returned to the government building; he then poured gas over himself and cried out "How do you expect me to make a living?" before setting

himself on fire (http://www.cbsnews.com/stories/2011/02/20/60minutes/
main20033404.shtml). The self-immolation of Bouazizi emerged as a symbol of protest, organizing local community members in protest against
the police atrocities, government corruption, rising food prices, and high
unemployment rates (in some of the towns where protests erupted, unemployment rates among college graduates were reported to be above
50%); Takriz responded to these localized street protests in Sidi Bouzid
by sending in Taks to report and mobilize the protests. With the increasing police atrocities to repress the protests, the lawyers called a strike, followed by the teachers. The Hacktivists Anonymous group (primarily its
subgroups AnonOps and Peoples Liberation Front) targeted and paralyzed
the Tunisian president's and parliament's websites in January 2011 under
the campaign "Operation: Tunisia" (http://en.rsf.org/the-new-media-be-
tween-revolution-11-03-2011,39764.html). The Chief Technology Officer
of Takriz, under the alias "Foetus," notes:

> We were online every day, and on the streets pretty much every day,
> collecting information, collecting videos, organizing protests, getting
> into protests . . . We met using Mumble [which is open-source, uses
> digital certificate authentication, and is regarded by Takriz as more
> secure than Skype]. We had minutes so people who couldn't make
> the meetings knew what was going on. We gathered information, by-
> passed censorship, channeled it on Facebook, scanned articles in the
> foreign media. We were in touch with the labor unions. We worked
> with everybody, we filled protests with people. (http://www.technolo-
> gyreview.com/web/38379/)

During this time period, sites such as Takriz and Nawaat emerged as discursive sites for circulating information, images, and videos, thus serving
as entry points for mobilizing community members, for enlisting participation, and for coordinating/informing about specific protest plans. These
sites of resistance hosted videos, Tweets, and Facebook links to dissemi-
nate information and to draw attention to the oppressions that were being carried out to thwart the possibilities of resistance. The government
responded to the online mobilizing of local communities through efforts
of censorship, blocking websites, orchestrating "cyber-attacks on Internet

activists, breaking into Facebook accounts and Facebook groups of activists, and deleting activist websites and blogs" (Reporters Without Borders, 2011a, 2011b); the censorship put forth by the government was bypassed through creative strategies that used Facebook. Furthermore, the censorship sparked additional participation in offline forms of protests.

When Bouazizi died, 5,000 people attended his funeral, further foregrounding the death of Bouazizi as the marker of the movement and as the voice of resistance. The death of Bouazizi, along with the protests in Sidi Bouzid, galvanized resistance across various pockets in Tunisia. The Tunisian government of Ben Ali responded by ordering additional police action, with snipers shooting protestors in their heads. However, as the violent police attacks spread, local citizen-journalists taking images of the violence through cell phone cameras started posting these images on Facebook and other social media sites (Pollock, 2011). Cell phone cameras played a vital role in documenting the police atrocities and in creating public awareness of these atrocities through dissemination; cell phone usage had grown dramatically over the last decade with approximately 95% of the population having cell phone subscriptions (Wagner, 2011). Citizen-journalists file-shared websites that were equipped with photos and videos, and they supplied videos to streaming websites. One particular image of a dead protestor with his brains spilling out was uploaded on YouTube and made rounds on Facebook, quickly spreading across Tunisia, being posted and re-posted online. Filmed by a medical school student at the hospital, the video was smuggled on a CD across the Algerian border and then streamed via MegaUpload. Takriz also forwarded the video to *Al Jazeera*. Images and videos taken on cellphones were uploaded on YouTube and Facebook, and were also circulated by Takriz on its Facebook page (http://www.facebook.com/takrizo?sk=wall#!/takrizo?sk=wall). These images and videos were effective in mobilizing protestors across Tunisia. In the face of the mounting protests, Ben Ali fled in January 2011. Facebook served as a site for complementing the resistive struggles on the ground. Noted Foetus, "Facebook is pretty much the GPS for this revolution. Without the street there's no revolution, but add Facebook to the street and you get real potential" (http://www.technologyreview.com/web/38379/).

That the economic and political contexts of the Tunisian protests are intertwined was demonstrated throughout the different stages of the Jasmine Revolution. The economic context of the Tunisian protests becomes visible in the following note posted by Takriz on their Facebook site:

> While all sectors of the economy was hit by the rapacity of the relatives of Ben Ali, it is obviously the big markets and the best in the country were targeted first. Thus, privatization has all been made illegally and total contradiction with the law and regulations. The first major victim of these operations is the Tunisian State, a State which has been completely gutted by Ben Ali and his entourage, and this, to secure his hold on the country by eliminating any dissenting voice and up to create from scratch a puppet opposition. The Committee of Public Hi Regarding the "business" which became the main activity of Ben Ali and his entourage, we present below a preliminary list of the wealth accumulated by Ben Ali and his family, and this, with an arrogance that sheds light on the mentality of these people who have no political conscience, who are convinced that Tunisia belongs to them and which substitute for the state. (http://www.facebook.com/takrizo?sk=notes&s=40#!/note.php?note_id=10150090741927262)

Articulated in the narrative of resistance are the everyday experiences of marginalization, juxtaposed in the backdrop of the corruption in the business practices of Ben Ali and his family. The exploitation of the economy is tied to the political corruption of the family. The note posted by Takriz specifically discusses the ways in which the privatization of the economy played out to serve the interests of the Ben Ali family. Privatization was carried out to benefit the interests of the family and its relatives, shaped within specific processes that minimized resistance and concentrated decision-making power within this entity.

Similar to the local contexts of the ongoing protests in Tunisia in the 2000s, there were ongoing labor, unemployment, and economy-related protests in Egypt throughout the decade. In 2008, the city of Mahalla in the Nile Delta witnessed large-scale protests in the textile sector. Industrial workers in textile factories planned a strike on April 6, 2008 (Pollock, 2011). The localized protests of the workers were also supported by a nationwide activist organizing led by Ahmed Maher, utilizing blogs, posters, and the Internet to generate support to plan a national shopping boycott and demonstrations in Cairo on April 6. Because of his organizing work with the April 6 protests, Maher was jailed and then later released. Upon his release, Maher announced that he was launching the "April 6 movement" and started gathering youth to mobilize for the movement. In starting to organize for the "April 6 movement," the leaders started learning from similar movement groups and training programs such as the Academy of Change, an Arabic online organization offering nonviolent civil disobedience guidelines, and Optor, a Serbian youth movement led by the Serbian revolutionary Ivan Marovic that was instrumental in overthrowing Slobodan Milošević. The April 6 movement sent one of its activists, Mohammed Adel, to train with the Center for Applied Nonviolent Action and Strategies (CANVAS) founded by Marovic, and Adel returned with a book on effective peaceful strategies of protest and a game called "A Force More Powerful" for teaching nonviolent resistance in regime transformations. The April 6 activists rewrote an Egyptian version of the game to train local activists. The April 6 movement formed a Facebook group to mobilize support, as well as built a blog, YouTube, Twitter, and web presence. The "copy, publish, share" strategy became the basic framework for the campaign, spreading word rapidly about the April 6 plans for protests. The social media sites became spaces for posting messages, for sharing videos, for documenting corrupt practices of the government and police, and through this process, raising large-scale awareness regarding what was going on in Egypt under the leadership of Mubarak. The visual depiction of events as well as the video recordings of live experiences became conduits for solidarity building and for drawing in participants. YouTube and Facebook increasingly emerged as platforms for sharing information about corruption and government and police atrocities. The government responded to the online participation of activist videos, photos, and voices of resistance by seeking to censor Facebook. Here is a note posting of the April 6 movement in response to the censorship:

> The online gathering place for young pepole poses a challenge to authorities. June 2, 2008

Right now, the government of Egyptian President Hosni Mubarak is considering blocking Facebook, the social networking website that has become a popular hangout for twentysomethings worldwide and a favorite venue for Egypt›s disaffected youth. The reason: In April, one group of young citizens mobilized 80,000 supporters to protest rising food prices. Facebook networking played a crucial role in broadening support and turnout for an April 6 textile workers› strike and protest. The Egyptian government, which has governed for 25 years under emergency law and doesn›t allow more than five people to gather unregistered, hit back hard, jailing young dissidents and torturing Ahmed Maher, a young activist who tried, unsuccessfully, to organize a second demonstration in early May. Despite these setbacks, the «Facebook movement» in Egypt is significant for several reasons. First, it challenges the perception that there is no prospect for independent, secular opposition in the country. The majority of Egyptians are under 30 and have known no other ruler than Mubarak. They have not seen real political parties because the government has long restricted opposition parties and free media. The Facebook movement engaged large numbers of youth for the first time. Second, the Web offers a safe political space—a role the mosque has traditionally played in Egypt. The Muslim Brotherhood has for decades been the only viable opposition. With Facebook, young secular people can communicate, build relationships and express their opinions freely. (Significantly, the Muslim Brotherhood opposed the successful April demonstration but supported the unsuccessful May event.) Every member in the 100,000-strong online community could be, at any given moment, a leader of a movement. Third, engaging Egypt›s youth is an important item on the agenda of Mubarak›s son, Gamal, as he works to gain support for his succession to power. As a young politician, Gamal established the Future Generation Foundation in 2000, which incubated many of the current leaders of the ruling National Democratic Party and the new Cabinet. Facebook activists and their supporters should be able to turn to this group for support. A few weeks ago, Belal Diab, a 20-year-old college student, interrupted one of the Egyptian prime minister›s speeches to protest the arrests of Facebook activists, shouting: «Look who are you fighting; it is us, the younger generation who stood with you and supported you!» Nevertheless, Facebook activists are being targeted by government-based media campaigns defaming the website and the youth activists who use it. The government also warns media not to talk about the phenomenon. I saw the heavy-handed efforts of the government while recording a TV show with Maher. During the taping, Egyptian police broke into the studio, threatened the station manager and forced the guest outside the room. What can be done to help this movement? The international community and the U.S. government should pressure the Egyptian government to support Internet freedom and keep Facebook accessible to Egyptians. One young activist, Ahmad Samih, is campaigning to gain local and international support to prevent the Egyptian government from blocking Facebook. So far, nearly 20 Egyptian human rights organizations are supporting this cause. International human rights organizations should publicly join in that show of support. Egyptian democrats are «Facebooking» their advocacy in order to escape heavy recriminations. It would be shameful for the international community not to stand up on their behalf against a government that seeks to deny them even that small space to express themselves. Otherwise, Mubarak›s self-fulfilling prophesy as the only alternative to the Muslim Brotherhood will continue to hold Egypt back from the democracy its people deserve. Sherif Mansour works at Freedom House, a human rights organization that has been monitoring political rights and civil liberties in Egypt since 1972. He can be reached at smansour@freedomhouse.org.

Voiced in the note is the articulation of the broader economic context of the protests. The note points to the rising food prices in Egypt and sets up the economic foundations for a framework of solidarity between the youth and the impoverished textile workers living in the margins. In mobilizing with the textile workers, the Facebook campaign offers a framework of solidarity, connecting the networks of resistance in both offline and online contexts. Online resistance complements the offline sites of political protests by garnering support, coordinating efforts, and drawing attention through news, information, images, and videos. The online spaces of Facebook become the sites for complementing the offline forms of resistance, often drawing attention to the protests on the streets and generating additional support. Simultaneously, the voices of resistance point toward the importance of maintaining these spaces of resistance in online contexts for alternative narratives to be articulated. The resistance, therefore, is mobilized in maintaining Facebook as a safe, discursive space for the voicing of opinions and thoughts freely. Calls are made to international solidarity networks to pressure the Egyptian government to respect Internet freedom. The voices of resistance are constituted around creating and fostering spaces for resistive articulations framed within the narratives of political rights and civil liberties. It is within this broader backdrop of online political participation and articulation of voices of resistance that the Egyptian revolution was mobilized.

On June 6, 2010, a young computer programmer, Khaled Said, was dragged to the streets by the police in front of a cybercafe in Alexandria and was beaten to death. Khaled's family stated that the police feared that he would share compromising videos of the police dealing drugs on You-Tube and Facebook. The death of Khaled triggered large-scale protests when his brother, Ahmed, shared images of his postmortem taken on a cell phone on Facebook. "We are all Khaled Said," noted a Facebook site remembering Khaled, which emerged as a space for mobilizing resistance, with over 1.5 million members. On seeing the images on his cell phone, a local activist, Hassan Mostafa called for protests outside the police station on his Facebook page. Multiple protests were organized, including a performance of a mock trial in front of the home of the Said family. Social media served as catalysts for spreading information about protests, for creating awareness, and for mobilizing specific strategies. Information about meetings was shared via Facebook. In instances where people didn't have access, site pages were printed and circulated. Text messages were sent to phones, and attachments were circulated via e-mail. Images and videos of protests were shared through Facebook and YouTube (see, for instance, http://youtu.be/7u1C79X88e4). Multiple media channels, therefore, were used complementarily in order to share information and plan strategies about the protests. Referring to the important role of Facebook, Mostafa noted, "Before this social-media revolution, everyone was very individual, very single, very isolated and oppressed in islands. But social media has

Figure 5.2. Uploaded by "mayyezayed." http://youtu.be/7u1C79X88e4

created bridges, has created channels between individuals, between activists, between even ordinary men, to speak out, to know that there are other men who think like me. We can work together, we can make something together" (http://www.technologyreview.com/web/38379/).

The online strategy of social change was accompanied by grassroots organizing activities on the ground, mobilizing resources for protests on the street. Facebook and other social media became means for seeking out transnational help through solidarity networks. For instance, the Egyptian activists reached out to activists across the border in Tunisia, who then utilized their long-standing networks with protest groups such as Indymedia and the Antifascist Network to share strategies of resistance that were carried out on the ground. For instance, one of the techniques widely used in the Egyptian movement of wearing black was adopted from the "Black Bloc," a well-established technique of wearing black to protect anonymity and increase impact. The knowledge shared through the online networks played a vital role in mobilizing resistance on the ground, both in terms of

Figure 5.3. Uploaded by "weareallkhaledsaid." http://youtu.be/KDmbK2oEobU

informing strategies as well as shaping attitudes toward specific issues related to the movement. The on-the-ground role of Facebook was visible in
wall writings in Egypt, thanking Facebook for the revolution; these images
then were posted, re-posted, and circulated through Facebook. Remembering the performance of silence in solidarity during the period after the
murder of Khaled, the "We are all Khaled Said" Facebook page provided a
video link (http://youtu.be/KDmbK2oEobU) to the performances of the
silent protests across Egypt along with the following description:

> Exactly one year ago, Khaled Said was murdered in front of his house.
> At the time, peaceful protests were met with violence from Mubarak's
> regime & his thugs. We then started doing silent stands, instead of
> protests, where young Egyptians dressed in black stood everywhere
> in Egypt silently & sad for what their country has become. This video
> was one of the first made for Khaled Said & has footage from our si-
> lent stands.

The video is accompanied by a song and mixes in footages of Khaled along with images of his tortured body, the bodies of other protestors, and images of silent protestors standing in opposition. Here's an excerpt from the English subtitle of the song that plays in the background:

How long are we scared for, it's time now

Time to change the injustice by stopping torture

We won't be scared, we won't kneel down.

No more cowards amongst us.

How long are we scared for, it's time now . . .

What are you waiting for? Why are you waiting?

Here is hope, get close to it . . .

Oh Egyptian, why do you accept to live in humiliation . . .

Amongst all humans you are humiliated alone . . .

You have taught and built civilization

Read Egypt's history if you want proof

Don't say how I can change

You are the force of change.

The voice of resistance expressed in the performance above points to the injustice that continues to be carried out in Egypt, and expresses defiance, noting that the time to stand up is now. The history of Egypt is offered as a lesson for change and as a source of inspiration. The empowerment of the citizens of Egypt experiencing torture and oppression is achieved through the offering of hope, and through the call to Egyptians to become the force of change. Dressed in black and standing in silence, Egyptians resist the culture of fear and repression that had been perpetuated by the Mubarak regime.

As the protests continued, police atrocities increased, and so did the efforts of blacking out the Internet. The administrator of the Arabic version of the "We are all Khaled Said" issued a call on January 14, asking the readers of his highly popular website whether they were going to take the streets on January 25, taking a cue from Tunisia. Simultaneously, he posted a Facebook event titled "January 25: Revolution against Torture, Corruption, Unemployment, and Injustice." Based on lessons learned from the Tunisian Jasmine Revolution, strategies were shared by the administrator with activists on the ground, announcing the sites of the protests. Simultaneously, on January 18, Asmaa Mahfouz, a 26-year-old protestor, issued a call for people to join her in protest at Tahrir Square to mark the death of four Egyptians who died by burning themselves, imitating the immolation of Bouazizi. Announcing her protest online, she gave out her address and her phone number; three people arrived at the protest before the armored cars of riot police descended. She was jailed and later released.

In her anger, she created a video blog and placed her protest online through YouTube and Facebook; the video went viral and later came to be known to the outside world as the "Vlog that Helped Spark the Revolution." In the vlog, Mahfouz, her head covered with a scarf, directly looks at the camera and passionately urges the viewer to participate; the vlog spread virally within Egypt, then to Saudi Arabia. Subsequently, through various networks, it found its way into the mainstream media channels globally. Here is an excerpt from the video:

> If you think yourself a man, come with me on January 25 . . . Come and protect me, and other girls in the protest. Sitting at home and just following us on the news or Facebook leads to our humiliation . . . go down to the street, send SMSs, post it on the Net, make people aware . . . Never say there's no hope! Hope only disappears when you say there's no hope. (http://youtu.be/SgjIgMdsEuk)

In the vlog, Mahfouz utilizes a personal narrative to invite the viewers to participate in action, simultaneously drawing upon the storytelling style of vlogs and turning a personal narrative into a political narrative. She also draws upon a cultural narrative that celebrates the role of men in protecting women to urge the viewer to come and protect her as she participates in protest. The cultural logic is drawn upon as a resource to issue a call to action. A series of actions are outlined as avenues for resistance, locally constituted within the dynamic contexts of culturally based narratives. Even as she directly looks into the camera in her video narrative, she does so wearing her head scarf, simultaneously disrupting the Eurocentric narrative that constructs Muslim women wearing head scarves as having no agency, and seeking to disrupt the broader logics of the structure. The video further goes on to ask for public participation on January 25:

> I'm making this video to give you one simple message: we want to go down to Tahrir Square on January 25th. If we still have honor and want to live in dignity on this land, we have to go down on January 25th. We'll go down and demand our rights, our fundamental human rights. (http://youtu.be/SgjIgMdsEuk)

January 25 is framed as the day for demanding the rights of the people, their fundamental human rights. The protests are presented as avenues for demanding the basic right of everyday Egyptians to their honor and to live a life in dignity. In the broader backdrop of fear that occupied political spaces of Egypt under the dictatorship of Mubarak and his police-military control, Mahfouz noted:

> So long as you come down with us, there will be hope. Don't be afraid of the government. Fear none but God. God says He will not change the condition of a people until they change what is in themselves. Don't think you can be safe anymore. None of us are. Come down with us and demand your rights, my rights, your family's rights. (http://youtu.be/SgjIgMdsEuk)

The references to rights are constituted within the broader framework of references to the rights of the family. Religious speech in the context of everyday living is invoked to allay the fears of Egyptians who had long been repressed by the dictatorship, with minimal opportunities for participation in public discursive spaces. The invocation of the religious narrative serves as an entry point to social change. The personal politics of social change and the personal choice to participate in processes of social change are constituted within a religio-politico-spiritual narrative of change. Reference to religion offers courage and hope amidst fear. Connecting this personal-political context in Egypt, also worth noting is the transformation in messaging strategies, with the shift from official Arabic language that is typical in political speeches to the messaging strategies on vlogs and other social media that draw upon the vernacular.

Within the broader backdrop of online and offline communication strategies mobilizing participation in protest, January 25 turned out to be a day of revolutionary protest participation in Egypt as large numbers of protestors gathered in Tahrir Square. Whereas social media, on one hand, served to gather people and mobilize them at sites of protest, on the other hand, images and videos of the protests taken by protestors and citizen-journalists were rapidly circulated on the web, thus creating both local as well as global forms of support. Activists borrowed connections to upload videos, then sent them to Tunisia to be uploaded on YouTube and Facebook. Networks between Egypt and London, Tunisia and Dubai served as spaces for sharing and distributing the videos of the protests. Responding to the protests and the large-scale circulation of the images of the protests, Mubarak shut down the Internet. The shutting down of the Internet prompted additional participation of protestors, with even more Egyptians stepping into the streets amidst the information vacuum. The complementary voices of resistance in both the online and offline worlds ultimately led to Mubarak stepping down in Egypt. The images shared on Facebook, YouTube, and blogs also created inspiration points for other movements across the Arab world.

Bolivia

The participation of indigenous groups in political processes to create entry points for social change was most visible during the election of Evo Morales to the presidency in Bolivia. The election of Morales built on decades of indigenous struggle to seek political legitimacy and opportunities for representation in discursive spaces, decision-making processes, and political structures in the mainstream, and accompanied by the political opportunity structures for indigenous participation that had been fostered by the multicultural neoliberal reforms in the 1990s under the Ley de Participación Popular (LPP) (Postero, 2005, 2007). Although indigenous communities constitute over 60% of the population in Bolivia, the representation of indigenous communities in the political processes constituted a marginal representation, with combined indigenous representation being less than 5% (Van Cott, 2003). The broader backdrop of the politics of Bolivia is framed within racist political structures that have perpetrated the marginalization of indigenous tribes from discursive spaces and simultaneously carried out economic reforms that have disenfranchised indigenous sectors from their traditional forms of livelihood.

Historically, Bolivian politics has been shaped by US client regimes that have established top-down agendas on political and economic domestic policies aligned with the interests of the US (Petras, 2004). In the backdrop of the top-down agendas imposed by the government in the form of the primarily middle-class National Revolutionary Party (MNR), Bolivia had developed a strong union of tin mine workers, bringing together the workers with left-wing peasants, students, and professions under the umbrella of the Central Obrero Boliviano (COB). Through its legislative assemblies, the COB had developed a socialist reform agenda of workplaces, land redistribution programs, and programs of social welfare. The strong organizing base of the COB paved the way for electoral politics and for the election of the left-based Unidad Democrática y Popular (UDP) in 1982, which, however, inherited the large-scale debts created during the dictatorship of Hugo Banzer, and found itself in the midst of battling hyperinflation. In the early elections that were called in 1985, a political coalition emerged on the Bolivian political landscape, which opened up to large-scale neoliberalization that was sweeping across Latin America at the time (Albo, 2008; J. A. Morales, 2008; Vargas, 2008). Starting in the mid-1980s, important structural reforms were carried out across Bolivia under Supreme Decree (DS) 21060 (J. A. Morales, 2008). Furthermore, beginning in the 1990s, Bolivia underwent large-scale capitalization reforms that led to the privatization of the various sectors through various structural adjustment programs (Roca, 1996).

The disenfranchisement of indigenous communities in Bolivia has played out through the historic relationships of production inherited from the Spanish, and through the systematic removal of indigenous communities from resource management policies and programs under foreign colonial and neocolonial interventions. In the 1980s, responding to the invasion of their lands and to the disenfranchisement of the indigenous sectors through industrialization projects, lowland indigenous people began to organize, narrating their difficult living situations and the on-slaught of the industrialization projects on their livelihood (Postero, 2007). This pattern of disenfranchisement of indigenous communities formed the backdrop of neoliberal reforms as the Bolivian state-borrowed loans from the International Monetary Fund (IMF) and correspondingly continued privatizing the economy and capitalizing natural resources under SAPs. In the 1990s, the program of neoliberalization of Bolivia was accomplished through the privatization of state enterprises under the framework of "capitalization," leading to the capitalization of five of the state's largest firms, including oil and gas, telecommunications, airlines, power generation, and railroads (Petras, 2004; Postero, 2005, 2007). In the 1990s, with their increasing disenfranchisement and the invasions of their land, indigenous communities organized the March for Territory and Dignity from the tropical lowlands to La Paz to demand the recognition of their culture and territories. These protests formed the basis for multicultural reforms that enabled community participation at local levels and simultaneously carried out the projects of economic liberalization that continued to disenfranchise indigenous communities through urbanization and resource exploitation (Postero, 2007).

The neo-imperial oppression of indigenous communities in Bolivia has been accompanied by the neoliberal policies of trade liberalization and privatization carried out by President Gonzalo Sánchez de Lozada, who led Bolivia from 1993, at the height of the establishment of the global neoliberal regime. Known widely as "Goni," the president implemented a variety of trade liberalization policies that sought to privatize public resources and turn these as sites of foreign direct investment. The widespread privatization of public resources paved the way for widespread resistance. In 2001, the "water wars" of Cochabamba marked the first series of local-national mobilization against the privatization of water, a resource that the people of Bolivia considered to be a public resource and hence beyond the scope of privatization (more on this in chapter six). This was also the backdrop for the growing efforts of local indigenous mobilizing among the *cocaleros* (coca growers), who were fighting the increasing imperial presence of US-led policies in Bolivia that targeted local coca growers and carried out violence on them. In October 2003, President Sánchez de Lozada announced his plans for the development of the newly found natural gas resources for the purposes of exporting to the US and Mexico through Chile, and opening up the gas resources to private foreign investment; the popular sectors rose up in resistance, resulting in protests across Bolivia in what came to be known as the "Gas Wars." The popular protest and organizing across Bolivia manifested in street protests, massive demonstrations, and blockades throughout the month of October; the president resigned and fled the country (Postero, 2004). Commenting on the climate of resistance in Bolivia in the period beginning from the "Water Wars" into the period of the "Gas Wars," Postero (2004) noted that the October revolution in Bolivia was shaped within the context of the large-scale disenfranchisement of the poor and the indigenous communities from the platforms of decision making, and the accompanying material inequities produced by the neoliberal policies. The uprising had a strong indigenous component, having been led by indigenous leaders Evo Morales and Felipe Quispe, and drawing on narratives of indigenous resistance and Andean warrior people. The indigenous sectors mobilized in coalition with the poor and the popular sectors, focusing on the disenfranchising effects of neoliberal policies such as privatization of public resources, the *Área de Livre Comércio das Américas* (ACLA) free trade agreements, and the opening up of the economy to foreign capital. Here is how Morales described the events of October 2003:

> This uprising of the Bolivian people has resulted not only from the issue of natural gas, of hydrocarbons, but from a collection of many issues: from discrimination and from marginalization, but fundamentally from the exhaustion of neoliberalism. The culprit responsible for so many deed, and also responsible for the uprising of Bolivian people, has a name: it is called neoliberalism. Now, with the recent events in Bolivia, I have realized that what matters is the power of an entire people, of an entire nation. For those of us who are convinced that it is important to defend humanity, the best support we can offer is to create the power of the people. (Morales, 2003, quoted in Postero, 2004, p. 208)

The neoliberalization of Bolivia provided the backdrop for the popular protests of the indigenous and peasant sectors. Amidst widespread disenfranchisement of the poor and rising unemployment, Evo Morales won the December 2005 election by an ample margin (J. A. Morales, 2008). A key component of the Morales campaign was the move to nationalize hydrocarbons, and the Morales government passed a nationalization decree in 2006, turning the various aspects of the industry ranging from exploration and prospecting to production and marketing into the hands of *Yacimientos Petrolíferos Fiscales Bolivianos* (YPFB).

The resistance of Morales to the politics of neoliberalism is played out in the efforts offered by him and the people he worked with in the indigenous sectors of Bolivia through their participation in political processes of decision making. The broader context of indigenous political participation is constituted in the backdrop of the long history of indigenous exploitation in Bolivia, accompanied by the erasure of indigenous communities from resource management processes and from decision-making frameworks that are quintessential in shaping the structures of environmental governance. A month after Bolivia's Gas War, Morales noted the following in an interview with Counterpunch (2003):

> The state should be in charge of the exploration, the industrialization, and the commercialization of hydrocarbons. This could be an economic solution for our countries, but meanwhile, these hydrocarbons are being stolen by transnational corporations. In Bolivia we are convinced that the gas is our property and we must defend it.

The economic solution of state-owned industrialization and commercialization processes is offered as an alternative to the neoliberal model of development that facilitates the stealing of hydrocarbons by TNCs. As a strategy of resistance to the neoliberal configuration of political organizing, Morales notes that gas is a public property and therefore should be defended collectively in the public domain. Furthermore, the top-down neoliberal forms of ownership and private property are resisted through alternative articulations of indigenous ownership and indigenous participation in resource management:

After more than 500 years, we, the Quechuas and Aymaras, are still the rightful owners of the land. We, the indigenous people, after 500 years of resistance, are retaking the power. This retaking of power is oriented towards the recovery of our own riches, our own natural resources such as the hydrocarbons. This affects the interests of the transnational corporations and the interests of the neoliberal system. Never the less, I am convinced that the power of the people is increasing and strengthening. This power is changing presidents, economic models, and politics. We are convinced that capitalism is the enemy of the earth, of humanity and culture. The US government does not understand our way of life and our philosophy. But we will defend our proposals, our way of life and our demands with the participation of the Bolivian people. (Morales, 2003)

The re-taking of the control that has been held in the hands of corporate and political powers emerges as the framework of indigenous resistance. The marginalization of indigenous communities of the Quechuas and the Aymaras from the platforms of decision making and governance becomes the axis on which indigenous resistance is organized, seeking to capture the spaces of ownership in the hands of the people. Capitalism is positioned as the enemy of the earth, humanity, and culture, and resistance is organized around the desire of the people to bring about changes in the economic model of organizing Bolivian society. Therefore, indigenous organizing is built on a framework of critique of the political and economic structures of neoliberalism.

The disenfranchisement of indigenous communities is the cornerstone of the speech "I believe only in the power of the people" recorded in 2003 after the ousting of Sánchez de Lozada (Morales, 2005):

What happened these past days in Bolivia was a great revolt by those who have been oppressed for more than 500 years. The will of the people was imposed this September and October, and has begun to overcome the empire's cannons. We have lived for so many years through the confrontation of two cultures: the culture of life represented by the indigenous people and the culture of death represented by the West. When we the indigenous people together with the workers and even the businessmen of our country fight for life and justice, the State responds with its "democratic rule of law."

What does the "rule of law" mean for indigenous people? For the poor, the marginalized, the excluded, the "rule of law" means the targeted assassinations and collective massacres that we have endured. Not just this September and October, but for many years, in which they have tried to impose policies of hunger and poverty on the Bolivian people. Above all, the "rule of law" means the accusations that we, the Quechuas, Aymaras, and Guaranties of Bolivia keep hearing from our governments; that we are narcos, that we are anarchists. This uprising of Bolivian people has been not only about gas and hydrocarbons, but an intersection of many issues: discrimination, marginalization, and most importantly, the failure of neoliberalism.

The struggle for power in Bolivia is framed through the tension between the desire for life among the indigenous people and the politics of death imposed by the West on Bolivia. Top-down oppression of the indigenous sector is carried out under the umbrella of the "rule of law." In the speech, Morales specifically discusses neoliberal policies and the marginalization of indigenous communities produced by these policies. He also discusses the ways in which the "rule of law" is utilized to stigmatize indigenous people, to impose top-down policies that generate hunger and poverty, and to carry out the targeted assassinations and massacres.

Neoliberalism is constituted in the discursive space as the site of resistance and social change (Morales, 2005):

> It must be said, companeras and companeros, that we must serve the social and popular movements rather than transnational corporations . . . When we speak of the "defense of humanity," as we do at this event, I think that this only happens by eliminating neoliberalism and imperialism . . . I believe in the power of the people . . . And now, with all that has happened in Bolivia, I have seen the importance of the power of a whole people, of a whole nation. For those of us who believe it is important to defend humanity, the best contribution we can make is to help create that popular power. This happens when we check our personal interests with those of the group. Sometimes,

> we commit to the social movements in order to win power. We need
> to be led by the people, not use or manipulate them.

The resistance of the popular movement in Bolivia is constituted against
the powers of neoliberalism and imperialism. The neoliberal reforms are
understood in relationship to TNCs and top-down forms of governance
that impose imperial agendas. The power of the people is seen in resistance
to neoliberalism and neoliberal policies. Local grassroots participation is
understood as the site of popular power, and popular power is understood
in terms of respecting the interests of the group. As opposed to the individualistic assumptions of neoliberalism, the collective needs of the group
are offered as alternative sources for driving political participation. Local
grassroots participation is defined in terms of the leadership that is offered
by the people rather than top-down efforts of co-opting their participation
or manipulating them through top-down agendas.

The local and national organizing in Bolivia then fosters spaces of resistance and transformative politics in a global scale (see, for instance, E.
Morales, 2008). Bolivia not only serves as a model for politics of resistance
on a global scale, but also emerges on the global arena as a resistive voice
that interrogates the processes of decision making and communication
within the structures of the international financial institutions (IFIs), including the World Trade Organization (WTO), International Monetary
Fund (IMF), and World Bank (WB). Morales, as leader of Bolivia, interrogates the decision-making structures and processes of the WTO, pointing out the differential access to WTO negotiations among developed and
developing countries. He further documents the hypocrisies in WTO negotiations where developed countries heavily subsidize their agricultural
and food companies nationally, and simultaneously utilize their power
in WTO negotiations to force developing countries to open up markets
to favor the big companies from developed countries (E. Morales, 2008):

> The WTO negotiations have turned into a fight by developed coun-
> tries to open markets in developing countries to favor their big com-
> panies.

> The agricultural subsidies in the North, which mainly go to agricul-
> tural and food companies in the US and Europe, will not only con-
> tinue but will actually increase, as demonstrated by the 2008 Farm
> Bill in the United States. The developing countries will lower tariffs
> on their agricultural products while the real subsidies applied by the
> US or the EU to their agricultural products will not decline.
>
> As for industrial products in WTO negotiations, developing countries
> are being asked to cut their tariffs by 40% to 60% while developed
> countries will, on average, cut their tariffs by 25% to 33%.

Morales, as a leader of a country that represents the developing world,
points out the hypocrisies in the policies of neoliberalism that use the
language of the free market to open up markets in the global South and
simultaneously utilize protectionist policies nationally that support agricultural and food companies in US and Europe through agricultural
subsidies. Rather than applying the logics of the free market, the powerful nations of the global North utilize their power over WTO to impose
top-down policies that favor TNCs from the global North and open up
markets in the global South for these TNCs. The incongruence of the logics of neoliberalism lies at the heart of the narrative of resistance that is
offered by the Bolivian state on the global stage.

The political organizing of global economic systems under the neoliberal configuration is questioned in terms of its inherent logics. Here is
another excerpt from the same article (E. Morales, 2008):

> Countries should prioritize the consumption of what we produce lo-
> cally. A product that travels half around the world to reach its destiny
> can be cheaper than other that is produced domestically, but, if we
> take into account the environmental costs of transporting that mer-
> chandise, the energy consumption and the quantity of carbon emis-
> sions that it generates, then we can reach the conclusion that it is
> healthier for the planet and for humanity to prioritize the consump-
> tion of what is locally produced.

What becomes evident in the excerpt is the emphasis on questioning the
value of individually directed consumption that satisfies the needs and

wants of the individual consumer. How the price of a commodity is calculated is noted amidst questions of value. The value of the commodity, in turn, is tied to questions of energy consumption and quantity of carbon emissions tied to the price of transporting the merchandise across the geographic spaces. The model of global flow of goods is countered with a model of local production that fulfills the needs of community members. Morales (2008) further goes on to note:

> Foreign trade must be a complement to local production. In no way can we favor foreign markets at the expense of national production.
>
> Capitalism wants to make us all uniform so that we turn into mere consumers. For the North there is only one development model, theirs. The uniform models of economic development are accompanied by processes of generalized acculturation to impose on us one single culture, one single fashion, one single way of thinking and of seeing things. To destroy a culture, to threaten the identity of a people, is the greatest damage that can be done to humanity. The respect and the peaceful and harmonic complementarity of the various cultures and economies is essential to save the planet, humanity and life . . .
>
> In the 21st century, a "Development round" can no longer be about "free trade", but is rather has to promote a kind of trade that contributes to the equilibrium between countries, regions and mother nature, establishing indicators that allow for an evaluation and correction of trade rules in terms of sustainable development.

The global free-trade model of neoliberalism is resisted through the positioning of the local market as the framework for seeking balance. The privileging of national and local production puts forth the local as the entry point to economic planning. The neoliberal model of development is clearly identified as a culturally situated Eurocentric model from the North. The uniform model of economic development is imposed top-down on the global South, thus leading to the destruction and erasure of cultures and the threatening of the identity of people. The "free trade" agendas of the "development round" are resisted by alternative suggestions for the development of trade rules that foster sustainable development. The article by Morales (2008) ends with the following conclusion:

> We, the governments, have an enormous responsibility with our peoples. Agreements such as the ones in the WTO have to be widely known and debated by all citizens and not only by ministers, businessmen and "experts". We, the peoples of the world, have to stop being passive victims of these negotiations and turn into main actors of our present and future.

The essential discursive formations of the WTO negotiation structures that privilege the powerful actors and the elite from the global North are rendered accessible through the call for popular participation in WTO negotiations. Rather than the discursive space being constituted through the participation of elite actors such as ministers, businessmen, and experts, a call is made for broader public participation in processes of decision making and development policy planning. Morales urges the people of the world to participate actively in the negotiations to shape the scope and nature of global policies, both for the present and the future. Similar voices of resistance are heard in the successful local indigenous organizing of The Confederation of Indigenous Nationalities of Ecuador (CONAIE) (Lucero, 2008; O'Connor, 2003), and in other parts of Latin America (Lucero, 2008).

Conclusion

Throughout this chapter, we discussed politically directed movements that have been specifically constituted as attempts to reshape and transform the social, economic, and political structures. These movements, organized across various spaces dispersed around the globe are connected around a broad theme of seeking transformations in political structures of organizing and governance. The desire for political change in structures of organizing originates from the concentration of structures in the hands of the elite. Accompanying this concentration of power in the hands of transnational elite is the simultaneous erasure of opportunities for participation for the poorer and indigenous sectors of the globe. The disenfranchisement of the poor is carried out through the absence of opportunities for the poor to be involved in systems and processes of decision making. The subalternity of the subaltern sectors, therefore, is constituted amidst the politics of erasure that is configured into existing processes of organizing of resources. Resistance, as expression of agency, seeks to transform the discursive spaces and the logics under which these discursive spaces are constituted in order to increase the political opportunities for participation among the popular and subaltern classes. As depicted in the examples presented throughout this chapter, the voices of resistance seek to carve out political processes and decision-making structures where communities can participate in making choices through deliberation and dialogue. As opposed to the neoliberal emphases on participation and community-based solutions, the voices of resistance configure communities as sites of resistance that seek to transform the consolidation of power in the hands of transnational elite. The language of community articulated through the voices of resistance fundamentally disrupt the narratives of community participation that emerge in neoliberalism in order to manage the neoliberal modes of governance by shifting public resources away from the state. The community that emerges at these sites of protest is a community that seeks to engage with the political processes of the state, with the goal of determining the ways in which these processes are shaped and engaging in these processes continuously in order to participate in decision making.

Resistance, Development, and Social Change

Introduction

Development is the key site of global neoliberal governance, serving as the reason for neoliberal interventions. The existence of neoliberalism, therefore, is dependent on the concept of development. The traditional markers of economic growth and efficiency within the framework of development are utilized to push the agendas of neoliberalization of the globe through structural adjustment programs (SAPs). The underlying logic of development-based neoliberal adjustments is founded on the premise that privatization and trade liberalization would lead to economic development by opening up the markets. It is assumed that the global establishment of "free" markets would enable the rational logic of effectiveness to take hold, leading to economic growth and to the trickling down of resources. Furthermore, the development logic of neoliberalism operates on the notion that the removal of barriers and regulations on entrepreneurial capacity would spark economic growth, thus improving the fundamental condition of the nation state. As depicted in the introduction to this book, inherent in the notion

Chapter Six

of neoliberalism as development is the contradiction in the conceptualizations of development, which are deployed to serve the interests of transnational capital and further impoverish the global South in imperial relationships of dependence. It is in this backdrop that we engage with three specific culture-centered sites of resistance: the Save Niyamgiri movement, the Cochabamba water wars, and the Narmada Bachao Andolan. Each of these sites of resistance present us with opportunities for listening to voices of resistance that challenge the top-down narratives of development built into the industrialization, privatization, and liberalization principles of neoliberal reforms.

Save Niyamgiri Movement

The Save Niyamgiri movement challenges the key top-down lessons offered by development experts under the modernization framework that puts forth industrialization, urbanization, and land redevelopment as solutions to underdevelopment and poverty. Historically, in the context of the tribal regions of India and specifically in the Orissa state, a geographic region that is rich in natural resources and minerals, the government has contracted out vast parts of tribal land to mining companies, resulting in the large-scale displacement of tribal populations. In almost all of these development projects, the politics of development has been carried out through the marginalization of tribal communities from discursive spaces, without tribal participation in decisions of resource management and utilization. The large-scale usurping of tribal land to carry out industrialization and mining projects under the framework of development has had a long history in post-independence India. Tribal communities have been systematically erased from their traditional forms of livelihood and traditional spaces of living as a result of these development projects.

Furthermore, the development of mining projects has been constituted amidst corrupt practices, with large discrepancies between the promises made to tribal community members and the actual opportunities and compensations offered to tribal community members once the projects have been built. The promises of employment to tribal community members that have often been offered as strategic tools to carry out the displacement projects have not been met, and even in instances where they have been met, have resulted in the employment of tribal community members as unskilled labor in the mines. It is in this backdrop of historic exploitation of tribal communities in Orissa (also referred to as the adivasis) that the Save Niyamgiri movement is situated. In 1997, the Orissa authorities had signed a contract with Sterlite India for the Niyamgiri mining project. In 2003, the Kalahandi District Administration sent out notices to people in the region, notifying them that their land was to be acquired for the purposes of building the refinery (Amnesty International, 2010). The local people were not consulted and this was in direct violation of Schedule V of the Indian constitution that protects tribal land. Under Schedule V, local authorities are required to consult community members through *Gram Sabhas* and *Gram Panchayats* before acquiring land in Schedule V areas. The Kalahandi District Collector's office sent out land acquisition notices to landowners in June 2002, noting that the District Administration was going to compulsorily acquire land for the refinery project; people that lost their land would be adequately compensated, and people that lost both their home and their land would be compensated as well as resettled. These letters were not sent to landless laborers whose livelihoods were going to be affected by the acquisition. People who had complaints were asked to register their complaints by June 22, 2002, and the public meetings were held on June 26, 2002. Within two weeks, the land acquisition had started. In September 2004, additional land was acquired by the District Administration and then transferred to the refinery.

In 2006, Sterlite, a subsidiary of the UK-based mining company Vedanta Aluminium built a refinery in Lanjigarh at the bottom of the Niyamgiri Hills of Orissa in India. Since the establishment of the refinery, there have been widespread reports of human rights violations as well as environmental pollution. In 2007, Vedanta Aluminium applied for expansion of the refinery. The refinery had been built on land that was earlier used by the adivasi communities in the area for farming, and it was compulsorily acquired from tribal communities in 2002 and 2004, displacing 118 families and forcing approximately 1,200 families to sell their farmlands to the refinery.

Since 2003, in the face of the top-down displacement projects that were carried out by the government in coordination with the mining company, the local tribal communities started organizing protests and participating in public demonstrations. Through these protests and public demonstrations, they presented the voices of resistance, drawing attention to the ways in which tribal community members were fundamentally absent from the policy platforms and discursive spaces that discussed the mining projects and the establishment of the mines. At the center of the protests was the articulation of the violations of local, national, and international laws that mandate tribal consultations, participation, and informed consent in projects that impact tribal communities. India's Panchayat Extension to Scheduled Areas Act (PESA) legislation enacted in 1996 mandates that prior recommendations through *Gram Sabhas* or *Panchayats* involving tribal community members at the appropriate level shall be conducted before granting mining leases in scheduled areas (Amnesty International, 2010). Between 2002 and 2009, throughout the entire period where decisions were made that in essence uprooted tribal communities from their spaces of livelihood, the tribal community members were not consulted. Consultation meetings and public hearings that were held regarding the mining project and the distillery were held in spaces that were difficult to reach. Publicity of the meetings and consultations was circulated in newspapers that were published in Oriya and English, and available in the cities. No efforts were made on behalf of the state government or the mining company officials to engage the local tribal community members in the discussions, and most of the tribal community members from the affected areas had not even heard of the consultations and public meetings.

In a report on the processes utilized in securing the land and setting up the mining and distillery projects, Amnesty International (2010) notes that officials of the District Administration and company representatives were present at the consultations, but no one from the Dongria Kondh communities that were affected by the mine site attended. The consent of the Dongria Kondh community members was not sought out; also, they were not involved in processes of decision making regarding the acquisition of the land and the setting up of the mining and the distillery projects.

Noting this absence of villagers from discursive spaces of decision making, N. S., a Dongria Kondh man, shared with the Amnesty researchers, "Please write to Vedanta Resources and ask them to go talk to the Dongria Kondh." Along similar lines, another Dongria Kondh participant, S. M., noted, "Our message to the company and Sarkar [the government] is simple. We will sit together, us Dongria people, and decide directly" (Amnesty International, 2010, p. 35).

In meetings with community members in the village council meetings for land acquisition, villagers were misinformed that they would each receive 100,000 Indian rupees for each acre of land in addition to jobs for every family member who sold land provided by the company. The dream sown among the indigenous community members was that the area would get supplies of electricity and water, and would soon turn into a Mumbai or Dubai. According to the official records, the District Administration assured the villagers that the proposed refinery would be directly beneficial to the local village as well as to the entire country; they suggested it would also generate job opportunities for the unemployed men and women. This articulation of information manipulation is evident in the resistive voices in the Amnesty International (2010) report:

> At no stage, they said, were they told that the refinery processes involved risks of substantial pollution. "We were not told that they will make alumina powder and send it elsewhere," said S. and K., two women, who attended two of the village council meetings: "We were later shocked to discover so many trucks bringing the bauxite and taking the powder away. We felt deceived, as we were not told that everything would be done here. The officials did not share in the *gram sabha* meeting or elsewhere that there would be so much dust, chimney smoke, noise, that our river would become dirty. We had never seen a refinery so had no experience or information on what life could be like staying so close to it." B. N., a man from Kenduguda, whose land was acquired to support the construction of the refinery's ash pond (see Chapter 5, Photo 10) and who lives close to the pond, said, "we were never told anything about an ash pond or what living next to it would be like." A. M., a man from Rengopalli, similarly explained that they were never given any information about the two red

mud ponds (see Chapter 5, Photos 11-13), one of which is now being built right next to his village, and they had not been given any information on what the red mud was made of and if it posed any risks to them. He also said that once this red mud pond was constructed it "will close access to the public road and make it difficult for our children to go to school." "The other road we can use is where they want to build the pillars for conveyor belt [linking the mine and refinery]. I am worried about things falling from the belt on to us." Other residents of from Rengopalli pointed out that their village would soon be stuck between the red mud pond and the proposed conveyor belt from the proposed bauxite mine site at Niyamgiri to Lanjigarh, but had been given no choice in the matter or alternatives. (p. 41)

Central to the voices of resistance was the articulation of the misinformation or absence of information in the community before the acquisition of the land and the building of the refinery. Pointing to their lack of access to structural resources of information, community members noted the manipulative strategies utilized by the administration to deceive them. They also noted within this context the environmental pollution caused by the refinery and the consequences of the environmental pollution for the families living in the area. Furthermore, the communities living on top of the Niyamgiri Hills had no representation in the village council meetings, and this became a key point of contention in the resistance. The use of oppressive top-down forces to displace the Dongria Kondh from their spaces of living is noted in the following narrative: "Once the village officer and the police came here. They did not give any notice to take away the land. Forcefully they built the road and the pipeline" (http://youtu.be/VJt59wb-NI6s). Here is another excerpt: "Our land on which we were farming was taken away forcefully by the company" (http://youtu.be/VJt59wbNI6s).

The discursive erasure of the Dongria Kondh from the modernist platforms of development where decisions were being carried out that impacted their lives was accompanied by the circulation of specific truth claims about development, simultaneously erasing alternative rationalities and narratives that were articulated by the Dongria Kondh. For the Dongria Kondh, the Niyamgiri Hills define the spiritual, cultural, social, and

Figure 6.1. Uploaded by "1takemedia." http://youtu.be/VJt59wbNI6s

economic aspects of livelihood. The central role of the Niyamgiri Hills to the lives of tribal community members is rendered visible in the following song (http://youtu.be/VJt59wbNI6s):

> Today I saw Niyamgiri mountains
> And my eyes have become holy
> The mountain looks so beautiful
> And the nightingale is singing
> Since ages, deer and antelopes and bears
> Have been living here.

The Niyamigiri Hills are considered sacred by the Dongria Kondh, the adivasi community dwelling and depending almost entirely on the forests for their livelihood. The Niyamgiri Hills constitute the economic, cultural, and social fabric of the Dongria Kondh, offering material and symbolic resources. Another protestor echoes the theme of the sacredness of the Niyamgiri Hills: "Yes Niyamgiri is our God. We live in the mountains and survive. We don't have any land on which we can produce and live. We are dependent on the mountain. We won't leave Niyamgiri." Similarly, laying claim to the historic ownership of the land by the adivasi community, a protestor shares: "We have been living here for generations, how can the government now just say that it is their land and decide to allow mining without talking to us?" (Amnesty International, 2010, p. 3).

What emerges as central to the articulation of resistance is the erasure of tribal voices from the processes of decision making. Laying claim to the land that is their home, the Dongria Kondh voices interrogate the frame of development offered by the government that usurps tribal land. The question of ownership is foregrounded to narrate the story of indigenous communities living on the land for generations. In the backdrop of the local resistance against Vedanta and its refinery, when in 2008, the Indian Ministry of Environment and Forests (MoEF) approved in principle a bauxite mining project involving the London-based Vedanta in the Niyamgiri Hills of Orissa, India, the indigenous people of this region rose up in concerted protest, raising their voices against the mining company, the Indian government, and the usurping of their land, and joining their efforts with several national and international actors that created entry points for exerting pressure.

These voices of resistance discuss the unhealthy effects of the mining operations understood through the lived experiences of the Dongria Kondh in the region. The everyday struggles of the Dongria Kondh were constituted amidst the effects of the mining operations. The "Niyamgiri, You are Still Alive" YouTube video (http://youtu.be/VJt59wbNI6s) includes experiences of community members, such as "We will not get any water even if we dig deep. It is only because of Niyamgiri that we get water" and "When we bathe, the skin itches. When we drink water, we get sores in our mouth." Voices of local community members from the area and their stories of suffering are recorded through mobile phones and uploaded on social networking sites (see, for instance, http://youtu.be/l_s6HhDAuAY). Videos, photographs, and audio recordings document the effect of the Vedanta operations in the region. Videos point to the red mud spill and document the toxic hazards, and then circulate the evidence through web-

Figure 6.2. Uploaded by "KBKNEWS." http://youtu.be/l_s6HhDAuAY

sites and online groups. Consider, for instance, the following posting on the Facebook group "Save Niyamgiri" (http://www.facebook.com/group.php?gid=31785088220):

> News from Samarendra "Vedanta's environmental crimes: red mud burst again 2 hours ago . . . the sludge has reached the company compound . . . protesters have filmed it in their mobiles . . . Please spread this news to others . . . this is second time the company has tried to cover up the whole toxic affair. Bloddy Vedanta, Once again showed his real face."

Photographs and videos circulated through Facebook and YouTube generated awareness about the effects of the refinery as documented through the tools available to local community members. These resources became sources for building the evidence base regarding the refinery and its effects on the community. The resistance of the local community of the Dongria Kondh is expressed in the form of the Niyamgiri Suraksha Samiti. Here is the voice of Lado Sikaka, a local leader (http://youtu.be/ipHmVee_uXw):

Vedanta has troubled us greatly. It is fighting with us for Niyamgiri. The company people try to lure us with schools and roads in our villages. They cannot trick us like that. We will do whatever it takes to save Niyamgiri. We have a right over the mountain. If they take Niyamgiri our world will be destroyed. We won't give up Niyamgiri for any price. Can they give us the wealth of Niyamgiri in return? Niyamgiri is not a pile of money. That mountain is our life. We won't flinch if you take our flesh but we won't tolerate Niyamgiri being dug up. They have bought Niyamgiri from the Govt. but it doesn't belong to the Govt. It belongs to the tribals . . . makes me so angry I get tempted to use the axe. We are not afraid of them because it is for Niyamgiri. They might outnumber us but every one of us will fight. We are not afraid of monsters like Vedanta.

Evident in the narrative is the resolve of the Dongria Kondh to stand up in resistance, and to struggle against the various means of control exer-

Figure 6.3. Uploaded by "niyamgiri." http://youtu.be/ipHmVee_uXw

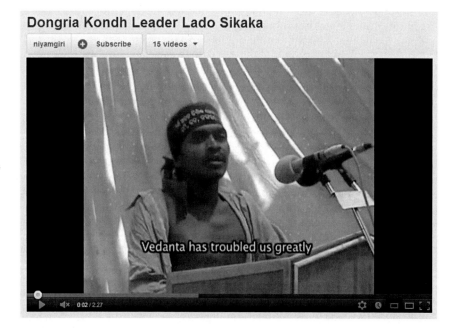

cised by the company hand-in-hand with the state and the district. The voice of Lado Sikaka challenges the dominant structures of articulation by foregrounding the right of the Dongria Kondh to Niyamgiri. It is in this backdrop that the leader expresses the will of his community to not give up Niyamgiri at any price.

Throughout 2009, there were protests organized by the "Niyamgiri Suraksha Samiti," and the images of these protests were shared through online resources (http://youtu.be/Dm8ljBHv61Y). In the videos of the protests, community members are depicted marching, voicing slogans such as "We won't be afraid for the sake of mother earth" and "We won't tolerate devastation in the name of development," and singing songs and performing dances in groups. Songs on Niyamgiri carry out the message of the movement. For example, the song "Gaon chorab nahin" ("We won't leave our village"), sung by local performers, depicts the conviction of the Dongria Kondh to not leave their land. Penned by Bhagwaan Majhi, an adivasi

Figure 6.4. Uploaded by "niyamgiri." http://youtu.be/Dm8ljBHv61Y

leader against bauxite mining in Kashipur, the picturization of the song in the backdrop of the lush, green Niyamgiri Hills, the plants and the trees, and the images of the mines and the aftermaths drive home through visuals the impact of the bauxite mining operations. The song is set to adivasi tune and is presented amidst adivasi art and animation depicting the different aspects of adivasi life in relationship to the mining operations. Here is an excerpt of the lyrics of the song (http://youtu.be/Q49PnMl3HH8):

> We will not leave our village
> Nor our forests
> Nor our mother earth
> We will not give up our fight!
> They built dams . . .
> Drowned villages and . . .
> Built factories
> They cut down forests

Figure 6.5. Uploaded by "actionaidcomms." http://youtu.be/Q49PnMl3HH8

Dug out mines
And built sanctuaries
. . . Without water, land, and forest, where do we go?
Oh God of development, pray tell us, how to save our lives?

Similarly, other performances, songs, videos, and films are circulated to create spaces for listening to the voices of resistance. Videos on different aspects of the mining operations and tribal resistance are widely circulated through social media. Simultaneously, reports are disseminated across various outlets to raise awareness. In a report written by Das and Padel (2010), Bhagaban Majhi, the leader of the Kashipur movement, is noted as saying:

> *Agya, unnoti boile kono?* (Sir, what do you mean by development?) Is it development to displace people? The people, for whom development is meant, should reap benefits. After them, the succeeding generations should reap benefits. That is development. It should not be merely to cater to the greed of a few officials. To destroy the millions of years old mountains is not development.

Performances on streets share the stories of the community and its experiences of loss. Protest participants carry axes as symbolic representations of resistance. Here is a portion of a speech given by a leader at the site of the protest march: "If they come with guns, we will pick our arrows, spears, and axes." Another leader says, "We won't allow mining and we will remain united. . . . We won't be afraid of death to save Niyamgiri. Die we may we won't leave Niyamgiri" (Das & Padel, 2010). The deviance of the protests against the top-down structures of development is shared in the weaving together of the movement with similar movements against mega-development projects, providing a broader backdrop for resisting the industrialization projects carried out in the name of development. Here is the voice of another leader at the protest site (Das & Padel, 2010):

> Today they have put whole of Orissa for sale while sitting in Bhubaneswar. Our struggle is against these ministers and officers in Bhubaneswar who decide which company will get what part of Orissa. Till today, Tata has not been able to lay a brick in Kalinga Nagar. Vedanta has not been able to set up its university in Puri. POSCO is not being

able to enter Dhinkia. None of the mega-projects announced by the government have been able to acquire land because people are protesting and resisting everywhere.

The protests in Niyamgiri are framed alongside other protests against mega-projects that are touted under the framework of development. It is this very framework of development that is interrogated, with critical questions being raised at the grassroots level. Solidarity across individual sites against projects of mega-development weave together the resistive elements of the movement into broader interconnected narratives that question the assumptions of development. Scholarly articles documenting the human rights violations, environmental hazards, and displacements of communities from their sources of livelihood offer entry points for disrupting the dominant structures of development planning (see, for instance, Das & Padel, 2010).

Critical to the growing movement against the Vedanta mining project was the solidarity that was being charted between the local activists, the national-level activists, and the activist networks at the global level. Tribal communities from the Niyamgiri area participated in concerted efforts of resistance. For instance, in May 2008, hundreds of Dongria Kondh traveled to Bhubaneswar, the capital of Orissa, to articulate their resistance to the mining project to be set up on their sacred mountain. The protest march was covered across several activist outlets and generated global-national-local networks of reporting, reaching a global audience. Here's a report excerpt from Survival International (2008), a global non-governmental organization (NGO) that works on issues of indigenous rights:

> Survival has launched a campaign targeting Vedanta, and is urging shareholders, including major British companies Standard Life, Barclays Bank, Abbey National and HSBC, as well as Middlesbrough and Wolverhampton Councils, to disinvest unless Vedanta abandons its plans.
>
> Survival's director Stephen Corry said today, "If Vedanta goes ahead with this mine, the Dongria Kondh will be destroyed. They cannot survive as a people without their land. The Norwegian government

has already sold its shares in Vedanta, and other investors should fol-
low suit, or face boycotts over their human rights record."

The offline sites of protest organized by tribal community members found
their way into mainstream discursive spaces through media reports, reports organized by local and national NGOs, and reports created by
global NGOs to organize campaign against Vedanta's mining project in
Niyamgiri. The resistive narratives voiced at the local sites are picked up
and re-narrated by NGOs and activists at other sites of protest, drawing
global attention to the unethical and coercive practices of Vedanta that
severely impacted the environment as well as the local cultural practices
of the Dongria Kondh.

Resistance is constituted in the disruption of those spaces of dominant discourses that serve the strategic functions of Vedanta. For instance,
when in 2009, the World Environment Foundation (WEF) announced its
Golden Peacock Award for best environmental management practices to
be awarded to Vedanta Alumina Limited, over 20 activists representing
environment and social action groups organized a protest at the opening
ceremony of the Global Convention for Climate Change being held at
Palampur Agricultural University. The activists carried banners stating,
"Stop greenwashing corporate crimes" and "Stop selling climate change,"
utilizing the space of the opening ceremony to disrupt the environmentally
conscious image of Vedanta by narrating the story of the Vedanta mining
project and the refinery plant. Documenting the oppressions carried out
by Vedanta on tribal communities, the displacement of tribal community members, the displacement of local livelihood, large-scale environmental abuse, health hazards, and the environmental effects of the distillery, the activists took over the microphone to note the hypocrisy of the
awards that conferred the prestige of being environmentally conscious to
a corporation that was destroying the environment in a local community
in Orissa. Distributing reports on the environmental and human rights
abuses of Vedanta, the activists also noted that these types of awards serve
as public relations strategies for corporations such as Vedanta to deflect
attention away from their environmentally disruptive practices and to
counter efforts of regulating the environmental abuses caused by compa-

nies like Vedanta. Here is an excerpt from a speech in Hindi by an activist who took over the microphone at the award ceremony to contest the narrative of environmental consciousness being offered by Madhav Mehra, the chairman of WEF:

> Vedanta is globally infamous for corporate crimes. A company that has made mockery of environment laws . . . Those who have paid to come to this convention should know why Norway Govt. banned Vedanta. We are here to protest against such incriminating companies being awarded by Madhav Mehra's organization . . . These are all entities who only stage drama in the name of environment and such awards are only meant to greenwash their crimes and set their images clean in public eye. We will not let it happen. WEF is a sham! What kind of environmental convention is this? What kind of environmentalists are these? If you come here for the people, to stop displacement, to save the mountains, to protect the glaciers, we welcome you! But kindly stop these festivities. (http://youtu.be/r_FYSGMwoII)

Figure 6.6. Uploaded by "niyamgiri." http://youtu.be/r_FYSGMwoII

As another activist seeks to take the microphone to translate the speech into English, she is stopped from doing so by the organizers. To this, the activist says, "They are not allowing me to speak in English because their delegates will understand what I am saying. They will see. The fact of the matter is that Vedanta Alumina Resources Limited has already bought people in this country, has already ruined the people in Niyamgiri and other parts of the country." At this point, she is elbowed off the stage, with the organizers stating, "Throw her off the stage," "Push her off." As the activists are being strong armed, one of them notes, "Don't touch us. There is camera rolling here." Amidst the end of the speeches and the protest, several participants at the WEF convention walked out of the opening ceremony. After being briefed, the Tibetan Prime Minister in exile, Samdhung Rinpoche, who was the chief dignitary at the event, walked out, along with many local schoolchildren in the area who were attending the event. The raw video footage of the ceremony along with the subtitles of the protest voices are circulated through the Niyamgiri YouTube channel and through Facebook sites. Although the mainstream media largely carried negative reports of the protests, framing the activists as disruptive, multiple activist groups circulated the message of those standing in opposition along with the videos of the protests through the Internet, utilizing social media, including YouTube, Facebook, and blogs (see, for instance, http://goldenpeacockawardsenvironment.wordpress.com/tag/mehra/).

The discursive presence of the voices of the Dongria Kondh at public sites of discussion disrupt the hegemony of the dominant structures that have traditionally narrated frameworks of development. The Belamba Public Hearing witnessed a concerted effort by the Dongria Kondh to resist the discursive erasures of the Dongria Kondh from the platforms of decision making and from the discursive articulations of policy making. Dongria Kondh voices foregrounded the struggles of the community and the effects of the mining and refinery operations on the community. The proceedings are available on YouTube (http://youtu.be/dSKAfx1mOUY). At the hearing, the tribal community members present discussed the hazardous effects of the refinery on the Vamsadhara River, and they resisted the plans for the expansion of the refinery. Here is the voice of Lado Majhi at the Belamba Public Hearing (quoted in Das and Padel, 2010):

> Niyamgiri is our Mother. Our life depends on the mountain. Can you pay five lakhs for one tree? Our *Sarkar* [Govt] should not sell out to a foreign company. Even if everyone else accepts the project, we can't allow mining on Niyamgiri.

At the heart of the narrative is the interrogation of the economic metric that drives development planning and programming. Lado Majhi interrogates the meaning of development by probing the very frameworks through which questions of value are assessed and through which values are assigned to specific projects. The value of the forests to the Dongria Kondh community members is tied to the meanings of the forests in the lives of the community and the sacredness of the forests amidst the cultural, social, spiritual, and economic spaces of everyday lives of tribal community members. Meanings emerge into the discursive spaces of development policy as sites of contestation; the meanings assigned to development through values of economic growth privileging the powerful owners of the mining operations are contested by the meanings of sustenance, nurturance, and sacredness held by the Dongria Kondh community members.

The local sites of activism are connected to the global platforms of activist politics through new media platforms such as web pages, bulletin boards, and discussion groups, through social media such as Facebook, and through audio-visual tools such as YouTube. For example, the Facebook page of the Save Niyamgiri movement seeks to organize public opinion and support through the connections and networking opportunities it offers across local and global spaces (http://www.facebook.com/#!/group.php?gid=31785088220). The Facebook page shares important news directly from the site, compiles a variety of media stories, and connects with videos that narrate through the voices of the tribal community members the experiences they face in the backdrop of the mining project, the threats to their life posed by Vedanta, the violence enacted by the corporation, and the state-sponsored police violence on tribal protests. It emerges as a site for sharing news and information about the movement, providing access to images and videos taken from field sites as communities participated

Figure 6.7. Uploaded by "niyamgiri." http://youtu.be/dSKAfx1mOUY

in their efforts of resistance. Videos of protests and police tortures from local spaces of protest emerged into the networks of solidarity through Facebook. Similarly, videos linking to documentaries on the resistance, videos of performances, and videos utilized by Vedanta for its public relations practices fostered networked sites of resistance. Websites such as "Foil Vedanta" (http://www.foilvedanta.org/articles/battles-over-bauxite-in-east-india-the-khondalite-mountains-of-khondistan/) offer information resources, environmental reports, links to articles, photographs, and steps for action. The online sites of protest became spaces for globalizing the voices of protest; amidst the increasing popularity of the YouTube channel of the Save Niyamgiri movement, it was hacked a day before the Vedanta's annual meeting in London. After the resurrection of the channel, the following video was created (http://youtu.be/_a_cbyhCCSg), challenging the structural processes through which grassroots participation was erased. The local-global solidarity networks of the movement emerged through the involvement of organizations such as Amnesty International and Survival International in documenting the corrupt practices of Vedanta and in developing campaigns in London and at other global sites that carried the message of the Save Niyamgiri movement. The local-national-global organizing of the movement was instrumental in pressuring the Indian government to refuse clearance to Vedanta (http://www.survivalinternational.org/tribes/dongria); along these very lines, the global solidarity networks pressured the Church of England, the Norwegian government, and investment firm Martin Currie to withdraw their funding from Vedanta. The resistance in Niyamgiri continues as villagers protest the toxic poisoning from the refinery and the red mud spills (see images of these protests by villagers of Rengopalli at http://www.facebook.com/#!/group.php?gid=317850882200); in this backdrop, Vedanta continues its ongoing strategies of exerting pressure on local and national political processes to secure access to the mining sites.

Similar to Save Niyamgiri movement, other movements have emerged across several sites of India, challenging the narratives of development pushed by the local, state, and federal governments in order to drive industrializing, mining, and corporatization projects through land acquisition and through the systematic displacement of the poor from their spaces of livelihood (Das & Padel, 2010). For instance, Lalgarh, a region in the West Midnapore district of West Bengal, has emerged as a site of resistance against state-sponsored violence and top-down programs seeking to displace tribal communities, reflective of large-scale resistance that has emerged across the Eastern corridor in India (Mike, 2009). Although the state of West Bengal, India, has historically experienced systematic efforts of rural resistance over the last four decades, the politics of resistance in Lalgarh erupted in response to specialized development projects that were being carried out by the state government of West Bengal that threatened to displace large sectors of populations from the region, and the continuing police harassment to thwart the protests of local community members. Lalgarh is home to rural communities that depend primarily upon agriculture as a means of living, and it has a large population of indigenous tribes. The struggles in Lalgarh are situated in the backdrop of broader struggles over land in Singur and Nandigram (Bhattacharya, 2009); fundamental to

Figure 6.8. Uploaded by "niyamgiri." http://youtu.be/_a_cbyhCCSg

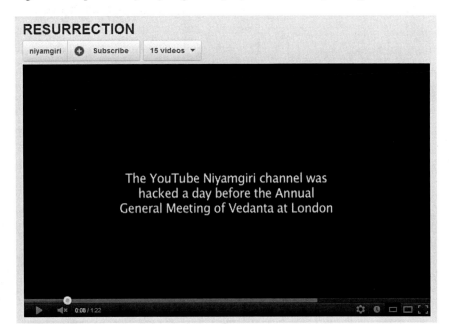

these struggles is the demand of impacted communities for representation and for opportunities for participation in decision-making processes and structures. Across the Eastern corridor of India, local voices of subaltern resistance have emerged in collectives as these voices have challenged the projects of large-scale displacement of indigenous and agrarian communities carried on in the name of development, and primarily in the form of mining, industrialization, and urbanization (Das & Padel, 2010; Navlakha, 2010). India has responded to these indigenous voices of protest through repressive mechanisms of state control, deploying the paramilitary and the police under the framework of anti-terrorist actions branded "Operation Green Hunt." Challenging the oppressions and police atrocities in Operation Green Hunt, several local movements, through their networks with national and global activists, have started identifying the atrocities carried out by these actions, documenting the forms of violence, exploitation, and oppression carried on in the name of Operation Green Hunt, and mobilizing resistance through online channels such as Facebook and

YouTube. These online resources also become conduits for documenting police atrocities and for bringing to the fore images, stories, and real-time videos of state-sponsored violence (see, for instance, the videos on the torture and harassment of the indigenous teacher Soni Sori at http://freesonisoriandlingaram.wordpress.com/category/soni-sori/ that serve as resources for mobilizing resistance against oppressions carried out on indigenous communities in India). Through these voices, local narratives of protest documenting the oppressions and exploitations carried out by the state-corporate nexus offer frameworks for dialogue in dominant discursive spaces of development.

Cochabamba

Yet another instance of grassroots protest is the demonstration organized by the residents of the Bolivian city of Cochabamba in 2000 against the high cost of privatized water sold by Aguas del Tunari, a subsidiary of Bechtel that took over the water systems of Bolivia through a World Bank-mandated privatization directive (Olivera, 2004). In their protests against the privatization of water in Cochabamba, the people of Bolivia took to the streets, battling the police and indefinitely blockading the regional highways and roads (Dutta, 2011; Olivera, 2004). The privatization of water resources in Cochabamba played out in the backdrop of water shortages faced by the people, World Bank directives of water privatization in the region, the passing of Law 2029 that declared the privatization of the water and the confiscation of wells and alternate forms of water use, and the signing of a forty-year contract with a consortium of enterprises named Aguas del Tunari. With majority of the interests in Aguas del Tunari held by US-based Bechtel, and including Bolivian companies with political linkages, it became clear that the privatization of water served the interests of the global and transnational elites, simultaneously putting large price tags on water for the poor. La Coordinadora (Coalition in Defense of Water and Life) emerged in response to (a) the inability of local community members to pay the rising price of water; (b) the privatization of water, which Cochabambinos believed was a natural gift and a public service; (c) the nature of government decision making; and (d) the erasure of the local community from decision-making structures that contracted out resources that belonged to the community without involving the community.

In their protest on January 12, 2000, La Coordinadora members blockaded traffic, busting car windows and forcing shops to close; this was followed by a town meeting in the plaza that demanded the government send a commission. Subsequently, resistance was expressed in the form of planning a peaceful demonstration that was publicized as the "takeover of Cochabamba," constituting the physical seizure of the main plaza, symbolically representing the coming together of the workers to make their own decisions. On February 4 and 5, 2000, marchers took over the streets of Cochabamba, setting up barricades and blockading the entire city. Subsequently, between April 4 and April 12, 2000, La Coordinadora organized protest marches in Cochabamba, with blockades cutting off the main highways and masses of protestors occupying the city centers in Cochabamba. Here is an excerpt from the writing of Oscar Olivera, a leader of La Cochabamba, whose name became synonymous with the "Water War," that appeared in the *Guardian* in 2006 under the title "The voice of the people can dilute corporate power":

> In Bolivia, we consider water to be a common good—a human right, not a commodity. It is central to life and all that it embraces. It is collective property, yet in another sense it belongs to no one. These ideas, which have their roots in indigenous people's thinking, are what mobilised working people, both in the countryside and in the cities. The struggle to take control of our water supplies in 2000 became known as the "water war" of Cochabamba. (http://www.guardian.co.uk/society/2006/jul/19/comment.guardiansocietysupplement)

What is evident in this narrative is the foregrounding of the indigenous belief that water is a natural resource and a common good, not a commodity that can be privatized. This fundamental idea that seeks to define the realm of ownership of water, suggesting that it is a collective property and yet belongs to no one, resists the neoliberalization of global natural resources that seeks to turn these resources into privatized commodities to be traded by transnational corporations (TNCs). The protests of Cochabamba against the World Bank-enforced mandate that sought to privatize water, pushed through by the relationships between the World Bank, Bechtel, and the national government of Bolivia, also symbolize protests against the fundamental principles of neoliberalism that define development in terms of the privatization of resources. Highlighting the commoditization of water as the enactment of multinational greed, an indigenous worldview is put forth to frame water as a collective resource. Even in the face of state-sponsored violence that sought to thwart the protest and unleashed terror on the citizens, the protests continued, ultimately forcing the government to cancel the contract.

In this article written during his visit to the World Development Movement conference in Britain, Olivera notes the following:

> This confrontation was against the logic that tries to turn everything into commodities. All over Latin America, people now see that multinationals are trying to take over our resources and our goods held in common ownership including gas and oil—for their own profit. They are mobilising to take them back. Many companies in Bolivia against which we are fighting are British. And the demonstrations are very passionate because it is about our survival.
>
> Here in Britain, people have to pay large amounts of money for water. Just as in Bolivia, privatisation deals are signed on the backs of the people. Privatisations are always in the financial interests of the water companies.
>
> There are many ways of commercialising water—not only where a public utility is privatised, but also when water is lost, or when it is polluted. Then people must buy bottled drinking water, which costs far more.
>
> People must be made aware that what multinationals and rich governments want is to turn water into a commodity. (http://www.guardian.co.uk/society/2006/jul/19/comment.guardiansocietysupplement)

Resources and goods held in common ownership, such as gas, oil, and water, have become subjects of commoditization in the hands of multinationals, and this notion of ownership of collective resources for private profiteering lies at the heart of the resistance movement in Bolivia. The local-global linkage of the resistance movement becomes apparent in the articulation that many of the corporations being fought are British; this information is presented alongside a depiction of the picture in Britain where people have to pay large amounts of money for water.

The alternative narrative of water as a public and collective resource lies at the heart of the mobilization in Cochabamba. The mobilization resists the privatization efforts underlying neoliberal expansionism. The story of Cochabamba then emerges on the landscape of the International Monetary Fund (IMF) and World Bank-imposed neoliberal policies as a story of resistance, placing an alternative rationality that interrupts the discursive articulations of neoliberalism that extend the reach and imperial control of TNCs through the privatization of collective resources. Marcela Olivera, sister of Oscar Olivera and an international liaison for La Coordinadora, noted the following during her April 19, 2010 interview with Amy Goodman on *Democracy Now* on the ten year anniversary of the "Water War":

> What happened ten years ago, it opened the doors to what we have right now and what we're going to have later. You know, if we have a president like Evo Morales, it's because the social movements in April 2000 opened a door for that to happen. And the message, I think, is that we are not—the Water War is not over. The conflict ten years ago was not just about water; it was about something else, especially what we call democracy. It was about who decides about the things that matter to us, that are important to us. And ten years later, we are in a point where we want to say it was not over, it's not over. We are still trying to not resist—you know, resist privatization, in this case, but to build something. And I think there's still a long ways to go.
>
> You know, we were—I feel like—personally, I feel like I was a very important part of the history, in that we changed a little bit the curse of what was going on. The lesson of the Water War is that nothing is definitive, that we always can change things. The system was privatized already here; we could put it back, we could break that, and we could get back the company into our hands, something that we never imagined that could happen. And this is something that Os-

car all the time says, that slogan that we always repeat on the streets, that the people, united, will never be defeated, it's something that we lived here in Cochabamba ten years ago, and it's something that we believe it can happen again and again and again.

We never thought we were going to win. Never. Never thought we were going to win. What we were doing, it was struggling for that minute and that second. I don't think in anybody's head was the fact, we're going to win this war. (http://www.democracynow.org/2010/4/19/the_cochabamba_water_wars_marcella_olivera)

The strength of the Cochabamba movement drew not only from the local participation in the processes of social change that involved diverse sectors from within the country, but also from the solidarity that the local movement built with transnational actors. The International Forum on Globalization (IFG), an organization that is made up of academics, activists, economists, and researchers, was invited to participate in a conference on water rights in Cochabamba in December 2000, to create partnership between the local citizens of Cochabamba and the international movement against corporate globalization. Based on the lessons learned from the Cochabamba "Water Wars," the network of local Cochabambinos and IFG drafted the "Declaration of Cochabamba":

Here, in this city which has been an inspiration to the world for its retaking of that right through civil action, courage and sacrifice standing as heroes and heroines against corporate, institutional and governmental abuse, and trade agreements which destroy that right, in use of our freedom and dignity, we declare the following:

For the right to life, for the respect of nature and the uses and traditions of our ancestors and our peoples, for all time the following shall be declared as inviolable rights with regard to the uses of water given us by the earth:

1. Water belongs to the earth and all species and is sacred to life, therefore, the world's water must be conserved, reclaimed and

protected for all future generations and its natural patterns respected.

2. Water is a fundamental human right and a public trust to be guarded by all levels of government, therefore, it should not be commodified, privatized or traded for commercial purposes. These rights must be enshrined at all levels of government. In particular, an international treaty must ensure these principles are noncontrovertable.

3. Water is best protected by local communities and citizens who must be respected as equal partners with governments in the protection and regulation of water. Peoples of the earth are the only vehicle to promote earth democracy and save water. (http://nadir.org/nadir/initiativ/agp/free/imf/bolivia/cochabamba.htm)

The right to water is narrated as a human right, and the ownership of water is situated within the agentic realms of the Earth and all species living on it. Countering the Eurocentric universals that have carried out the agendas of privatizing global resources under the individualistic framework of ownership of individual property, the voices of resistance emerging from Cochabamba articulate a collective universal emanating from the global South. Here the depiction of human right springs from voices of the people from the global South, drawing from localized cultural narratives rooted in cultural values in the global South that disrupt the privatizing logics of transnational hegemony. The language of "rights," which has played an important role in global logics of neoliberal governance, is taken up by the discourses of resistance in Bolivia to offer a resistive framework for collective rights.

The collective struggle of the local communities in Bolivia in the movement against the privatization of water disrupts the hegemonic discourses of neoliberalism that seek to privatize all forms of collective resources and embed these resources into global markets for competition. The claim that water is a collective resource is offered as a knowledge claim narrated through the local struggles of Cochabamba participants who seek to impact global policies that dictate the everyday practices of human beings in their relationships to water. Specific frameworks of knowledge rooted in the cosmologies of the global South disrupt the violence embodied in the privatizing logics of Eurocentric values that drive neoliberal reforms globally.

Simultaneously, the narratives of harmony and respect for nature are offered as universals that counter the neoliberal agendas of water privatization and the reductionist treatment of water under neoliberal frameworks of governance as a resource to be managed. More specifically, the declaration argues that water is a public trust that needs to be guarded by all levels of government against efforts of privatization, commodification, or trade for commercial purposes. The legal-political framework of water ownership removes it from the realm of policy making and program planning under neoliberal governance that seek to restrict its uses among those with resources. The proposal for a universal treaty at a global level stands in resistance to claims of privatization that underlie the neoliberalization of collective resources such as water. In this backdrop of the consolidation of power in the hands of TNCs as a means for commoditizing water and turning it into a commodity to be purchased in the market, the paradigms of "earth democracy" and "save water" emerge as alternative frameworks of organizing that privilege the local ownership of water and other natural resources. Resisting the consolidation of decision making and management control in the hands of TNCs, the declaration foregrounds the agency and vital role of local communities in deciding how water is managed and regulated. Democracy as understood in the language of the global South is constituted in the agency of everyday people from the global South and in their active participation in decisions related to the management and regulation of natural resources at a local level. This theme of collective public ownership of public resources is then played out also in the following water and gas wars in Bolivia, and fostered a climate that led to the election of the *Movimiento al Socialismo* (MAS) in the general elections in 2005. The "Narmada Bachao Andolan" in India carries the same theme of local ownership and decision making that emerges so strongly in the Cochabamba movement.

Narmada Bachao Andolan (NBA)

The Narmada Bachao Andolan (NBA) is a movement in India that offers a framework for resistance against the building of mega-dams on the river Narmada, a struggle started in 1987 that offers leadership for global movements of resistance against neoliberal policies of development that privilege the building of dams as a solution to issues of development. The offline resistance of the movement primarily draws upon strategies of non-violent resistance, fasts, protest marches, sit-ins, and noncooperation, and is complemented by web-based strategies put forth by groups such as the "Friends of River Narmada" (www.narmada.org), a website dedicated to the cause of the NBA, and to the broader global struggle against the construction of mega-dams on rivers. The website of Narmada opens with the following introduction:

> The construction of large dams on the River Narmada in central India and its impact on millions of people living in the river valley has become one of the most important social issues in contemporary India. Through this website, we the friends of the Narmada valley and its people hope to present the perspective of grassroots people's organisations on the issue. Read an introduction to the issue.
>
> The Friends of River Narmada is an international coalition of organisations and individuals (mostly of Indian descent). The coalition is a solidarity network for the Narmada Bachao Andolan (Save the Narmada Movement) and other similar grassroots struggles in India. (http://www.narmada.org/)

Evident in the narrative is the linkage of the international coalition with the grassroots movement at the local site. Essential to the impact of the struggles is the solidarity between the local and global, circulating the stories of the local struggles at global sites and generating support in disparate contexts and at disparate levels.

Also at the heart of the online presence is the desire to recognize and represent the local voices of community organizers and community activists in their resistive struggles to transform the inequities written into the dominant structures. The image accompanying the text on the front page is the image of a rally in Khandwa organized in 2008, representing visually the collective agency of local communities in coming together to resist their displacement. The Friends of River Narmada coalition further goes on to explain its identity:

> The struggle against the construction of mega-dams on the River Narmada in India is symbolic of a global struggle for social and environmental justice. The Friends of River Narmada is an international coalition of individuals and organizations (primarily of Indian descent). In particular, we are a support and solidarity network for the *Narmada Bachao Andolan* (Save the Narmada movement) which has been fighting for the democratic rights of the citizens of the Narmada Valley. (http://www.narmada.org/about-us.html)

Once again, worth noting here is the framing of the local struggle for justice amid a global framework of struggles for social and environmental justice. Therefore, the local resistance against the construction of dams on the Narmada River becomes the exemplar for global struggles against the construction of mega-dams, offering entry points for solidarity and collective action. The agency of the Friends of River Narmada is depicted in relationship with the localized agency of the Narmada Bachao Andolan that is fighting for the democratic rights of the citizens of the Narmada Valley through various forms of localized participation.

The NBA has emerged on the discursive spaces of Indian public policy as a key site of contestation, resisting the state discourses of development by foregrounding the voices of local communities that have been displaced and continue to be threatened to be displaced by the building of the dam. This recognition and representation of the displaced voices counters the mainstream narratives and processes of development decision making that have traditionally operated by systematically erasing the voices of subaltern communities that have been rendered as targets and/or recipients of development policies and programs (Dutta, 2011). Questioning the authenticity (truth/falsity) of statements issued by the state and national governments to justify the building of the project, the voices of resistance narrated in the NBA point toward the gaps between the promises made by the project and the reality of the inequalities and oppressive effects on subaltern communities produced by the project. The question of development once again emerges onto the discursive space as a marker of contestation; the mainstream ideas of development that are pushed in the dominant structures are actively resisted by the subaltern frames of meaning. The notion of symbolic resistance is reiterated in the principles:

- that the Narmada Valley Development Project (NVDP) has been conceived without adequate participation from the people who are going to be affected;

- that many dams of the NVDP are not viable solutions to many of the problems (power, drinking water, flood control, irrigation) they set out to solve, and that there needs to be a greater emphasis on the search for alternative solutions from all concerned (Government, NGOs, people);

- that the construction and planning of many dams of the NVDP has disrupted (and will potentially disrupt) the lives of millions of people without just and adequate compensation;

- that the people of the Narmada Valley are waging a just and legitimate struggle to assert their right to life, livelihood, and participation in their own development;

- that while the country can ask for sacrifices from its people, such people must be justly and adequately compensated for the sacrifices that they are thus making;

- that while the country can ask for sacrifices from the people of the Valley for the greater cause of national progress, the burden of sacrifice should be distributed across the nation, and not be restricted to a specific group of people;

- that the NVDP is merely an example of a much bigger problem that is manifesting itself across the country: the Union Carbide disaster in Bhopal, the Enron controversy in the Dabhol Power Project in Maharashtra, the controversy over the Cogentrix project, the forgery of Environmental Clearances by Ernst & Young;

the controversy over the construction of the Bangalore-Mysore highway, the human rights abuses over the port construction at Maroli, and the list goes on.

- that the struggle in the Narmada Valley consequently throws up much deeper issues about the developmental choices being followed in India and elsewhere, and that there needs to be a much wider debate of these choices;

- that the *Narmada Bachao Andolan* is a symbol of hope for people's movements all over the world that are fighting for just, equitable, and participatory development. (http://www.narmada.org/about-us.html)

The frames represented in the principles of the Friends of Narmada draw attention to the fundamentally inequitable nature of the communicative processes through which development decisions are made, excluding the subaltern sectors that are impacted by the policies and programs that are put forth under the framework of development. The principles also highlight the lack of participation of the displaced communities in the processes of decision making, and in the specific outcomes that result from these processes. The logic of development is interrogated by contesting the value of mega-dams to the everyday lives of the people who reside in the valley. The rights of the subaltern sectors are juxtaposed in the backdrop of the corporate-state nexus that push development projects and carry out exploitations and oppressions of the subaltern classes through these development projects. The depiction of the struggle in Narmada then offers a framework for situating other global struggles on choices of development, symbolizing an alternative framework of development as envisioned by peoples' movements from the grassroots.

The interrogation of the dominant framework of development continues to reverberate through the various facets of the online site. For instance, deconstructing the claim made by the national and state governments that the Sardar Sarovar Project (SSP) would address issues of development by offering drinking water and by bringing irrigation water to drought-prone areas of Gujarat, a document prepared by the "Free the Narmada Cam-

paign" notes the social classes that will benefit from the project the (http://
www.narmada.org/sardar-sarovar/faq/whopays.html):

> Cities, rich farmers, industry, politically powerful lobbies, not the
> people from drought prone areas. (See Map; link to http://www.nar-
> mada.org/sardar-sarovar/faq/map.html) Before the water can reach
> Kachchh and Saurashtra, it will have to negotiate-literally-the water-
> intensive cash-crop growing, politically powerful districts of Vado-
> dara, Kheda, Ahmedabad, Gandhinagar and Mehsana. Against their
> own directives, the authorities have allotted Vadodara city a sizeable
> quantity of water. Sugar-mills, water-parks, golf-courses, and five-star
> hotels are already positioning themselves at the head of the canal, and
> many have already been issued licenses.

Development emerges as the site and axis of contestation. Worth noting
in the voices of resistance is the reframing of the role of dams in perpetuating local-global inequities hidden in the claims of pro-poor policies of
development. Asking the questions of who will benefit turns the scrutiny
onto the dominant structures of development that often use the language
of helping the poor to develop solutions that disenfranchise the poor as
they concentrate resources and wealth in the hands of the rich.

The document specifically deconstructs the arguments that the SSP
would provide drinking water to communities in need and offer irrigation water for the drought-prone communities in the Kachchh, Saurasthra,
and Northern Gujarat. It points out that no money in the SSP project has
been spent on drinking water and that the project will actually provide
minimum water to the drought-prone areas, instead making the drought
problem worse by diverting money from meaningful and effective local
solutions. Also, the voices of resistance that come together in the NBA
point out the violations of the Narmada Water Disputes Tribunal (NWDT),
documenting the lived experiences of displaced communities who have
not been compensated by the government, and sharing the stories of families whose homes are submerged as a result of the dams. The promises
of development and progress are set in relationship to the experiences of
marginalization by displaced communities who were not even consulted
as the project was set in motion. The communicative erasures of commu-

nities that were and continue to be severely affected by the mega-dams lie at the heart of the struggles of resistance. It is in the backdrop of these communicative erasures that the online site becomes a space for narrating the voices of local protests and struggles. Consider, for instance, the following story on a march held by dam oustees in October 2009 in the Khandwa district:

> The oustees said that there is large scale corruption in the Harda area of the Indira Sagar dam and rehabilitation grants put into hundreds of personal savings accounts in the post offices and banks have been taken out and pilfered by middlemen and people related to the Company. Officers and middlemen are demanding thousands of rupees to give oustees their entitlements. The oustees also expressed shock that the NHDC has erased the water level marks in the Indira Sagar dam last month so that the public can no longer know what the water-level in the dam is. They said that this is part of a conspiracy to flood the area, and increase the water level above 260 meters which has been fixed by the High Court at the present. The oustees also stated that on one hand, the adult sons of farmers will have to be given 2 ha. of agricultural land each, and on the other the draw-down land of the dam will have to be distributed to each land-less oustee family, so that the livelihoods of the oustees are replaced. They said that all the affected villages will have to be surveyed and provided compensation and rehabilitation entitlements and they strongly oppose the exclusion of the 41 affected villages of the Indira Sagar dam. The oustees also opposed the terror being perpetrated in the area by the contractor who has taken the contract for the fisheries in the Indira Sagar dam, and his armed men. Routinely villagers are being beaten up, even if they fish only for their personal consumption. The oustees declared that they would continue to fish for their food and no Government and contractor can stop them from doing so. They also demanded that the contract for fisheries should be given to the oustees next year, and the present contract with the private contractor should be discontinued. (http://www.narmada.org/nba-press-releases/october-2009/28Oct.html)

In this depiction of the local struggle, the voices of the oustees challenge the terror perpetrated by the state under the name of development. The voices also question the specific mechanisms and processes through which the compensations are given out, this pointing out the oppressions and inequities that are built into the processes of compensations. Corruption and mishandling of settlement money are foregrounded, pointing out the multiple instances where displaced peoples have not received compensation. Attention is drawn to the removal of markers of the water level, which local communities see as a strategy for flooding the area.

Based on its local politics of change, the NBA has become symbolic of a global struggle for environmental and social justice, emerging as a space for the articulation of local voices of communities at the margins of development that have been rendered silent precisely through the marginalizing discourses of development. The decade-long protest against the Sardar Sarovar reservoir has become an exemplar of people's movements, foregrounding in narratives of development the voices of those whose lives and lifestyles are erased by projects carried out in the name of development. The proposed hydroelectric projects on the Narmada River in western India are hotly contested, once again through the voices of protest that articulate alternative narratives. Attending to the local politics of resistance, the NBA has grounded its struggle against the dams in the villages along the Narmada valley, mobilizing indigenous communities to resist displacement, and simultaneously foregrounding these stories of resistance as inspiration and guidance at global sites of struggle (Routledge, 1993). On one hand, the online presence of solidarity emerges as an entry point for solidarity; on the other hand, the struggle itself becomes an exemplar of strategies of social change.

In narrating their dissent, local communities of organizers refer to cultural logics of resistance, drawing from the rich narratives of India's freedom struggle against the British. "Satyagraha," the strategy of nonviolent noncooperation that became a key political strategy of resistance in India's freedom struggle, emerges as a key form of protest. In the call for satyagraha in 2000, a peaceful form of protest through persistence,

an NBA invitation notes the following (http://www.narmada.org/events/
satyagraha-2000/invitation.html):

> On this backdrop of constant struggle and challenge to the displace-
> ment and submergence, the height of the dam remained the same
> this year, despite the repeated efforts of Gujarat government to get
> the work on the dam restarted beyond 88 meters. However, though
> the height remains the same, last year the rains were below average.
> This year, the average rainfall would bring in the greater submergence
> than that of last year. There would be more destruction of houses and
> farms during this monsoon. The people have decided to challenge the
> imposition of unjust submergence, displacement by the government
> and demand for the complete review of the dam.
>
> People will be observing the monsoon-long Satyagraha again this
> year as part of Satyagraha 2000, which will be launched on July 15,
> at Jalsindhi, Domkhedi and other villages in the valley. The details
> of the Satyagraha will be announced on the first day of Satyagraha
> in the valley. This time, along with the struggle, we will also pursue
> the constructive work (*navnirman*), surveying with the villagers the
> resources of the adivasi area, with village mapping and participating
> in the daily village chores or in the work of the people's school (*je-
> evanshala*).
>
> Once again, the struggle is round the corner and at this decisive hour,
> we wish you to be with us, as comrade-in-arms, friends and wit-
> ness to this non-violent assertion of the rights of the people of this
> country. The people in the Narmada valley once again call unto you
> to join in the Satyagraha and strengthen the resistance in the valley
> against the displacement and destitution. The struggle in the valley
> is a joint endeavour of us all against the repression and destruction
> in the name of development.

The call for protestors to join in the local struggle of the displaced and submerged communities is articulated within specific demands that are made
by community members, asking the government to conduct a complete
review of the dam and to prevent the forced submergence of villages. Locally situated historico-cultural narratives of *satyagraha* are introduced in

order to craft out spaces for the enactment of agency. Culturally located concepts such as *navnirman* (constructive work) and *jeevanshala* (people's school) are put forth to offer subaltern rationalities of sustenance that challenge the neoliberal frameworks of development imposed by the dominant structures. Constructive work provides an alternative rationality of development. On a similar note, the concept of people's school democratizes the spaces of learning and seeks to place legitimacy within the lived contexts of learning in subaltern frameworks. Conducting chores in the village, engaging in constructive work, and participating in people's schools become strategies of resistance that draws from the cultural logic of protest in the historical context of India. Every day practices of participation emerge into the global sites as strategies for protest against the hegemonic top-down frameworks of development.

During the protests throughout the monsoon seasons, as the water continued to rise, protestors continued to carry out their resistance by standing in the waters, articulating their resistance in "facing the water." In the monsoon seasons of 1999 and the subsequent years, the protestors from the displaced and submerged villages along with several activists from around the country started off the protests with songs, performances, and slogans. An effigy of the Demon of the Dam in Narmada was submerged in the river, and a mahua tree was converted into a "tree of resolve," nailing the names of the villages that have been submerged by the dam and symbolically narrating the protest of the communities to assert their right on the land on which they have lived for generations (NBA, 2000). The images, voices, and narratives of the protests are then posted and re-posted online, creating entry points to solidarity, and urging actions elsewhere in the globe (see, for instance, http://www.narmada.org/images/haripics/harikrishna.pictures1.html). During the Domkhedi satyagraha in 1999, after breaking her fast, Medha Patkar, a leader of the NBA, gave the following speech (http://www.narmada.org/events/satyagraha-2000/medha.statement.html):

> We will be confronting the submergence, (which is bound to come at any time) in the spirit of dedication and sacrifice. We will stay put resolutely at the centres of Satyagraha, in every house, wishing that

the water may not rise—yet ready to sacrifice the life. We wish that the Mother Narmada shall remain free, flowing, even if we have to sacrifice. We will see how many and who all would come and from where to be with us.

The government shall not play the game of "saving the lives" after it had fully prepared to submerge the entire valley. No false promises. If that happens, we would confront their design. We will decide about the strategy, policy accordingly and will not leave them scot free this time.

The time has come to raise question on the judicial process through which the life and resources of the people in the valley are being taken away. Why not question it? After all the objective of such process is justice, and not certainly injustice. This is a part of the system created by human beings. It is not only the matter of abstract theory but the questions are being raised out of the actual reality.

The impending submergence would violate the stipulations of the Narmada Water Disputes Tribunal (NWDT) and the orders of the Court itself as there is no land or resettlement. At this juncture we will have to think of the justice and injustice. How come it cannot be? We are raising the issues, following the path of constitution and legal propriety, so that the judicial system should not be proved unjust due to the machinations of the power holders, so that the dignity and position of the judiciary should be intact.

The satyagraha becomes a site of protest, questioning the unfair and inequitable judicial processes that marginalize the subaltern sectors. The readiness to sacrifice life emerges as a strategy for resistance, turning on its head the role of the government in building the dam and in submerging villages that are home to many of the protestors. In seeking to foster a just system of decision making and arbitration, the satyagraha draws attention to the unfair and inequitable processes through which those in power have created specific policies and programs to displace the subaltern margins from their rightful spaces of livelihood. The protest marches, performances, songs, and fasts (*dharna*) are accompanied by interventions within legal and juridical structures requesting for transparency, for additional information on studies conducted on the benefits and drawbacks of the dams, and exerting the rights of displaced communities under legal configurations to forms of resettlement. Several cases filed in courts seek to fill the discursive spaces of jurisdiction with the voices of the poor from displaced and submerged communities (see Figure 6.1).

The protests carry out the demand for resettlement by highlighting through performances the stories of removal of the subaltern sectors in the region from their homes. Letter writing campaigns directed at ministers, as well as direct forms of protest that seek out opportunities of dialogue with political actors, are additional strategies of resistance, with online forums and discussion groups requesting participation through online channels such as e-mail and websites. As the state responded to the ongoing protests with the use of violence through *lathi* charges (attacks with police sticks) and arrests, the protestors responded with innovative strategies of protests such as "machali satyagraha" (catching and eating the fish from the river as divine blessings) and "jan sunwai" (public hearings) (NBA, 2009). These innovative strategies draw from local cultural frameworks and offer entry points for the enactment of agency. Culture emerges at the site of global struggle in resistance to neoliberalism. As opposed to neoliberal conceptualizations of multiculturalism and diversity, cultural logics in movements such as the NBA operate in global discursive sites as resistive strategies for disrupting neoliberal assumptions and everyday strategies of neoliberalism. The market logics of neoliberalism that imperialize development frameworks are resisted by the local logics of communities built on autonomy and self-reliance.

In this context of resistance against global neoliberalism, the movement communicates how local struggles against globally powerful stakeholders can indeed bring about change, thus offering an exemplar for constituting resistance against the global projects of mega-dams. The narrative of resistance is centered on the key role of agency, noting how displaced people came together for resistance:

> The struggle of the people of the Narmada valley against large dams
> began when the people to be displaced by SSP [Sardar Sarovar Project]

Figure 6.9. Image from the Chimalkhedi satyagraha in 2007.

began organizing in 1985-86. Since then the struggle has spread to encompass other major dams in various stages of planning and construction chiefly Maheshwar, Narmada Sagar, Maan, Goi and Jobat. Tawa and Bargi Dams were completed in 1973 and 1989 respectively have seen the affected people organize post-displacement to demand their rights. (http://www.narmada.org/nvdp.dams/)

The movement became a model for organizing. The history of the struggle served as a backdrop to the movement's modern struggles amidst Narmada valley politics. Current issues faced by the movement are presented in the form of press releases by NBA. The webpage includes an archive of press releases that document the different aspects of the struggle against structural forces.

For the Friends of Narmada website, localized processes of capacity building focus on the exchange of information regarding resources, policies, strategies, and tactics, which then are shared in multiple discursive platforms as entry points for transformation. This capacity building is achieved in a plethora of platforms and flows in numerous ways, serving a multitude of functions simultaneously, drawing upon multiple intersections of collaborations. It is this simultaneity of capacity building that demonstrates the ways in which resources flow in communicative platforms of global activist organizations. For instance, one aspect of capacity building of the project focused on providing resources about the movement to global stakeholders. In this context, the website serves as a repository of information, contributing to the capacity of global movements of resistance by documenting the steps, stages, successes, and failures of the movement. This presentation of resources offers opportunities for interested parties to learn about the movement and develop their own information resources regarding the movement. The archives of pictures and press releases provide insights regarding the lessons learned from the movement and become learning tools for other groups interested in similar issues. These resources also become points of solidarity building for other movements, connect these movements with each other, and provide networks of solidarity among movements.

Furthermore, this global-level activism is mobilized for local purposes. For instance, the website discusses the ways in which global publics could participate in protesting the building of the dam by signing petitions on the Web, by participating in virtual hunger strikes, and by participating in rallies and protest marches in their respective locations. In this way, globally dispersed local publics are mobilized for a local cause. The activist capacity of individual local actors is mobilized at the global level to support the capacity of a specific local movement. Ultimately, online resources serve as platforms for community capacity building and for mobilizing resistance.

Conclusion

What we learn through the voices from the global South that co-construct the narratives of resistance against neoliberal definitions of development is the expression of local agency of communities in the global South in actively redefining the meanings of development. Resisting the depiction of communities in the global South as passive, participants narrate their stories of active meaning making and participation in processes of change directed at altering social structures. These voices question the dominant narratives of development that are utilized to carry out top-down interventions through the participation of the state, national, and transnational corporations. Meanings of development narrated through SAPs are interrogated in terms of the effects they produce, and the agendas and actors that they serve. The Save Niyamgiri, Cochabamba, and Narmada Bachao Andolan movements are all constituted around defining the key terms in the dictionary of development, pointing toward the ways in which these terms have carried out the interests of the dominant sectors, and marginalizing the poorer sectors from the global South. The linkages of the North and the South, the local and the global, also emerge in Global Exchange, an education and action resource center that builds networks of resistance to globalization politics by empowering communities locally and connecting them to global solidarity networks (http://www.globalexchange.org/mission). Also, the IFG carries out the theme of offering alternatives through networks of resistance (http://www.ifg.org/about.htm):

> The International Forum on Globalization (IFG) is a North-South research and educational institution composed of leading activists, economists, scholars, and researchers providing analysis and critiques on the cultural, social, political, and environmental impacts of economic globalization. Formed in 1994, the IFG came together out of shared concern that the world's corporate and political leadership was rapidly restructuring global politics and economics on a level that was as historically significant as any period since the Industrial Revolution. Yet there was almost no discussion or even recognition of this new "free market," or "neoliberal" model, or of the institutions and agreements enforcing this system—the World Trade Organization (WTO), the International Monetary Fund (IMF), the World Bank, the North American Free Trade Agreement (NAFTA) and other such bureaucracies. In response, the IFG began to stimulate new thinking, joint activity, and public education about this rapidly rising economic paradigm.
>
> Unique in its diversity, depth, and breadth, the IFG works through an active international board of key citizen movement leaders; a small,

dedicated staff; and a network of hundreds of associates representing regions throughout the world on a broad spectrum of issues. Our work is closely linked to social justice and environmental movements, providing them with critical thinking and frameworks that inform campaigns and activities on the ground.

The IFG produces numerous publications; organizes high-profile, large public events; hosts many issue-specific seminars; coordinates press conferences and media interviews at international events; and participates in various other activities that focus on the myriad consequences of globalization. During the last few years, the IFG has launched a pioneering program that focuses on alternative visions and policies to globalization that are more equitable, just, democratic, accountable, and sustainable for people and the planet.

Essential to the organizing of the IFG is the creation of participatory spaces for discussions of evidence and for sharing of information to assess the impact of globalization processes. Because globalization processes are fundamentally carried out through the presentation of information as evidence to justify neoliberal policies, a key function of the IFG in fostering spaces for articulations of alternatives is to deconstruct the underlying logics and assumptions that are carried out in globalization. This function of deconstructing the underlying logics of neoliberal policies also lies at the heart of the Oakland Institute, a think tank that publishes evidence-based analyses on globalization policies (http://www.oaklandinstitute.org/node/468):

> The Oakland Institute is dedicated to creating a space for public participation and democratic debate on key social, economic, environmental, and foreign policy issues that affect our lives. By becoming a member of The Oakland Institute, you are building the foundation for a democratic and peaceful future.
>
> The Oakland Institute accepts no funding from corporations or governments. Your tax-deductible donations allow us to conduct independent research, analysis, and advocacy to facilitate democratic participation in critical social, economic, environmental, and foreign policy decisions that affect our quality of life.

> When you join the Oakland Institute you have the satisfaction of underwriting open discussion of critical issues. Free trade agreements, new technologies such as genetic engineering, and governmental funding priorities to challenge growing hunger and poverty, call for vigorous public discussion of the pros and cons. The Oakland Institute is providing a progressive perspective on such critical issues that are currently greatly under-reported and largely neglected by the mainstream media.

Fostering democratic spaces for discussion and creating open forums where public discussions and public participation offer entry points for conversations on key global issues, the Oakland Institute voices resistance to neoliberal policies by disrupting the closure of discursive spaces and sites. As depicted in the examples of the IFG and the Oakland Institute, voices of resistance against neoliberalism seek to thwart the top-down exploitative impact of neoliberal policies by resisting the minimization of discursive spaces for informed participation under the manipulative and constraining strategies deployed by the transnational hegemony. The politics of change of alternative to dominant logics of development is accomplished by critically interrogating the manipulative strategies, the public relations ploys, the misrepresentation of information, and the erasure of discursive sites of contestation that are essential to the logics of neoliberalization.

Similarly, organizations such as Focus on the Global South create legitimate entry points for the articulations of alternative frameworks of development and for the teaching, research, and applications of the alternative ideas. For instance, deglobalization, one of the flagship offerings of Focus on the Global South, seeks to build an alternative framework for economic systems (http://www.focusweb.org/content/paradigm-deglobalisation):

> It is in response to the growing clamor for alternatives to the current system of global governance that Focus has elaborated the strategy of deglobalisation as the guiding paradigm for its programmatic work in the next three-year period.

> Deglobalisation is not a synonym for withdrawing from the world economy. It means a process of restructuring the world economic

and political system so that the latter builds the capacity of local and national economies instead of degrading it. Deglobalisation means the transformation of a global economy from one integrated around the needs of transnational corporations to one integrated around the needs of peoples, nations, and communities.

We cannot talk about construction without deconstruction, reintegration without disintegration. Today there are many experiments in alternative economics, for example local currency systems, participatory budgeting such as that practised in Porto Alegre, or ecological communities like Gaviotas in Colombia. The reigning god, however, is a jealous one that will not take lightly challenges to its hegemony. Even the smallest experiment or alternative to the dominant model is stopped, weakened, or co-opted. Peaceful coexistence between different systems, a pro-corporate one and a pro-people one, is, unfortunately, not an option.

Thus the deglobalisation project must have two prongs, two logics that are in synergy: deconstruction and reconstruction or recreation.

Evidence of the effects of globalization including poverty, unemployment, rising inequality, and economic stagnation are presented to create a discursive opportunity for the articulations of openings. Drawing out the possible spaces of resistance against the deglobalization processes, the voices from the global South articulate the importance of a collective resistance that is simultaneously deconstructive as well as co-constructive. In conclusion, the voices of resistance foregrounded through the examples and cases presented in this chapter offer critiques of the power and control exerted by transnational hegemony through the narrative of development, and simultaneously foster spaces for democratic participation to enable the alternative stories of development voiced through the participation of people and communities who have been historically erased from discursive spaces.

Epilogue: Voices in Motion

Introduction

The final chapter summarizes the key points articulated throughout the book regarding alternative rationalities that challenge neoliberal forms of global governance. Through the re-presentations of voices of resistance from the global margins, I discuss the ways in which a global politics of resistance can contribute to social transformations and transformations in structures of oppression and exploitation. The alternative rationalities that are voiced by the various disenfranchised sectors of the globe who co-construct their voices in dialogue offer a framework for organizing a global politics of resistance, which is at once local and is simultaneously global in nature. This global-local network of resistance disrupts the political and economic hegemony of neoliberalism by interrogating the assumptions that make up the neoliberal logic, and through these interrogations, attempting to render visible alternative forms of organizing social, cultural, political, and economic systems.

Through the images, participatory articulations, community-based mobilizing efforts, global protest

Chapter Seven

275

marches, performances, and narratives circulated through social media, the voices that co-construct a global politics of resistance throughout the pages of this book present an ongoing and emerging framework of organizing that outlines a politics of social change. What are the key threads then that run through these voices of social change that emerge at various sites of the globe? What are the moments of harmony between these voices? What are their points of departure? What are the lessons they offer about the expressions of human agency in conversations with cultural scripts that seek to transform the inequitable structures of local, national, and global policies? How do the voices that emerge in the pages of this book conceptualize the politics of social justice and the constitutive communicative processes that define the parameters of political participation in transformative endeavors?

Voices in Conversation

Although they represent diverse sectors of the globe with diverse worldviews, the voices of resistance across disparate geographic spaces of the globe offer mutually engaging entry points of conversation, articulating the intersections of culture, structure, and agency in the enactment of change. The cultural contexts of local communities offer value-based frameworks and symbols for enacting agency, putting forth alternative rationalities of organizing that challenge the structures of neoliberalism. As I participated in co-constructing my understandings of these global protests in writing this book, I came away impressed by the synergistic relationship between these different voices from different parts of the globe as they build on each other to narrate values and frameworks of resistance to the neoliberal colonization of the globe and global resources. In the following sections, I briefly summarize some of the key threads that run through these local processes of resistance, seeking to offer some meta-theoretical insights about the processes of change that are voiced in the stories of resistance.

Interpenetration of Issues

The global challenge to neoliberalism offered at local sites is articulated in the form of discursive moves that draw out the inter-penetration of issues; for instance, resistance constituted around issues of development (such as the Save Niyamgiri movement) is intertwined with resistance organized around issues related to the environment, which in turn is intertwined with resistance around issues of economic and political justice. The voices of activism from the global South and the global North inter-penetrate each other, joining in solidarity and finding spaces of intersections around these various issues that serve as the entry points of mobilizing against neoliberal forms of governance. Material and symbolic markers of resistance from the global South find entry points in voices of resistance in the global North and vice versa. Simultaneously, these voices from South and North collaborate on developing shared frames of resistance as they draw upon mutual resources, issues, and structures to build networks of solidarity. Given the expansive role of neoliberalism in controlling various aspects of political, economic, social, and cultural life globally, at the heart of the global resistance against neoliberalism is the articulation of the intersections among the different issues and the inter-related relationships among these issues. Political struggles against corporate takeover of the environment, land, political spaces, economic spaces, and frameworks of development are all intertwined in their resistance against the consolidation of power in the hands of transnational hegemony.

In many of these voices of social change, resistance against neoliberal governance emerges as the impetus for the protests, foregrounded in the narratives of the protests. In the voices of resistance from the global South (take, for instance, the example of resistance in Bolivia against water privatization and the privatization of the gas sector), neoliberalism emerges as a concept around which the voices of resistance identify the identity of the organizing processes. In these instance, voices of protestors specifically identify neoliberalism, define it, and articulate its consequences, mapped out in relationship to the issues that are central to the processes of organizing. For example, voices of social change in the global South specifically identify the deleterious effects of neoliberalism on local economies, ways of life, and cultures, and this becomes the entry point to the protests. In other instances, although neoliberalism is not explicitly identified in the language of the protests, specific dimensions of neoliberalism such as privatization, liberalization, and so forth emerge within the frames of protest as rallying points for the protests. In yet other instances, such as in the case of the Arab Spring, underlying issues of unemployment and rising food prices lay at the heart of the protests; therefore, resistance to neoliberal governance is narrated in expressions of anger at the unemployment and the rising price of food, which is manifested in organizing directed at transforming political structures.

The voices of resistance that emerge within local, national, and global discursive spaces also note the inter-relatedness of the issues that are the subjects of the protests, and organize around these inter-related issues. Resistance emerges in a global network of interconnected nodes, where narratives embodied in local voices connect with other narratives from local voices from elsewhere, forming an interconnected web of voices of resistance. The local emerges at the site of the global through its politics of authenticity; it is this very localized authenticity narrating alternative rationalities of organizing that emerges on global discursive sites, rendering these sites impure (Dutta & Pal, 2010; Godalof, 1999). Connections are expressed in the penetration of voices of solidarity from globally dispersed sites into local sites of protest and vice versa. For instance, the messages of protest from Egypt find their way into messages of protest in Wisconsin. Activists from the Arab Spring offer inspiration for the protestors in Wisconsin, symbolically emerging in the slogans, posters, and chants. Similarly, the messages of the Occupy movement find resonance in the protests in Egypt as the protestors continue to offer their criticism of the global concentration of power in the hands of the wealthy. Some of the activists from Egypt appeared in a general assembly at Occupy Wall Street in Liberty Square. More recently, in early 2012, large numbers of people took to the streets in Nigeria to protest the erasure of oil subsidies; solidarity with the local protests were held at several Occupy sites, constituting an Occupy Nigeria group that marched to the Nigerian embassy and continued raising the issue within the Occupy movement (Swagler, 2012).

In line with the politics of protest that connects local actors across a variety of issues, the networks of resistance spread out horizontally, organizing around various issues that emerge as the outcomes of neoliberal governance (Castells, 1998, 1999, 2001). For instance, both the building of the Keystone XL Tar Sands pipeline and the Occupy Monsanto protests are intertwined with the underlying resistance against corporate power and the concentration of political decision making in the hands of corporate power. As a result, protestors against the Tar Sands pipeline find solidarity from protestors in the Occupy movement. Simultaneously Occupy protests are planned out that offer resistance against the Tar Sands pipeline, thus leveraging solidarity across issue areas to create a broader network of protest. Similarly, the protests against the consolidation of power in the hands of agro-TNCs (transnational corporations) in the form of the Occupy Monsanto movement are constituted within the broader framework of the Occupy narrative that seeks to disrupt the concentration of power and decision-making capacities on global and national policies in the hands of TNCs. This notion of networking of issues is embodied in the Occupy movement, as the movement emerges as a loose network of protests that are organized around the broad theme of corporate power in national and global governance structures, played out through the several different Occupy protests and Occupy sites around different issues, emerging as nodes of action.

Complementary Uses of Communication Channels and Platforms

Although social scientific studies as well as public debates of communicative processes of resistance have largely been shaped by questions and debates that relate to the role of social and online media in processes of change, the voices of resistance narrated throughout the chapters presented in this book point toward the complementary uses of communicative processes, resources, infrastructures, and channels (Aelst & Walgrave, 2004; Bailey, Cammerts, & Carpentier, 2008; Carpentier, 2007; Couldry & Curran, 2003; Coyer, Dowmunt, & Fountain, 2007; Dutta-Bergman, 2004c; Garrido & Halavais, 2003). Face-to-face performative strategies and forms of direct action on the streets are complemented by the information dissemination and community mobilization functions of social media (Ferrel, 2001). As protests take place on the streets, the voices of the protests narrated at community events, sit-ins, nonviolent demonstrations, and noncooperation performances get taken up across social media and circulated, urging for action. Participants at the sites of direct action record their narratives through audio, video, and written accounts and share them through various online media. In instances of subaltern resistance where the voices of resistance are performed at distant local sites—far removed from the global centers of decision making where policies are configured and carried out—there are alternative narratives offered, which are alternative understandings of policies and programs that find expression through mediated forms of protest and create entry points at other remote sites of operation of global capital (Aelst & Walgrave, 2004; Bailey et al., 2008; Carpentier, 2007; Couldry & Curran, 2003; Coyer et al., 2007; Garrido & Halavais, 2003; Reed, 2005; Zoller & Dutta, 2008a, 2008b). The voices of resistance of the indigenous activists in the "Save Niyamgiri movement find points of solidarity with activists organizing in London against Vedanta, at the shareholder meeting of Vedanta. The complementarity of communicative channels and infrastructures carry forth the messages of change and resistance to global sites, creating entry points for solidarity and for complementary forms of direct action. Various forms of complementary direct action in this sense are complementarily organized through complementary functions of communicative channels and processes.

Culture as De-construction/Culture as Co-construction
The cultural-centeredness of the projects of social change is intrinsically tied to their active participation in the deconstruction of the cultural roots and values embodied in the universal narratives of rationality embodied in Eurocentric formulations of neoliberal governance. Culture emerges as a marker for returning the gaze at the imperial undertones of neoliberalism, offering localized forms of participation, recognition, and representation that then become the very bases for offering alternative rationalities of organizing. Furthermore, through the networks of solidarity, cultural values from hitherto marginalized spaces that are not recognized

as capable of participation in dominant discursive spaces of neoliberalism emerge onto discursive sites. That the ideals of democracy and liberty are configured through specific rationalities of the market embodied
in Eurocentric values becomes evident throughout the various voices of
social change articulated from the global South and that then find their
ways in the discursive spaces of culture in the global North. From resistive
voices in EZLN and *La Vía Campesina*, we hear about the hypocrisies in
the languages of liberty and democracy that are used by neoliberalism to
thwart opportunities for popular participation. In the voice of Evo Morales, we hear stories of manipulative processes in World Trade Organization (WTO) decision-making structures that erase voices from the global
South. In the voices of indigenous activists Soni Sori and Linda Kodopi,
we hear voices of resistance that talk back to the Indian state amidst the
immense violence (encounters, murders, rapes, arrests, tortures, etc.) that
has been unleashed by the state on its indigenous people in order to create openings for mining and industrialization projects on tribal land (see
the Facebook group at http://www.facebook.com/#!/groups/freelingaand-
soni/). In these voices of resistance, participation is reframed in terms of
privileging local voices and their localized understandings of collective
ownership of resources and harmonious relationships of communities
with nature, explicitly standing in resistance to the top-down neoliberal
policies of the state that seek to co-opt participation to carry out corporate agendas and to shift entrepreneurial accountability into the level of
communities by diverting resources away from state-supported programs
(Freire, 1973). As opposed to participation serving as a conduit for development as configured within the dominant structures (Chambers, 1983,
1994a, 1994b, 1994c, 1997; Cleaver, 1999; Dutta & Basnyat, 2008a, 2008b,
2008c, 2010), the narratives of participation articulated in the voices of
resistance stand precisely in resistance, seeking to bring about changes in
the unjust practices of the dominant structures and redistribute the upward transference of resources.

These frames of local participation amidst cultural logics of human
livelihoods find their ways into global sites of protests through the international conferences against neoliberalism, through the World Social

Forums, and through global movements of protest at the Western sites of neoliberalism as embodied in the Occupy protests and protests at the global summits of the powerful transnational actors. As Occupy protestors in the US carry out their resistance against corporate giants such as Monsanto through localized forms of protests embodied in Occupy Monsanto, they embody their resistance in carrying out the themes of protest that are raised from the global South. Similarly, the cultural narratives of regulating corporate governance emerge into global structures to articulate alternative rationalities that call for popular participation in seeking to control the realms of operation of corporations. In threads of the Occupy movement that question the logic of displacements of homeowners from their homes, we hear the resonance of voices from the global South that seek to occupy natural spaces as homes of indigenous communities, refusing to be displaced from their traditional livelihoods because of projects of development seeking to serve corporate greed and state-sponsored elite agendas.

Reflexivity as Vigilance

The all-encompassing power of neoliberalism lies in its capacity to be flexible and to co-opt local participation and agency within frames of control through the deployment of terms such as democracy, participation, and community involvement. Neoliberalism captures the global landscape through the precise policies of democracy and participation, where the contours of democracy and participation are constituted within specific agendas of corporate control and shifting resources away from public funds and resources. For instance, in the face of the local forms of resistance in Egypt and Tunisia, neoliberal forms of global capitalism responded to the voices of resistance by seeking to co-opt these voices within the narratives of democracy and civil society, constituted in the ambits of neoliberal desires.

The reflexive capacity of resistance precisely lies in the returning of the gaze at these co-optive moves that are constituted within dominant structures. These reflexive voices are evident in the voices of activists who point toward the hypocrisies of US expression of support for dissent in the uprisings in Egypt amidst US exercise of control of dissent against corporate control of government and juridical structures in the Occupy movement. Similarly, US articulation of support for the resistive performances across the Arab world is interrogated in the backdrop of the active role of the US in supporting military regimes by supplying these regimes with arms. Protests organized in the US against arms supplies to Egypt disrupt the hegemonic frame of neoliberalism that construct Egypt within the framework of democracy to expand the realms of control on Egypt.

The narratives of democracy circulated by the state (such as in the examples of India and the US) are disrupted by the voices of resistance that document the images and stories of police atrocities, exploitation, and oppression at the sites of resistance to neoliberalism. Resistive voices document corporate-police-state nexus in efforts to thwart the voices of resistance and to erase the everyday evidences that are gathered by activists and shared with other actors through online and offline networks. Even as the hypocritical structures of neoliberal governance attempt to control voices of resistance through the use of force and simultaneously parade around concepts of democracy and participation, the local narratives of resistance reflexively interrogate the rhetoric of the state, and through their vigilance, render visible the structures of oppression that carry out the interests of the neoliberal hegemony couched in the language of dialogue and openness. The meta-narrative of resistance points toward the resilience of stories of transformation that emerge into discursive sites in spite of the state-based apparatuses of control. The meta-discourses of communication as a site of neoliberal oppression crystallize in the local frames of community members; therefore, communicative elements of resistance are directed at addressing policies that minimize opportunities for participation, recognition, representation, and articulation. In the context of India, for example, specific forms of activist organizing targeting the sedition act[1] resist an act that utilizes the language of terrorism to thwart opportunities for resistance.

Deconstructing Epistemic Structures

The voices of resistance narrated throughout the pages of this book challenge the logics of superiority embedded within the structures of neoliberalism; they also challenge the opaqueness of the decision-making processes within the dominant structures that render these structures and their ensuing processes invisible to the very communities that are affected by the decisions taken within these structures. When projects of development, for instance, are carried out on the ideas of altruism, the fundamental meanings of development, progress, and economic growth are interrogated. The voices of activists in the Save Niyamgiri movement bring to question the logic of development that is used to justify the large-scale displacement of tribes under the narrative of development. When projects of displacement are carried out to justify industrialization under the name of economic growth, the underlying assumptions of economic growth and who benefits from such growth are questioned. Assumptions of development under the expectations of trickle-down economics are brought to question by pointing out the large-scale economic inequities that are created by neoliberal reforms alongside the articulations of the rising unemployment, rising food prices, and the increasing impoverishment of the poor. More fundamentally, the epistemic structures are challenged by voices of resistance through the interrogation of the political and economic interests served by these epistemic structures. Academic sites of knowledge production become the sites of interrogation, with the critical gaze being turned toward practices in anthropology, geography, ethno-botany, pharmacy, and so forth, in the context of the imperial functions served by specific forms of funded projects. For instance, the US military-backed mapping project, Mexico Indigena, which was supposedly funded by the US military with the face of promoting indigenous empowerment in the context of the land reforms in Mexico that sought to promote privatization came under intense scrutiny by local indigenous activists and later by the academic community because of the accusation that the mapping project was being carried out as a method of surveillance for gathering intelligence for the US government (Mychalejko & Ryan, 2009). Similarly, economists at elite financial institutions that have played key functions in pushing the neoliberal regime are interrogated for their complicity in promoting mechanisms for concentrating wealth in the hands of few, often simultaneously benefitting personally through projects of economic liberalization.

The assumptions embodied in policies and juridical structures are questioned by the voices of resistance that co-construct alternative narratives throughout the various examples I have shared with you. For example, when Occupy activists in Atlanta occupy the home of a war veteran who is threatened to be evicted from her home by the bank that owns her mortgage, Occupy activists interrogate the assumptions of the banking/mortgage industry and the decision-making structures in juridical processes in the US that disenfranchise citizens. Similarly, the Occupy narratives that seek to re-occupy court systems challenge the juridical processes within court systems that favor those with access to power. It is in this backdrop that bottom-up processes of participation in legal structures seek to enact the rights of local communities at the margins.

The top-down decision making embodied in legal and political processes is interrogated and simultaneously resisted through grassroots participation in these processes. Occupy activists, for instance, draw attention to the influential role played by the lobbying industry in shaping policies and the implementation of these policies in the US. The Occupy K-Street component of the movement draws attention to the powerful role of the lobbying industry in shaping public policy (http://www.facebook.com/OccupyDC; Kingkade, 2011). In one specific example, the story of an influential lobbying firm is shared through social media, documenting a memo of the firm directed at big banks on Wall Street where the firm outlines its strategies for discrediting the Occupy movement (Larsen & Olshansky, 2011). Documents such as these circulated through the alternative epistemic structures of the processes of social change also render visible the political and legal processes that are deployed by powerful economic and political actors in discrediting social change efforts by utilizing communicative processes that are explicitly directed at discrediting resistance. Similarly, images of police atrocities being carried out in the US to control protests across the US are juxtaposed against the public diplomacy narratives crafted by Hillary Clinton and Barack Obama in the context of the Arab Spring, thus rendering visible the hypocrisies in neoliberal knowledge claims.

Voices of resistance in the Keystone XL Tar Sands campaign document the revolving door between Keystone XL lobbyists and the US Department of State, and in doing so, point out the ways in which the structures of political decision making have been taken over by powerful economic interests. Similarly, activists in the Save Niyamgiri movement in Orissa, India, draw attention to the greenwashing strategies and tactics of Vedanta by disrupting the sites of public relations knowledge production by organizations such as the World Environment Fund that serves as public relations tools of Vedanta by presenting it with an environmental award. Voices of resistance against Operation Green Hunt document the atrocities carried out by the Indian state on indigenous communities, and in doing so, disrupt the knowledge claims made by the Indian state about its democracy (see, for instance, http://www.outlookindia.com/article.aspx?265964 or the Facebook campaign One Million Strong against Operation Green Hunt at http://www.facebook.com/#!/groups/1msaogh/).

The deconstruction of the dominant epistemic structures and their dominant aesthetics, the very assumptions that play into these structures, and the value claims that constitute the logics of these structures lies at the heart of the politics of social change. Voices of resistance, therefore, are put forth on this framework of deconstruction, calling for alternative articulations of knowledge organized on the principles of sustenance, social justice, equity, and nurturing of the planet. In voices of resistance in the works of Shiva and the Navdanya movement, we come across the articulations of concepts such as "earth democracy," which offer entry points for conceptualizing the relationships of human beings with food, agriculture, and with nature (Bello, 2001). Alternative forms of epistemic claims create openings for change by organizing forms of resistance at the margins that seek to establish counter-hegemonies that are built on alternative values and frameworks for judging and establishing truth. The politics of redistribution of resources is situated alongside the processes of transformation seeking to create spaces for recognition and representation (Fraser & Honneth, 2003).

Conclusion

In conclusion, throughout the various stories that have emerged in the voices of resistance across the various sites of the globe, we attend to the quests for human dignity and for the opportunity to have a say in local, national, and global policy platforms. This fundamental search for human dignity to have a voice is shared in the letter written to civil society organizations of India by Soni Sori and shared on the Facebook and Wordpress sites organizing for her freedom (http://freesonisoriandlingaram. wordpress.com/):

> This if for all social workers intellectuals, NGOs, human rights organisations, women's commission and citizens of India, an abused and helpless tribal woman, is asking you to answer her why she is being brutally tortured and she wants to know.
>
> That by giving me current, by stripping me naked, or by brutally assaulting me inserting stones in my rectum- will the problem of Naxalism end ? Why so many atrocities on women? I want to know from all countrymen
>
> 1. When I was being stripped, that time I felt someone should come and save me and it did not happen. In Mahabharata , Draupadi's honour was saved when she called upon Krishna Whom should I have called , I was given to them (police) by the court . But now, I will not say that save my honour as I have nothing left. Yes, I want to know from all of you that why was I Tortured?
>
> 2. Police officer, S. P Ankit Garg after stripping me says that "you are a whore, a bitch, who pleases naxal leaders by selling your body and they come to your house every day and night. We know everything, "he said adding that ". You claim to be a good teacher, but you sell yourself even in Delhi. What's your status anyways, you think the big stalwarts will support such an ordinary woman like you". Why will a police officer say this? Today history is witness that whenever there is war in country or any other conflict, women have contributed a lot to the nation. Jhansi Lakshmi Bai fought with the Britishers, did she sell herself ? Indira Gandhi as the prime minister of India, she

governed the country, did she sell herself? Today all the women who are working in their respective areas are they selling themselves? All of us are bound with each other in unity and support, then why no one is coming to help me? I would like to have an answer from you?

In the voice of Sori, the erased subaltern talks back. She returns the gaze of the dominant structures that have perpetuated the violence and atrocities on her body. It is through her gaze that she re-writes a narrative of resistance, re-scripting her ownership of discursive sites of democratic governance, staking her claim on the sites of representation. In Sori's voice, we hear the implicit call for an alternative narrative that disrupts the hypocrisies and violence written into the script of the neoliberal state. Sori's voice is joined by activist groups across India who share the video documenting her torture on YouTube (http://youtu.be/a5lO6cEcUeI), and organize through letters, petitions, and messages on social media, protesting the awarding of a recognition by the state to the police officer who tortured

Figure 7.1. Uploaded by "Kamayaninumerouno." http://youtu.be/a5lO6cEcUeI

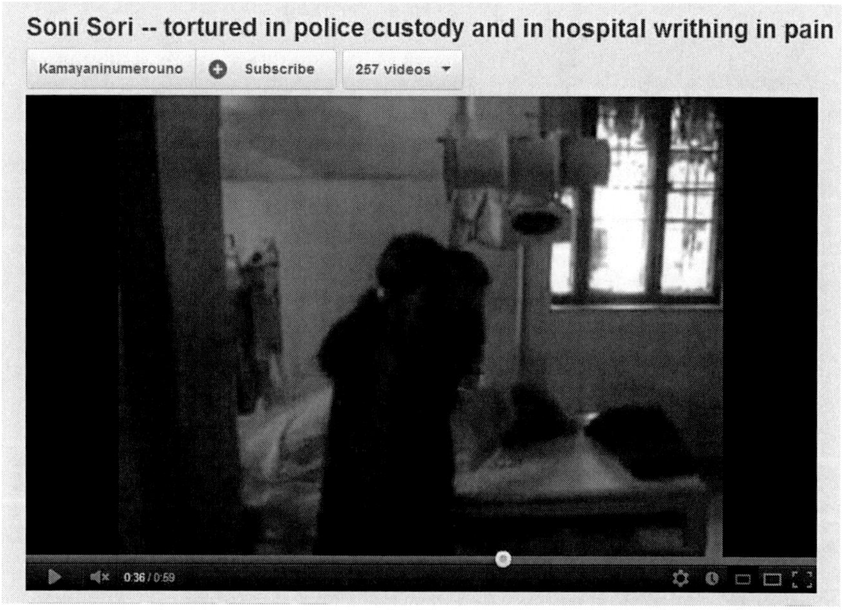

Sori and had developed a track record for torturing tribal community members in the region.

Figure 7.2. Poster calling for the masses to "Stand up for Soni Sori" (http://www. facebook.com/#!/photo.php?fbid=10150526829646608&set=a.429686291607.2170 59.692416607&type=1&theater).

I began this book by setting up the platform for the thesis of the culture-centered approach, empirically documenting the dramatic shrinkage of communicative spaces of participation and dialogue ironically through the very projects of participation and dialogue amidst neoliberal reforms that are being carried out globally. Even as the opportunities for public participation and voice are being dramatically limited, the voices of resistance from across the globe share with us their stories of everyday struggles through which they seek to open up these sites and spaces to opportunities for participation and for the expression of alternatives to the narrowly constructed neoliberal framework of governance driven by greed, desire for wealth accumulation, and privileging of private property. It is my hope that as you have listened to these various voices of resistance across the globe, you have come across the tremendous potential in the diversity of human thought and human constructions of narratives to offer us with hope, through alternative narratives of harmony, sustenance, solidarity, collective ownership, and relationships of mutual support.

Voices
Mohan J. Dutta
West Lafayette, January 26, 2012 (Indian Republic Day)

In your voices,
I hear the stories
Of conviction,
courage, and hope.

In your voices,
I hear the calls
For friendship
And protest.

In your voices.
I hear the anger
At the injustices,
abuses, and oppressions.

In your voices,
I hear the dreams,
songs and poems
That imagine a better world.

Notes

1. The sedition act has been largely used across India more recently in order to brand activists resisting neoliberal policies as Maoist and to place them in jail. For many activists, the sedition act uses state-based control mechanisms to erase voices of dissent.

References

Aelst, Van P., & Walgrave, S. (2004). New media, new movements? The role of the Internet in shaping the "anti-globalization" movement. In W. van de Donk, B. Loader, P. Nixon, & D. Rucht (Eds.), *Cyberprotest: new media, citizens, and social movements* (pp. 97-122). London: Routledge.

Agacino, R., & Escobar, P. (1997). Empleo y pobreza: Uncomentario sobre la experiencia chilena. *Revista Aportes* 2(5), 1-24.

Albo, X. (2008). The "long memory" of ethnicity in Bolivia and some temporary oscillations. In J. Crabtree & L. Whitehead (Eds.), *Unresolved tensions Bolivia: Past and present* (pp. 13-34). Pittsburgh, PA: University of Pittsburgh Press.

Algranati, C., Seoane, J., & Taddei, E. (2004). Neoliberalism and social conflict: The popular movements in Latin America. In F. Polet (Ed.), *Globalizing resistance: The state of struggle* (pp. 112-135). London: Pluto Press.

Alvesson, M., & Deetz, S. (2000). *Doing critical management research.* Thousand Oaks, CA: Sage.

Amnesty International. (2010). *Don't mine us out of existence: Bauxite mine and refinery devastate lives in India.* London: Amnesty International.

Anuradha, R.V., Taneja, B., & Kothari, A. (2001). *Experiences with biodiversity policy making and community registers in India.* London: International Institute for Environment and Development.

Appadurai, A. (1990). Disjuncture and difference in the global cultural economy. *Public Culture, 2,* 1-24.

Artz, L. (2006). On the material and the dialectic: Toward a class analysis of communication. In L. Artz, S. Macek, & D. Cloud (Eds.), *Marxism and communication studies: the point is to change it* (pp. 5-51). New York: Peter Lang.

Ayres, J. M. (1999). From the streets to the Internet: The cyber-diffusion of contention. *Annals of the American Academy of Political and Social Science, 566,* 132-143.

Ayres, J. M. (2001).Transnational political processes and contention against the global economy. *Mobilization, 6,* 55-68.

Bailey, O., Cammerts, B., & Carpentier, N. (2008). *Understanding alternative media.* Maidenhead: Open University Press.

Banerjee, S., & Linstead, S. (2001). Globalization, multiculturalism and other fictions: Colonialism for the new millennium? *Organization, 8*(4), 683-722.

Banerjee, S., & Prasad, A. (2008). Introduction to the special issue on critical reflection on management and organizations: A postcolonial perspective. *Critical perspectives on international business, 4,* 90-98.

Bardhan, N., & Weaver, C. K. (Eds.). (2011). *Public relations in global cultural contexts.* New York: Routledge.

Basu, A., & Dutta, M. (2008a). Participatory change in a campaign led by sex workers: Connecting resistance to action-oriented agency. *Qualitative Health Research, 18,* 106-119.

Basu, A., & Dutta, M. (2008b). The relationship between health information seeking and community participation: The roles of motivation and ability. *Health Communication, 23,* 70-79.

Basu, A., & Dutta, M. (2009). Sex workers and HIV/AIDS: Analyzing participatory culture-centered health communication strategies. *Human Communication Research, 35,* 86-114.

Bello, W. (2001). *The future in the balance: Essays on globalization and resistance.* Oakland, CA: Food First Books.

Bennett, W. L. (2003a). New media power: The Internet and global activism. In N. Couldry & J. Curran (Eds.), *Contesting media power* (pp. 17-37). Lanham: Rowman & Littlefied Publishers Inc.

Bennett, W. L. (2003b). Branded political communication: Lifestyle politics, logo campaigns, and the rise of global citizenship. In M. Micheletti, A. Follesdal, and D. Stolle (Eds.), *The politics behind products* (pp. 1-33). New Brunswick, NJ: Transaction Books.

Bennett, W. L. (2004). Communicating global activism: Strengths and vulnerabilities of networked politics. In W. van de Donk, B. Loader, P. Nixon, & D. Rucht (Eds.), *Cyberprotest: New media, citizens, and social movements* (pp. 123-146). London: Routledge.

Beverley, J. (1999). *Subalternity and representation: Arguments in cultural theory.* Durham, NC: Duke University Press.

Beverley, J. (2004). *Testimonio: On the politics of truth.* Minneapolis: University of Minnesota Press.

Bhattacharya, A. (2009). Singur to Lalgarh via Nandigram: Rising flames of people's anger against displacement, destitution and state terror. Retrieved from http://www.no2displacement.com/attachments/121_Lalgarh%20Book.pdf

Bhattacharya, T. (2012). Standing up to Indiana's attack on our unions. Retrieved from http://socialistworker.org/2012/01/25/standing-up-to-indianas-attack

Boal, A. (1979). *Theatre of the oppressed.* New York: Urizen Books.

Boal, A. (1992). *Games for actors and non-actors.* New York: Routledge.

Boal, A. (1995). *The rainbow of desire: The Boal method of theatre and therapy.* New York: Routledge.

Boal, A. (1998). *Legislative theatre: Using performance to make politics.* London: Routledge.

Braverman, H. (1974). *Labour and monopoly capital.* Chicago: University of Chicago Press.

Brecher, J., Costello, T., & Smith, B. (2000). Globalization from below: The power of solidarity. Cambridge, MA: South End Press.

Broadfoot, K. J., & Munshi, D. (2007). Diverse voices and alternative rationalities: Imagining forms of postcolonial organizational communication. *Management Communication Quarterly, 21,* 249-267.

Brown, W. (2005). Edgework: Critical essays on knowledge and politics. Princeton, NJ: Princeton University Press.

Burawoy, M. (1979). *Manufacturing consent.* Chicago: Chicago University Press.

Burt, J. M., & Mauceri, P. (2004). Introduction. In J. M. Burt & P. Mauceri (Eds.), *Politics in the Andes: Identity, conflict, reform* (pp. 1-14). Pittsburgh, PA: University of Pittsburgh Press.

Buzzanell. P. (2000) (Ed.) *Rethinking organizational and managerial communication from feminist perspectives.* Thousand Oaks, CA: Sage.

Carawan, G., & Carawan, C. (1963). *We shall overcome: Songs of the southern freedom movement.* New York: Oak Publications.

Carpentier, N. (2007). Theoretical frameworks for participatory media. In N. Carpentier, P. Pruulmann-Vengerfeldt, K. Nordenstreng, M. Hartmann, P. Vihalemm, B. Cammaerts, & H. Nieminen (Eds.), *Media technologies and democracy in an enlarged Europe* (pp. 105-122). Tartu: Tartu University Press.

Castells, M. (1996). *The rise of network society.* Oxford: Blackwell.

Castells, M. (1997). *The power of identity.* Oxford: Blackwell.

Castells, M. (1998). *End of millennium.* Oxford: Blackwell.

Castells, M. (1999). *Information technology, globalization, and social development.* Geneva, Switzerland: United Nations Research Institute for Social Development.

Castells, M. (2001). *The Internet galaxy: Reflections on the Internet, business and society.* Oxford: Oxford University Press.

Chambers, R. (1983). *Rural development: Putting the last first.* Lagos: Longman.

Chambers, R. (1994a). The origins and practice of participatory rural appraisal. *World Development, 22*(7), 953-969.

Chambers, R. (1994b). Participatory rural appraisal (PRA):Analysis and experience. *World Development, 22*(9), 1253-1268.

Chambers, R. (1994c). Participatory rural appraisal: Challenges, potentials, and paradigms. *World Development, 22*(10), 1437-1454.

Chambers, R. (1997). *Whose reality counts? Putting the last first.* London: Intermediate Technology Publications.

Cheney, G., & Cloud, D. (2006). Doing democracy, engaging the material: Employee participation and labor activity in an age of market globalization. *Management Communication Quarterly, 19*(4), 501-540. doi:10.1177/0893318905285485

Choi, C. (1995). Transnational capitalism, national imaginary, and the protest theater in South Korea. *Boundary 2, 22*(1), 235-261.

Clair, R. P. (193. The use of framing devices to sequester organizational narratives: Hegemony and harassment. *Communication Monographs, 60,* 113-136.

Cleaver, F. (1999). Paradoxes of participation: Questioning participatory approaches to development. *Journal of International Development, 11*(4), 597–612.

Cleaver, H. (1998). The Zapatista effect: The Internet and the rise of an alternative political fabric. *Journal of International Affairs, 51*(2), 621-640.

Cloud, D. (1994). The materiality of discourse as oxymoron: A challenge to critical rhetoric. *Western Journal of Communication, 58,* 141-163.

Cloud, D. (2005). Fighting words: Labor and the limits of communication at Staley, 1993 to 1996. *Management Communication Quarterly, 18*(4), 509-542.

Cloud, D. (2006). Change happens: Materialist dialectics and communication studies. In L. Artz, S. Macek, & D. Cloud (Eds.), *Marxism and communication studies: The point is to change it* (pp. 53-70). New York: Peter Lang.

Cloud, D. (2007). Corporate social responsibility as oxymoron: Universalization and exploitation at Boeing. In S. May, G. Cheney, & J. Roper (Eds.), *The debate over corporate social responsibility* (pp. 219-231). New York: Oxford University Press.

Coburn, D. (2000). Income inequality, social cohesion and the health status of populations: The role of neoliberalism. *Social Science & Medicine, 51,* 135-146.

Coburn, D. (2004). Beyond the income inequality hypothesis: Class, neo-liberalism, and health inequalities. *Social Science & Medicine, 58,* 41-46.

Cockburn, A., St. Clair, J., & Sekula, A. (2000). *Five days that shook the world: Seattle and beyond.* London: Verso Press.

Cohen-Cruz, J., & Schutzman, M. (Eds.). (2006). *A Boal companion: Dialogues on theatre and cultural politics.* New York: Routledge.

Collinson, D. (1994). Strategies of resistance: Power, knowledge and subjectivity in the workplace. In J. M. Jermier, D. Knights, & W. R. Nord (Eds.), *Resistance and power in organizations* (pp. 25-68). London: Routledge.

Collinson, D. (2002). Managing humor. *Journal of Management Studies, 39,* 269-288.

Conquergood, D. (1986). Between experience and meaning: Performance as paradigm for meaningful action. In T. Colson (Ed.), *Renewal and revision: The future of interpretation* (pp. 26-59). Denton, TX: Omega.

Couldry, N., & Curran, J. (2003). The paradox of media power. In N. Couldry & J. Durran (Eds.), *Contesting media power* (pp. 3-15). Lanham: Rowman & Littlefield Publishers Inc.

Counterpunch. (2003). An interview with Evo Morales legalizing the colonization of the Americas. *Counterpunch.* Retrieved from http://www.counterpunch.org/2003/12/02/an-interview-with-evo-morales-on-the-colonization-of-the-americas/

Coyer, K., Dowmunt, T., & Fountain, A. (2007). *The alternative media handbook.* London: Routledge.

Das, S., & Padel, F. (2010). Battles over Bauxite in East India: The Khondalite mountains of Khondistan. Retrieved from http://www.foilvedanta.org/articles/battles-over-bauxite-in-east-india-the-khondalite-mountains-of-khondistan/

De, K. (2009). Lalgarh: An icon of adivasi defiance. *Racism and national consciousness news/commentary.* Retrieved from http://racismandnationalconsciousnessnews.wordpress.com/2009/01/03/lalgarh-an-icon-of-adivasi-defiance-koustav-de/

de Sousa Santos, B. (2008). *Another knowledge is possible: Beyond Northern epistemologies.* London: Verso.

de Sousa Santos, B., Nunes, J. A., & Meneses, M. P. (2008). Introduction: Opening up the canon of knowledge and recognition of difference. In B. de Sousa Santos (Ed.), *Another knowledge is possible: Beyond Northern epistemologies* (pp. ix-lxii). London: Verso.

della Porta, D. (2009). Global justice movement organizations: The organizational population. In D. della Porta (Ed.), *Democracy in social movements* (pp. 16-43). London: Palgrave Macmillan.

della Porta, D., & Diani, M. (2006). *Social movements: An introduction.* Malden, MA: Blackwell Publishing.

della Porta, D., Kriesi, H., & Rucht, D. (Eds.). (1999). *Social movements in a globalizing world.* London: Macmillan.

Dellacioppa, K. Z. (2009). *This bridge called Zapatismo: Building alternative political cultures in Mexico City, Los Angeles, and beyond.* Lanham: Lexington Books.

Denzin, N. (2003). *Performance ethnography: Critical pedagogy and the politics of culture.* New Delhi: Sage Publications.

Deshpande, S. (2007). *Theatre of the streets: The Jana Natya Manch experience.* New Delhi: Jana Natya Manch.

Desmarais, A. (2007). *La Vía Campesina: Globalization and the power of peasants.* Halifax: Fernwood Publishing.

DeSouza, R., Basu, A., Kim, I., Basnyat, I., & Dutta, M. (2008). The paradox of "fair trade": The influence of neoliberal trade agreements on food security and health. In Zoller, H., & Dutta, M. (Eds), *Emerging perspectives in health communication: Interpretive, critical and cultural approaches* (pp. 411-430). Mahwah, NJ: Lawrence Erlbaum Associates.

Dhadda, S. (2010). Interview with Achyut Yagnik. In B. de Sousa Santos (Ed.), *Voices of the world* (pp. 236-254). London: Verso.

Diani M. (2000a). The Relational Deficit of Ideologically Structured Action: Comment on Mayer Zald. *Mobilization, 5,* pp. 17-24.

Diani M. (2000b). Simmel to Rokkan and Beyond: Elements for a Network Theory of (New) Social Movements. *European journal of social theory, 3,* pp. 387-406.

Diani M. (2003a). Networks and social movements: A research programme. In M. Diani M. & D. McAdam (Eds.), *Social movements and networks* (pp. 299-319). Oxford: Oxford University Press.

Diani M. (2003b). Leaders or brokers? In M. Diani M. & D. McAdam (Eds.), *Social movements and networks* (pp. 105-122). Oxford: Oxford University Press.

Doha, L. (2008). Saskatchewan First Nations protest pipeline. *First Nations Drum.* Retrieved from http://firstnationsdrum.com/2008/10/saskatchewan-first-nations-protest-pipeline/

Donk, W. V., Loader, B., Nixon, P., & Rucht, D. (2004). *Cyberprotest: New media, citizens, and social movements.* London: Routledge.

Duggan, L. (2003). *The twilight of equality?: Neoliberalism, cultural politics, and the attack on democracy.* Boston, MA: Houghton Mifflin Company.

Dutta, M. (2006). Theoretical approaches to entertainment education: A subaltern critique. *Health Communication, 20*(3), 221-231.

Dutta, M. (2007). Communicating about culture and health: Theorizing culture-centered and cultural-sensitivity approaches. *Communication Theory, 17*(3), 304-328.

Dutta, M. (2008a). Participatory communication in entertainment education: A critical analysis. *Communication for Development and Social Change: A Global Journal, 2,* 53-72.

Dutta, M. (2008b). A critical response to Storey and Jacobson: The co-optive possibilities of participatory discourse. *Communication for Development and Social Change: A Global Journal, 2,* 81-90.

Dutta, M. (2008c). *Communicating health: A culture-centered approach.* London, UK: Polity Press.

Dutta, M. (2009). Theorizing resistance: Applying Gayatri Chakravorty Spivak in public relations. In Ø. Ihlen, B. van Ruler, & M. Fredriksson (Eds.), *Social theory on public relations.* New York: Routledge.

Dutta, M. (2011). *Communicating social change: Culture, structure, agency.* New York: Routledge.

Dutta, M. (in press a). A culturally centered approach to communication for social change. In S. Melkote (Ed.), *Development communication and directed change: A reappraisal of theories and practices.* Singapore, Singapore: AMIC.

Dutta, M. (in press b). A culture-centered critique of global public relations. In K. Sriramesh (Ed.), *Cultural theories of public relations.* New York: Routledge.

Dutta, M., & Basnyat, I. (2008a). Interrogating the Radio Communication Project in Nepal: The participatory framing of colonization. In H. Zoller & M. Dutta (Eds), *Emerging perspectives in health communication: Interpretive, critical and cultural approaches* (pp. 247-265). Mahwah, NJ: Lawrence Erlbaum Associates.

Dutta, M., & Basnyat, I. (2008b). The Radio Communication Project in Nepal: A critical analysis. *Health Education and Behavior, 35*(6), 459-460.

Dutta, M., & Basnyat, I. (2008c). A critical response to participatory hegemony. *Health Education and Behavior. 35*(6), 472-473.

Dutta, M., & Basnyat, I. (2010). The Radio Communication Project in Nepal: Culture, power and meaning in constructions of health. In L. K. Khiun (Ed.), *Liberalizing, feminizing and popularizing health communications in Asia* (pp. 151-176). Burlington, VT: Ashgate.

Dutta, M., & Basu, A. (2007a). Health among men in rural Bengal: Approaching meanings through a culture-centered approach. *Qualitative Health Research, 17,* 38-48.

Dutta, M., & Basu, A. (2007b). Centralizing context and culture in the co-construction of health: Localizing and vocalizing health meanings in rural India. *Health Communication, 21*(2), 187-196.

Dutta, M. & Pal, M. (2010). Dialog theory in marginalized settings: A subaltern studies approach. *Communication Theory, 20*(4), 363-386.

Dutta, M., & Pal, M. (2011) Public relations and marginalization in a global context: A postcolonial critique. In N. Bardhan & C. K. Weaver (Eds.), *Public relations in global cultural contexts* (pp. 195-225). New York: Routledge.

Dutta-Bergman, M. (2004a). Poverty, structural barriers and health: A Santali narrative of health communication. *Qualitative Health Research, 14*, 1-16.

Dutta-Bergman, M. (2004b). The unheard voices of Santalis: Communicating about health from the margins of India. *Communication Theory, 14*(3), 237-263.

Dutta-Bergman, M. (2004c). Complementarity in consumption of news types across traditional and new media. *Journal of Broadcasting and Electronic Media, 48*, 41-60.

Dutta-Bergman, M. (2004d). An alternative approach to entertainment education. *Journal of International Communication, 10*, 93-107.

Dutta-Bergman, M. (2005a). Civil society and communication: Not so civil after all. *Journal of Public Relations Research, 17*(3), 267–289.

Dutta-Bergman, M. (2005b). Theory and practice in health communication campaigns: A critical interrogation. *Health Communication, 18*(2), 103–12.

Dutta-Bergman, M. (2005c). Operation Iraqi Freedom: Mediated public sphere as a public relations tool. *Atlantic Journal of Communication, 13*(4), 220-241.

England, K., & Ward, K. (2007). *Neoliberalization: States, networks, peoples*. Malden, MA: Wiley-Blackwell.

Escobar, A. (1995). *Encountering development: The making and unmaking of the Third World*. Princeton, NJ: Princeton University Press.

Escobar, P. (2003). The new labor market: The effects of the neoliberal experiment in Chile. *Latin American Perspectives, 30*(5), 70-78.

Ezzamel, M., Willmott, H., & Worthington, E. (2001). Power, control and resistance in the factory that time forgot. *Journal of Management Studies, 38*, 1053-1078.

Farmer, P. (1988a). Bad blood, spoiled milk: Bodily fluids as moral barometers in rural Haiti. *American Ethnologist, 15*, 131-151.

Farmer, P. (1988b). Blood, sweat, and baseballs: Haiti in the West Atlantic system. *Dialectical Anthropology, 13*, 83-99.

Farmer, P. (1992). *AIDS and accusation: Haiti and the geography of blame*. Berkeley, CA: University of California Press.

Farmer, P. (1999). *Infections and inequalities: The modern plagues*. Berkeley, CA: University of California Press.

Farmer, P. (2003). *Pathologies of power: Health, human rights and the new war on the poor*. Berkeley, CA: University of California Press.

Ferree, M. M., & Tripp, A.M. (2006). *Global feminism: Transnational women's activism, organizing, and human rights*. New York: New York University Press.

Ferrel, J. (2001). Reclaim the streets. In J. Ferrel (Ed.), *Tearing down the streets: Adventures in urban anarchy* (pp. 131-141). New York: Palgrave.

Foster, S. (Ed.). (1996). *Corporealities: Dancing knowledge, culture and power.* New York: Routledge.

Fraser, N., & Honneth, A. (2003). *Redistribution or recognition? A political-philosophical exchange.* London: Verso.

Freire, P. (1973). *Education for critical consciousness.* New York: Continuum.

Frey, L., & Carragee, K. (Eds.). (2007). *Communication activism: Communication for social change.* Creskill, NJ: Hampton Press.

Gabriel, Y. (1999). Beyond happy families: A critical reevaluation of the control-resistance-identity triangle. *Human Relations, 52,* 179-203.

Ganesh, S., Zoller,H., & Cheney,G. (2005). Transforming resistance, broadening our boundaries: Critical organizational communication meets globalization from below. *Communication Monographs, 72,* 169-191.

Garrido, M., & Halavais, A. (2003). Mapping networks of support for the Zapatista movement. In M. McCaughey & M. D. Ayers (Eds.), *Cyberactivism: Online activism in theory and practice* (pp. 165-184). New York: Routledge.

George, S. (2001). *The global citizen's movement: A new actor for a new politics.* Conference on reshaping globalization. Central European University: Budapest.

Gershman, J., & Irwin, A. (2000). Getting a grip on the global economy. In J. Y. Kim, J. V. Millen, A. Irwin, & J. Gershman (Eds.), *Dying for growth: Global inequality and the health of the poor* (pp. 11-43). Monroe, ME: Common Courage Press.

Giroux, H. (2003). *The abandoned generation: Democracy beyond the culture of fear.* New York: Palgrave Macmillan.

Giugni, M. (2002). Examining cross-national similarities among social movements. In J. Smith & H. Johnston (Eds.), *Globalization and resistance: Transnational dimensions of social movements* (pp. 13-29). New York: Rowman & Littlefield Publishers.

Giugni, M. (2004). *Social protest and policy change: Ecology, antinuclear, and peace movements in comparative politics.* Lanham: Rowman & Littlefield Publishers.

Giugni, M., McAdam, D., & Tilly, C. (1999). *How social movements matter.* Minneapolis: University of Minnesota Press.

Godalof, I. (1999). *Against purity: Rethinking identity with Indian and Western feminisms.* New York: Routledge.

Gomez-Pena, G. (1993). *Warrior for Gringostroika.* St Paul, MN: Graywolf Press.

Gomez-Pena, G. (1996). *The new world border.* San Francisco: City Lights.

Gomez-Pena, G. (2000). *Dangerous border crossers.* London: Routledge.

Gottfried, H. (1994). Learning the score: The duality of control and everyday resistance in the temporary-help service industry. In J. M. Jermier, D. Knights, & W. R. Nord (Eds.), *Resistance and power* (pp. 102-127). New York: Routledge.

Grignou, B., & Patou, C. (2004). Attac(k)ing expertise: Does the Internet really democratize knowledge? In W. van de Donk, B. Loader, P. Nixon, & D. Rucht (Eds.), *Cyberprotest: New media, citizens, and social movements* (pp. 164-179). London: Routledge.

Guha, R. (1988). The prose of counter-insurgency. In R. Guha & G. Spivak (Eds.), *Subaltern studies* (pp. 37-44). Delhi, India: Oxford University Press.

Guidry, J., Kennedy, M., & Zald, M. (2000). *Globalizations and social movements.* Ann Arbor, MI: University of Michigan Press.

Harvey, D. (2001). City and justice: Social movements in the city. In D. Harvey (Ed.), *Spaces of capital: Towards a critical geography* (pp. 188-207). London: Routledge.

Harvey, D. (2005). *A brief history of neoliberalism.* London: Oxford University Press.

Harvey, D. (2006). *Spaces of global capitalism: Toward a theory of uneven geographical development.* London: Verso.

Hashmi, S. (2007). The first ten years of street theatre: October 1978-October 1988. In S. Deshpande (Ed.), *Theatre of the streets: The Jana Natya Manch experience* (pp. 11-16). Delhi: Jana Natya Manch.

Indigenous Environmental Network. (2009). Energy justice in Turtle Island, North America. *Indigenous Environmental Network.* Retrieved from http://www.ienearth.org/docs/StatementonTarSandsandthePipelineFinal/index.html

Indigenous Environmental Network. (2011). Native American and Canadian First Nations to take part in largest acct of civil disobedience to stop Keystone XL Pipeline. Retrieved from http://www.ienearth.org/news/native-american-and-canadian-first-nations-to-take-part-in-largest-act-of-civil-disobedience-to-stop-keystone-sl-pipeline.html

Institute of Science in Society. (2008). Mass protests against GM crops in India. *Institute of Science in Society.* Retrieved from http://www.i-sis.org.uk/gmProtestsIndia.php

Jermier, J. M., Knights, D., & Nord, W. R. (1994). Introduction. In J. M. Jermier, D.

Johnston, H. (2009). Protest cultures: Performance, artifacts, and ideations. In H. Johnston (Ed.), *Culture, social movements, and protest* (pp. 3-29). Burlington, VT: Ashgate.

Johnston, H., & Noakes, J. (2005). *Frames of protest: Social movements and the framing perspective.* Lanham: Rowman & Littlefield Publishers.

Kabeer, N. (1994). *Reversed realities: Gender hierarchies in development thought.* London: Verso.

Khagram, S., & Levitt, P. (Eds.). (2008). *The transnational studies reader: Intersections and innovations.* New York: Routledge.

Kim, I. (2008). *Voices from the margin: A culture-centered look at public relations of resistance*. (Unpublished doctoral dissertation). Purdue University, West Lafayette, IN.

Kim, I., & Dutta, M. J. (2009). Studying crisis communication from the subaltern studies framework: Grassroots activism in the wake of Hurricane Katrina. *Journal of Public Relations Research, 21, 142-164.*

Kingkade, T. (2011). Occupy DC protestors take over K Street, Dozens arrested. *Huffington Post.* Retrieved from http://www.huffingtonpost.com/2011/12/07/occupy-dc-protesters-k-street-arrested_n_1135084.html

Knights, & W. R. Nord (Eds.), *Resistance and power in organizations* (pp. 1-24). New York: Routledge.

Kuruganti, K. (2011). "Monsanto Quit India" day marked across the country. *Alliance for Holistic and Sustainable Agriculture.* Retrieved from http://www.kisan-swaraj.in/2011/12/13/monsanto-quit-india-day-marked-across-the-country/

Langer, E. D., & Muñoz, E. (2003). Eds.) *Contemporary indigenous movements in Latin America.* Wilmington, Delaware: SR Books.

Larsen, J., & Olshansky, K. (2011). Lobbying form's memo spells out plan to undermine Occupy Wall Street. *MSNBC TV.* Retrieved from http://openchannel.msnbc.msn.com/_news/2011/11/19/8884405-lobbying-firms-memo-spells-out-plan-to-undermine-occupy-wall-street

Lucero, J. A. (2008). *Struggles of voice: The politics of indigenous representation in the Andes.* Pittsburgh, PA: University of Pittsburgh Press.

Martin, R. (1998). *Critical moves: Dance studies in theory and politics.* London: Duke University Press.

Marx, K. (1967). *Capital.* (S. Moore & E. Aveling, Trans.). New York: International Publishers.

Mayo, M. (2005). *Global citizens: Social movements and the challenge of globalization.* London: Zed Books.

McAdam, D., McCarthy, J., & Zald, M. (1996a). *Comparative perspectives in social movements: Political opportunities, mobilizing structures, and cultural framings.* Cambridge: Cambridge University Press.

McAdam, D., McCarthy, J., & Zald, M. (1996b). Introduction: Opportunities, mobilizing structures and framing processes. In D. McAdam, J. McCarthy, & M. Zald (Eds.), *Comparative perspectives in social movements: Political opportunities, mobilizing structures, and cultural framings* (pp. 1-20). Cambridge: Cambridge University Press.

McAdam, D., Tarrow, S., & Tilly, C. (2001). *Dynamics of contention.* Cambridge: Cambridge University Press.

McChesney, R. W. (1997). *Corporate media and the threat to democracy.* New York: Seven Stories Press.

McChesney, R. W. (1999). *Rich media, poor democracy: Communication politics in dubious times.* Urbana, IL: University of Illinois Press.

McKie, D., & Munshi, D. (2005). Connecting hemispheres: A comparative review of 21st century organizational communication in Australia/New Zealand and the United States. *Review of Communication, 5,* 49-55.

McKinley, T. (2004). Economic policies for growth and poverty reduction: PRSPs, neoliberal conditionalities and "post-consensus" alternatives. Paper presented at the International Conference on "The economics of new imperialism." New Delhi, India.

Meyer, D., & Whittier, N. (1994). Social movement spillover. *Social Problems, 41*(2), 277-298.

Mike, E. (2009). Revolution in India: Lalgarh's hopeful spark. Retrieved from http://kasamaproject.org/2009/07/11/sam-shell-lagarhs-hopeful-spark/

Millen, J., & Holtz, T. (2000). Dying for growth, part I: Transnational corporations and the health of the poor. In J. Y. Kim, J. V. Millen, A. Irwin, & J. Gershman (Eds.), *Dying for growth: Global inequality and the health of the poor* (pp. 177-223). Monroe, ME: Common Courage Press.

Millen, J., Irwin, A., & Kim, J. (2000). Introduction: What is growing? Who is dying? In J. Y. Kim, J. V. Millen, A. Irwin, & J. Gershman (Eds.), *Dying for growth: Global inequality and the health of the poor* (pp. 3-10). Monroe, ME: Common Courage Press.

Miller, M. J. (2006). Biodiversity policy making in Costa Rica: Pursuing indigenous and peasant rights. *The Journal of Environment Development, 15*(4), 359-381.

Miller, P., & Rose, N. (2008). *Governing the present.* Cambridge, MA: Polity Press

Miraftab, F. (2004). Public-private partnerships: The Trojan Horse of neoliberal development? *Journal of Planning Education and Research, 24,* 89-101.

Moghadam, V. (2009). *Globalization and social movements.* Lanham, MD: Rowman & Littlefield.

Morales, E. (2003). Bolivia, the power of the people. Speech delivered at a conference entitled *En Defensa de la Humanidad (In defense of humanity).* Mexico City. Translated by Bruce Campbell. Retrieved from http://www.americas.org

Morales, E. (2005). I believe only in the power of the people. *Znet.* Retrieved from http://www.zcommunications.org/contents/39041/print

Morales, E. (2008). On the WTO's round of negotiations. *Znet.* Retrieved from http://www.zcommunications.org/contents/53009/print

Morales, J. A. (2008). Bolivia in a global setting: Economic ties. In J. Crabtree and L. Whitehead (Eds.), *Unresolved tensions Bolivia: Past and present* (pp. 217-237). Pittsburgh, PA: University of Pittsburgh Press.

Mosley, P. (2001). Attacking poverty and the "Post-Washington consensus." *Journal of International Development, 13*(3), 307–14.

Mumby, D. K. (2005). Theorizing resistance in organizational studies: A dialectical approach. *Management Communication Quarterly, 19,* 19-44.

Munshi, D. (2005). Through the subject's eye: Situating the Other in discourses of diversity. G. Cheney & G. Barnett (Eds.), *International and Multicultural Organizational Communication* (pp. 45-70). Cresskill, NJ: Hampton Press Inc.

Munshi, D., & Kurian, P. (2007). The case of the subaltern public: A postcolonial investigation of corporate social responsibility's (o)missions. In S. May, G. Cheney, & J. Roper (Eds.), *The debate over corporate social responsibility* (pp. 438-447).

Murphy, A. G. (2001). The flight attendant dilemma: An analysis of communication and sensemaking during in-flight emergencies. *Journal of Applied Communication Research, 29,* 30-53.

Mychalejko, C., & Ryan, R. (2009). US military funded mapping project in Oaxaca: Geographers used to gather intelligence? *Z Magazine, 22,* 17-22.

Naples, N., & Desai, M. (2002). *Women's activism and globalization: Linking local struggles and transnational politics.* New York: Routledge.

Navarro, V. (1999). Health and equity in the world in the era of "globalization." *International Journal of Health Services, 29*(2), 215-226.

Navdanya. (2009). *Bija Vidyapeeth: The international college for sustainable living.* New Delhi: Navdanya. Retrieved from http://www.navdanya.org/attachments/Bija%20Vidyapeeth%20a%20historical%20glance%20copy.pdf

Navlakha, G. (2010). Days and nights in Maoist heartland. *Economic & Political Weekly, 45*(16), 38-47.

NBA. (2000). Satyagraha launched in Jalsindhi and Domkhedi with resolve to confront the waters. *NBA.* Retrieved from http://www.narmada.org/nba-press-releases/july-2000/satyagraha.launched.html

NBA. (2009). Displaced people will converge in Bhopal: Moral victory for the struggle in the Narmada valley. *NBA.* Retrieved from http://www.narmada.org/nba-press-releases/november-2009/06Nov.html

Nixson, F., & Walters, B. (2003). *Privatization, income distribution and poverty: The Mongolian experience.* Sydney: Asia-Pacific Press.

O'Connor, E. (2003). Indians and national salvation: Placing Ecuador's indigenous coup of January 2000 in historical perspective. In E. D. Langer & E. Muñoz (Eds.), *Contemporary indigenous movements in Latin America* (pp. 65-80). Wilmington, Delaware: SR Books.

Olivera, O. (2004). *Cochabamba: Water war in Bolivia.* Cambridge, MA: South End Press.

Olivera, O., & Lewis, T. (2004). *Cochabamba: Water war in Bolivia*. Cambridge, MA: South End Press.

Padhi, R., Pradhan, P., & Manjit, D. (2010). How many more arrests will Orissa see? *Economic and Political Weekly, 45*(10), 24-26.

Pal, M. (2008). *Fighting from and for the margin: Local activism in the realm of global politics*. (Unpublished doctoral dissertation). Purdue University, West Lafayette, IN.

Pal, M., & Dutta, M. (2008a). Public relations in a global context: The relevance of critical modernism as a theoretical lens. *Journal of Public Relations Research, 20*, 159-179.

Pal, M., & Dutta, M. (2008b). Theorizing resistance in a global context: Processes, strategies and tactics in communication scholarship. *Communication Yearbook, 32*, 41-87.

Payer, C. (1974). *The debt trap: The IMF and the Third World*. New York: Monthly Review Press.

Peeples, J., & Deluca, K. (2006). The truth of the matter: Motherhood, community, and environmental justice. *Women's Studies in Communication, 29*, 59-87.

Peet, R. (2003). *Unholy trinity: The IMF, the World Bank, and the WTO*. London: Zed Books.

Petras, J. (2004). Bolivia: Between colonization and revolution. Retrieved from http://canadiandimension.com/articles/1997

Pezzullo, P. (2004). Toxic tours: Communicating the "presence" of chemical contamination. In S. Depoe, J. Delicath, & M. Aepli Elsenbeer (Eds), *Communication and public participation in environmental decision making* (pp. 235-254). New York: State University of New York.

Pollock, J. (2011). How Egyptian and Tunisian youth hacked the Arab spring. *Technology Review*. Retrieved from http://www.technologyreview.com/web/38379/

Postero, N. (2004). Articulation and fragmentation: Indigenous politics in Bolivia. In N. G. Postero & L. Zamosc (Eds.), *The struggles for indigenous rights in Latin America*. Brighton, Portland: Sussex Academic Press.

Postero, N. (2005). Indigenous responses to neoliberalism: A look at the Bolivian uprising of 2003. *PoLAR: Political and Legal Anthropology Review, 28*, 73-92.

Postero, N. (2007). *Now we are citizens: Postcolonial politics in postmulticultural Bolivia*. Stanford, CA: Stanford University Press.

Prasad, A. (1997). The colonizing consciousness and representations of the Other. In P. Prasad, A. J. Mills, M. Elmes, and A. Prasad (Eds.), *Managing the organizational melting pot: Dilemmas of workplace diversity*. Thousand Oaks, CA: Sage.

Prasad, A. (2003). The gaze of the other: Postcolonial theory and organizational analysis. In A. Prasad (Ed.), *Postcolonial theory and organizational analysis: A critical engagement* (pp. 3-43). New York: Palgrave Macmillan.

Prasad, A. (2006). The Jewel in the crown: Postcolonial theory and workplace diversity. In P. Prasad, A. J. Mills, E. Michael, and A. Prasad (Eds.), *Handbook of Workplace Diversity*. Thousand Oaks, CA: Sage.

Prasad, P. (1997). The protestant ethic and the myths of the frontier: Cultural imprints, organizational structuring and workplace diversity. In P. Prasad, A. J. Mills, M. Elms, and A. Prasad (Eds.), *Managing the organizational melting pot: Dilemmas of workplace diversity* (pp. 129-147). Thousand Oaks, CA: Sage.

Prasad, A., & Prasad, P. (2002). Otherness at large: Identity and difference in the new globalized organizational landscape. In I. Aaltio-Marjosola & A. J. Mills (Eds.), *Gender, Identity and the Culture of Organizations* (pp. 57-71). London: Routledge.

Putnam, R.(1993). *Making democracy work: Civic transitions in modern Italy*. Princeton, NJ: Princeton University Press.

Putnam, R. (1995). Bowling alone: America's declining social capital. *Journal of Democracy, 6*, 65-78.

Reed, T. V. (2005). *The art of protest: Culture and activism from the civil rights movement to the streets of Seattle*. Minneapolis: University of Minnesota Press.

Reporters Without Borders. (2011a). World Report—Tunisia. Retrieved from http://en.rsf.org/spip.php?page=surveillance&id_article=39747

Reporters Without Borders. (2011b). The new media: Between revolution and repression—Net solidarity takes on censorship. Retrieved from http://en.rsf.org/the-new-media-between-revolution-11-03-2011,39764.html

Robertson, R. (1992). *Globalization: Social theory and global culture*. London: Sage.

Robins, K. (2000). Encountering globalization. In D. Held & A. McGrew (Eds.), *The global transformations reader: An introduction to the globalization debate* (pp. 195–201). Malden, MA: Blackwell.

Roca, C. F. T. (1996). Bolivia: Crisis, structural adjustment, and democracy. In A. E. F. Jilberto & A. Mommen (Eds.), *Liberalizing the developing world* (pp. 161-177). New York: Routledge.

Rootes, C. (2002a). The europeanisation of environmentalism. In R. Balme, D. Chabanet, & V. Wright (Eds.), *L'action collective en Europe/Collective Action in Europe* (pp. 377-404). Paris: Presses de Sciences Po.

Rootes, C. (2002b). Global visions: Global civil society and the lessons of European environmentalism. *Voluntas, 13*, 411-429.

Rootes, C. (2004). Environmental movements. In D. A. Snow, S. A. Soule, & H. Kriesi (Eds.), *The Blackwell companion to social movements* (pp. 608-640). Oxford: Blackwell.

Rothman, F., & Oliver, P. (1999). From local to global: The anti-dam movement in southern Brazil. *Mobilization: An International Quarterly, 4*, 41-57.

Rothman, F., & Oliver, P. (2002). From local to global: The anti-dam movement in Southern Brazil, 1979-1992. In J. Smith & H. Johnston (Eds.), *Globalization and resistance: Transnational dimensions of social movements* (pp. 115-149). New York: Rowman & Littlefield Publishers.

Sachs, J. (2005). *The end of poverty: Economic possibilities for our time*. New York: Penguin.

Sassen, S. (1998). *Globalization and its discontents*. New York: The New York Press.

Sastry, S. J., & Dutta, M. J. (2011a). Public health, global surveillance and the "emerging disease" worldview: A postcolonial appraisal of PEPFAR. *Health Communication*.

Sastry, S. J & Dutta, M. J. (2011b). Postcolonial constructions of HIV/AIDS: Meaning, culture,

Schulz, M. (1998). Collective action across borders: Opportunity structures, network capacities, and communicative praxis in the age of advanced globalization. *Sociological perspectives, 4,* 597-610.

Scott, J. C. (1985). *Weapons of the weak: Everyday forms of peasant resistance*. New Haven, CT: Yale University Press.

Shapiro, L. (2011). Wisconsin protests draw thousands of workers fighting for key union rights. *Huffington Post*. Retrieved from http://www.huffingtonpost.com/2011/02/21/wisconsin-protests-_n_826246.html?ref=wisconsin-protests

Sharma, A. (2008). *Logics of empowerment: Development, gender, and governance in neolilberal India*. Minneapolis, MN: University of Minnesota Press.

Shiva,V. (2001). Democratizing biology: Reinventing biology from a feminist, ecological, and Third World perspective. In M. Lederman & I. Bartsch (Eds.), *The gender and science reader* (pp.447-465). London: Routledge.

Shiva, V. (2008). Biodiversity, intellectual property rights, and globalization. In B. de Sousa Santos (Ed.), *Another knowledge is possible: Beyond Northern epistemologies* (pp. 272-287). London: Verso.

Shiva, V. (2010). Press statement on Bt. Brinjal and GM foods. Retrieved from http://www.navdanya.org/news/81-press-statement-on-bt-brinjal-a-gm-foods

Shiva, V., & Bedi, G. (2002). *Sustainable agriculture and food security: The impact of globalization*. New Delhi: Sage Publications.

Sklair, L. (1995). Social movements and global capitalism. *Sociology, 29,* 495-512.

Smith, J. (2002). Globalizing resistance: The Battle of Seattle and the future of social movements. In J. Smith & H. Johnston (Eds.), *Globalization and resistance: Transnational dimensions of social movements* (pp. 207-228). New York: Rowman & Littlefield Publishers.

Smith, J. (2004). Transnational processes and movements. In D. A. Snow, S. A. Soule, & H. Kriesi (Eds.), *The Blackwell companion to social movements* (pp. 311-335). Malden, MA: Blackwell Publishing.

Smith, J., & Johnston, H. (2002). Globalization and resistance: An introduction. In J. Smith & H. Johnston (Eds.), *Globalization and resistance: Transnational dimensions of social movements* (pp. 1-10). New York: Rowman & Littlefield.

Snow, D. A., & Benford, R. D. (1992). Master frames and cycles of protest. In A. Morris & C.M. Mueller (Eds.), *Frontiers of social movement theory* (pp. 133-155). New Haven, CT: Yale University Press.

Snow, D. A., & Benford, R. D. (1998). Ideology, frame resonance, and participant mobilization. *International Social Movement Research, 1,* 197-218.

Snow, D. A., Rochford, B., Worden, S. K., & Benford, R. D. (1986). Frame alignment processes, micromobilization, and movement participation. *American Sociological Review, 51,* 464-481.

Sotirin, P., & Gottfried, H. (1999). The ambivalent dynamics of secretarial "bitching": Control, resistance, and the construction of identity. *Organization, 6,* 57-80.

Sperling, V., Ferree, M. M., & Risman, B. (2001). Constructing global feminism: Transnational advocacy networks and Russian women's activism. *Signs: Journal of Women in Culture and Society, 26,* 1155-1186.

Spivak, G. C. (1988). Can the subaltern speak? In G. Nelson L. Grossberg (Eds.), *Marxism and the interpretation of culture* (pp. 120-130). Urbana: University of Illinois Press.

St. Clair, A. (2006a). The World Bank as a transnational expertise institution. *Global Governance, 12*(1), 5-18.

St. Clair, A. (2006b). Global poverty: The co-production of knowledge and politics. *Global Social Policy, 6,* 57-77.

Starr, A. (2005). *Global revolt: A guide to the movements against globalization.* London: Zed Books.

Stoller-McAllister, J. (2005). *Mexican social movements and the transition to democracy.* Jefferson, NC: McFarland and Co.

Survival International. (2008). Tribe stages mass protest against British company Vedanta. Retrieved from http://www.survivalinternational.org/news/3294

Swagler, M. (2012). General strike rocks Nigeria. *Socialist Worker.* Retrieved from http://socialistworker.org/2012/01/12/general-strike-rocks-nigeria

Swiderska, K., Daño, E., & Dubois, O. (2001). *Developing the Philippines' Executive Order No. 247 on access to genetic resources.* London: International Institute for Environment and Development.

Tar Sands Action. (2011a). Breaking: New Obama hire, Broderick Johnson, was Keystone XL lobbyist. *Tar Sands Action.* Retrieved from http://www.tarsandsaction.org/page/7/

Tar Sands Action. (2011b). Sec. of State Clinton on three Sunday talk shows- will hosts end the media blackout of State Department corruption scandal? *Tar Sands Action.* Retrieved from http://www.tarsandsaction.org/page/7/

Tarrow, S. (2005). *The new transnational activism.* New York: Cambridge University Press.

Treaty One First Nations. (2008). Canadian indigenous community to deliver message to Obama. Retrieved from http://groups.yahoo.com/group/Racism_Against_Indigenous_Peoples/message/11235

Tretheway, A. (1997). Resistance, identity, and empowerment: A postmodern feminist analysis of clients in a human service organization. *Communication Monographs, 64,* 281-301.

Tretheway, A. (2000). A feminist critique of disciplined bodies. In P. M. Buzzanell (Ed.), *Rethinking organizational and managerial communication from feminist perspectives* (pp.177-208). Thousand Oaks, CA: Sage.

Van Cott, D. L. (2003). From exclusion to inclusion: Bolivia's 2002 elections. *Journal of Latin American Studies, 35,* 751-775.

Vargas, C. (2008). The perverse effects of globalization in Bolivia. In J. Crabtree and L. Whitehead (Eds.), *Unresolved tensions Bolivia: Past and present* (pp. 238-254). Pittsburgh, PA: University of Pittsburgh Press.

Wagner, B. (2011). "I have understood you": The co-evolution of expression and control on the Internet, television, and mobile phones during the Jasmine revolution in Tunisia. *International Journal of Communication, 5,* 1295-1302.

Waltz, M. (2005). *Alternative and activist media.* Edinburgh: Edinburgh University Press.

Weber, M. (1988). *The protestant ethic and the spirit of capitalism.* New York: Charles Scribner and Sons.

World Bank. (2000a) Transforming development: New approaches to developing country-owned poverty reduction strategies. Retrieved from http://www.worldbank.org/poverty/

World Bank. (2000b). Draft guidelines for participation in PRS and IPRS in the ECA region. Retrieved from http://www.worldbank.org/participation/ECAPRSPs.htm

World Bank. (2000c). *Poverty reduction strategy process.* Retrieved from http://www.worldbank.org/poverty/strategies/backgr.htm

World Bank. (2001). Nicaragua to receive US$4.5 billion under the enhanced HIPC initiative, World Bank and IMF open way for debt relief [Press release]. News Release No: 2001/188/S, World Bank.

World Bank. (2002). *Poverty reduction strategy source book.* Retrieved from http://siteresources.worldbank.org/INTPRS1/Resources/383606-1205334112622/13839_chap7.pdf

Yearley, S. (1994). Social movements and environmental change. In M. Redclift & T. Benton (Eds.), *Social theory and the global environment* (pp. 150-168). London: Routledge.

Yearley, S. (1996). *Sociology, environmentalism, globalization.* London: Sage.

Yearley, S., & Forrester, J. (2000). Shell, a sure target for global environmental campaigning? In R. Cohen & S. M. Rai (Eds.), *Global social movements.* New Brunswick, NJ: The Athlone Press.

Zoller, H. M. (2003). Health on the line: Identity and disciplinary control in employee occupational health and safety discourse. *Journal of Applied Communication Research, 31*(2), 118-139.

Zoller, H. M. (2004). Dialogue as global issue management: Legitimizing corporate influence in the Transatlantic Business Dialogue. *Management Communication Quarterly, 18*(2), 204-240.

Zoller, H. (2005). Health activism: Communication theory and action for social change. *Communication Theory, 15,* 341-364.

Zoller, H. (2006). Suitcases and swimsuits: On the future of organizational communication. *Management Communication Quarterly, 19,* 661-666.

Zoller, H., & Dutta, M. (2008a). Introduction: Communication and health policy. In H. Zoller & M. Dutta (Eds.), *Emerging perspectives in health communication: Interpretive, critical and cultural approaches* (pp. 358-364). Mahwah, NJ: Lawrence Erlbaum Associates.

Zoller, H., & Dutta, M. (2008b). Afterword: Emerging agendas in health communication and the challenge of multiple perspectives. In H. Zoller & M. Dutta (Eds.), *Emerging perspectives in health communication: Interpretive, critical and cultural approaches* (pp. 449-463). Mahwah, NJ: Lawrence Erlbaum Associates.

Zoller, H., & Ganesh, S. (2012). Dialogue, activism, and democratic social change. *Communication Theory, 22,* 66-91.

Index